Granite and Gravity

GRANITE AND GRAVITY

IN THIS LIFE, PREPARE FOR THE NEXT

Vivian Elani

Sacred Stories
PUBLISHING

Granite and Gravity
Copyright © 2016

All rights reserved.

This book or part thereof may not be reproduced in any form, stored in a retrieval system, or transmitted in any form by any means-electronic, mechanical, photocopy, recording, or otherwise without prior written permission of the publisher, except as provided by United States of America copyright law.

The information provided in this book is designed to provide helpful information on the subjects discussed. This book is not meant to be used, nor should it be used, to diagnose or treat any medical condition. The author and publisher are not responsible for any specific health needs that may require medical supervision and are not liable for any damages or negative consequences from any treatment, action, application, or preparation, to any person reading or following the information in this book.

References are provided for information purposes only and do not constitute endorsement of any websites or other sources. In the event you use any of the information in this book for yourself, the author and the publisher assume no responsibility for your actions.

Books may be purchased through booksellers or by contacting Sacred Stories Publishing.

Granite and Gravity: In This Life, Prepare For The Next

Vivian Elani

Tradepaper ISBN: 978-1-945026-19-5

Electronic ISBN: 978-1-945026-20-1

Library of Congress Control Number: 2016947253

Published by Sacred Stories Publishing, LLC
Delray Beach, FL
www.sacredstoriespublishing.com

Printed in the United States of America

To my husband, my soul mate.

At a time when life was an unstable ladder –

Afraid to take another step
For the rung might break
And the hands
That worked so hard can only grasp
At the sides

Trying for something to hold
Filling only with splinters
Falling to an unknown destiny.

Then the darkness of your eyes swirled
Around to match the midnight of my heart
Enclosing in a misty shadow the torn hands and empty soul.

For my destiny was beside the
One who would change my life
And the mystery

That prompted my spirit to grow
Is still the mystery
That protects my flesh
And entangles my fears

With stable hands.

-Vivian Carbonetti, February 18, 1985

Preface

ALMOST TWO DECADES BEFORE he would be named chief engineer of the Brooklyn Bridge, John Roebling found himself on an East River ferry impacted in the ice. It is said that his time spent stranded between New York and Brooklyn on that winter day ignited in him the notion that a bridge spanning the river was a crucial step in the city's civil engineering. A safe and sturdy connection between Brooklyn and Manhattan was necessary and when finally given the chance, Roebling forged the passageway with masterful architecture and insight that is still revered today.

Cruelly, Roebling would never see the bridge stretch across the East River. In the initial survey of the site, Roebling sustained an injury, whose complications would take his life.

In Roebling's passing, his son, Washington, took over as chief engineer. Armed with his father's innovative vision and meticulous planning, Washington completed the bridge in 1883.

The Brooklyn Bridge is a marvel of architectural balance. Arguably the most vital aspect of the bridge's integrity is the anchorages that secure its cables. Washington referred to the execution of these anchorages as a governing of, "granite and gravity". Although he was speaking in technical terms, Washington provides quite a dimensional phrase.

Washington worked to forge a union between the granite masonry's own mass and the gravitational force that descended upon them. In a broader, spiritual sense, we are often tasked with navigating immense forces in our own lives. How we harness these forces and how we find congruence among them often dictates the stability of our relationships, our level of confidence and our capacity for personal growth.

It was this phrase and this sentiment that sparked the first inspirations for this novel and has since given rise to the story of Flora and Nathan.

Aria

(Earth names, Anna and Olivia)

Soul World: Anticipation

ARIA LOOKED DOWN FROM THE SKY. This was *the* pivotal moment for her soul group. Their future lives together would be determined by how Flora proceeded from this particular point in her life. Flora was lying in her darkened bedroom, staring into space. She had suffered a long, painful childbirth, ending with the death of her son.

Her seamstress and friend, Olivia, was on her way up the stairs to speak to Flora. Nathan, her husband, told Olivia that Flora would not speak to anyone—wouldn't even look into his eyes. So Olivia took it upon herself to see Flora. Maybe she could help Flora.

Olivia took each step tentatively; hand on the banister, looking down at her feet. She stopped periodically and sighed, shaking her head. At one point, she stopped and turned her head to look down the stairs, causing Aria's energy to come to a standstill.

Being a soul, Aria had the ability to peek into the future, but the future was uncertain. If the outcome of the meeting with Olivia and Flora was positive, Aria knew that Flora would be on the correct life path. But predicting the future was difficult. She had been through all the combinations of actions that Flora would execute as a result of this conversation. However, there were too many variables to perform an accurate forecast, so Aria just gave up.

I was naïve to think that this would be easy. When the Council of Souls asked Aria to orchestrate her soul group's next life, she readily agreed. However, this task proved to be more difficult than expected.

As Flora muttered, "What am I to do?" Aria's light-blue energy swirled around in anticipation and suspense.

Flora

June 1878: Lost Again

WHAT SHALL I DO? FLORA ASKED HERSELF over and over again as she rocked her frail, battered body back and forth in bed. She tossed the heavy blankets aside and kicked them away until they dropped onto the hardwood floor of her stuffy and unkempt bedroom. She looked at the items cluttered on her vanity: the used handkerchiefs that littered the floor and the wide-open armoire that revealed the chaos of dresses, parasols, and boots inside. Dust motes swirled in the slivers of sunlight that escaped through the cracks of her drawn curtains. Every painting that hung on the walls seemed menacing in the dim light. The farm scenes of cows, sheep, and chickens that she had once regarded with a sense of comfort now seemed unnatural and eerie.

Flora struggled to get out of bed, tentatively walked over to the vanity, and sat down. The pain throughout her body felt as if she had been tossed from a carriage and trampled by horses. She had never given the process of childbirth much thought before her labor started. But once it did, she was terrified and confused. The pain and hallucinations she had both during and afterwards would not soon be forgotten.

Slowly and quietly, she opened the top drawer of the vanity and found it: the necklace that she had hidden. The necklace that her mother gave to Flora when she was a little girl. The mother who supposedly died giving birth to Flora. "Oh," Flora said. "I almost followed in her footsteps." But her mother couldn't have died during childbirth. What really happened to her—and why? She studied the white and purple beads of the necklace carefully before putting it back in its hiding place.

For the second time in her life, she just didn't know what to do next. The first was when her father passed away some ten years ago. She felt as lost now as she did then.

"I've come back to where I started," she said aloud in the darkness. "Lost again." She sighed as her eyes rested on her favorite painting—two ships sailing through the Hudson River Valley with a vibrant sunset about to burst upon the sky over the mountains. It used to hang in the dining room in her father's house across from Washington Square Park. She sold that house several years ago and moved to the top floor of the building she owned on 23rd Street. Now, she had her reservations about the move. Her choice to marry Nathan, who purchased that painting for her, was also called into question. Every swift and confident decision that she had ever made now seemed incorrect. She gazed upon the artwork. Each one of those decisions had led her to today.

Flora heard a soft knock on the door and slowly turned her head away from the painting in time to see it crack open. One of the seamstresses that worked in her hat shop, Olivia, opened the door wider and stepped into the room. She looked paler and even thinner than usual. Her brown hair was drawn into a tight bun behind her head. The lightweight, cotton-gray dress, which Flora fitted to her petite body several weeks ago, seemed loose. Olivia's face changed to one of concern as soon as her eyes adjusted to the poor lighting in Flora's bedroom.

"Flora, you shouldn't be out of bed," Olivia gasped as she rushed over. She gently assisted Flora back into bed, picked up the blankets from the floor, and arranged and smoothed them out. She retrieved a hairbrush from the vanity and gently brushed and braided Flora's long, brown hair. Olivia's calming presence quieted Flora's mind, giving it a needed respite. When satisfied, Olivia finally settled into the chair next to Flora's bed and placed her hand in Flora's.

After a few more moments of silence, Olivia said, "Flora, why won't you talk to anyone? You're scaring all of us. Nathan. . . ."

With the mention of Nathan's name, Flora's grip tightened onto Olivia's hand. She turned her head away from Olivia and attempted to stop the tears that inevitably started their course down her face and onto her already-damp pillow. Her mind spun out of control, thinking about her son—lost just hours after a delivery that almost killed her. Thoughts of her husband, Nathan, abandoning her kept running through her brain. The intense chatter in her mind was nonstop. Nightmares invaded her usual peaceful slumber and were too much to bear.

Each dream worse than the next—her father, evicting a poor woman and children from his deplorable tenement housing—standing at her father's side in some dark alley to meet with the managers of his drug ring—waiting in the cab as he stopped off to see how his prostitutes were fairing. Each dream ended with her father shaking her, telling her to "stop, stop, stop!" But these dreams couldn't be true. She never witnessed these events; however, she couldn't discount the kernel of truth in each one.

"Flora," said Olivia. "Please, tell me what pains you so. I mean . . . you're suffering from something more than your physical ailments. Flora, look at me."

Flora turned to Olivia, looked into her soft brown eyes, and said, "I don't have the strength, Olivia. This is too much to handle." That was all Flora could say before sobbing once again.

Olivia took a cool cloth and did her best to calm Flora down before gently saying, "Flora, you'll not be able to pretend that you're unaffected by this like you've done during other crises in your life. You'll have to feel and face this pain. You'll need to rely on and trust the people that love you. Tell me—what can I do to help?"

"Nothing," Flora replied in a small voice.

"Flora, please tell me something. When you were feverish and hallucinating, you spoke of your father. Is that the source of your pain?" Olivia questioned.

"I don't know," replied Flora, shaking her head from side to side slightly. "No, I do know. He left me, Olivia. He left me with this terrible guilt and anger. He left me a fortune that leaves me feeling dirty, and no matter how many good deeds I try to do with it, I continue to feel stained. His unrelenting greed caused many people misery. It was just so easy to not think about it. But now . . . now, it's all I can think of. Now, I know. I know that I . . . I. . . ."

"Hate him?" Olivia said, finishing the sentence that Flora couldn't. As she said the words, Flora nodded in agreement.

"Then you must feel that hatred. Admit that you hated him. Then, find your peace with him. You shouldn't feel guilty for his deeds. You have to start talking again. Keeping it all within yourself will end up killing you. Everyone is worried sick."

"I'm afraid of what I'll say to him," Flora whispered.

"Him? You mean say to Nathan?"

"Yes," Flora replied, looking down at the pattern on her blanket.

"Tell me: what are you afraid to tell him?"

"Olivia," said Flora with fresh tears in her eyes. "It's my fault that I lost the baby. During the whole pregnancy, I thought that it wasn't meant to be. A premonition." Flora paused and wiped her eyes with a handkerchief.

"You feel guilty about that?" Olivia asked.

"Yes, guilt that I may not have wanted this child at all. And now I see my guilt reflected back to me in Nathan's eyes."

"Flora, I've known many women who have lost their babies. They all believe that they're at fault, that they deserved this as punishment for something. Most women question whether or not they wanted the child they are, or were, carrying, for many different reasons. What you're feeling is normal."

"Really, Olivia? Are you telling me the truth?"

Olivia leaned forwards and grasped Flora's hand again. "Of course I am. Most women know when their pregnancy isn't right. They have a 'premonition' that something's wrong."

They sat in silence for several minutes while Flora digested what Olivia had said.

"Olivia, let me be alone now. I understand now what I must do."

Aria
(Earth names, Anna and Olivia)

Soul World: Splitting Energy

ARIA EMPATHIZED WITH FLORA'S PAIN AND misery. Aria felt badly for having to put Flora through such an ordeal. It was needed, and even the Council of Souls had agreed with her. But it didn't really make Aria feel better.

Aria thought back to when the Council had given her this task of orchestrating her soul group's lives. At the time, it seemed so easy, but now, she realized how difficult it was to balance the soul's energy within a human form. She studied how soul energy influences human life. How it's an undercurrent of their emotions, sitting deep within them. But all of that studying was worthless when attempting to oversee lives without the practical experience that someone like her teacher had.

Flora's intuition was correct. She wasn't meant to have a child at all. The only reason she was pregnant was so that she would lose the baby. This was purposely done in order to disrupt her life, set off this emotional crisis, and force her to face all of which she had denied for so long. It was up to her now to overcome this impediment. If not, her soul would remain stagnant. If she succeeded, her soul would elevate to a higher understanding. This process of graduating from one level of enlightenment to another required dedication, patience, and many, many lives of trial and error.

Before getting this assignment, most of Aria's soul mates were living their lives in Boston or Provincetown, Massachusetts. Her human form was quietly working as a seamstress in London. She wasn't paying much attention to the life she was living on Earth but was, instead, concentrating on her studies in the Soul World. She was proficiently splitting her energy between the Sky and the Earth.

While living a human life, part of the soul energy is always left behind to hibernate. But when souls become more advanced, the part that was left behind during an incarnation can actually stay awake and converse with other souls. Part of them can study their lessons while the other part of them is on Earth. Their energy is efficiently split between two realms.

She was deeply absorbed in what she was reading when Teacher interrupted.

That's when it all started.

"Aria, the Council would like to see you."
"Me?" Aria asked.
"Yes, Aria, you."
Odd. She had never met with the Council except when she returned from a life. The Council of Souls was a group of extremely advanced souls, but they didn't sit in judgment. They didn't actually plan lives nor did they use their power to exert control over souls. Their responsibility was to perform the life review. Questions asked during the review were based upon lessons that were supposed to be learned. However, the Council didn't make a decision about where the soul stood in its advancement. The Council and teachers only guided, prompted, and supported the soul's work. Aria didn't know how her advancement was actually determined; it just happened.

These thoughts caused her to become immediately concerned. It hadn't escaped anyone's attention that Aria had been progressing a little faster than everyone else in the soul group. If the group became too imbalanced, it was vulnerable to being split and merged with other groups upon the Council's discretion.

"Aria, why are you being so slow?" Teacher asked. "Please keep up with me."

"I'm sorry; I'm just wondering why the Council wants to see me."

She and Teacher stood silently in front of the Council. It was an intimidating scene: several Council members placed around both Aria and Teacher. They were silent, motionless purple orbs of light and energy. Aria looked over at Teacher, into her deep-blue center, but Teacher wouldn't return her gaze. Finally, Councilor Creek broke the silence. "Aria, tell us: why didn't you choose to hibernate like your other soul mates?"

"Hibernating doesn't suit me. I've too many things that I want to meditate about and study."

"Yes," Councilor Creek continued, "we noticed that you seemed to have outpaced your soul mates. Since you're more advanced, it only makes sense that you don't feel the need to hibernate."

Aria's uneasiness increased. She didn't want to leave her soul group, but would do whatever the Council deemed best.

Councilor Pedor interjected, "We see that during your life in Eyam, during the Great Plague, you tended to many children. You owned a large piece of land just outside of town and went into London to bring back orphaned children. How many children did you raise?"

Aria looked down and said in a small voice, "About twenty."

"Twenty-two, to be exact," said Councilor Pedor.

"Why, Aria," Councilor Creek asked, "did you feel so compelled to feed, clothe, and educate so many children? Why would you open your heart again? Some of these children caused you great distress and heartache."

"During that lifetime, I had an incredible urge to help as many children as I could."

Councilor Pedor looked intensely at Aria and asked again why she took responsibility for so many children.

"Councilor Pedor," Aria pleaded. "You understand why. Why must I speak of it?"

"Aria, please answer," Teacher prompted.

"Because," Aria responded, reluctantly, "I had seven of my own children." Aria began to feel a little "human" and wondered if the Council was manipulating her energy. "My beautiful children." She sighed. "We had a farm with the most incredible sheep in Eyam Village. My husband and I were very successful wool traders. I made the children and my husband clothes and—and we were very happy."

"Then, all of my children died of the plague. Each one got sick very quickly, as did my husband. I buried all of them and wondered why I was still alive. Staying in the empty house was unbearable, so I stayed with my husband's sister in town. We all mourned together, the entire town. Everyone had lost family. For a long time, I didn't know what to do. One day, I took a walk to see the house where I used to live. It seemed like just a house, not a home, now that it was empty. As I walked up the hill, an old woman appeared from behind me. I whirled around and came face-to-face with this old, wrinkled woman in a dirty, torn dress. We looked at each other for a moment, and then she took a step towards me, pointed her dirt-encrusted finger at me, and said very clearly, 'This is what you get for having more than you need!' I suddenly became faint and crumpled to the ground. It was almost as if she had cast a spell upon me. After I regained my composure, I stood up and looked around, but she was gone."

Aria paused for a moment and then continued, "After that, I was a person with a different perspective on life. I no longer felt sorry for myself and turned my mourning into something else. After the quarantine was lifted, my empty home was changed into one filled with children who needed a family as much as I did."

"Aria," Councilor Pedor said, "on several occasions, we've seen you recover from extreme loss with dignity; you turned your tragedy to success. We believe that you have a future as a teacher."

Aria was shocked. She thought that she was far, far from ever being considered future teacher material.

"We would like to give you an assignment," Councilor Lux stated. "You're to assist your soul mates in planning their next lives. Teacher has conveyed to me that it will be in New York City. You're to be present in their lives, but how you orchestrate the lives is up to you. You may use your teacher for advice. You won't have to stand at the Council with your soul mates when they return from this life in Manhattan, so you must keep Teacher up-to-date."

"Are you comfortable splitting your energy between the Sky and Earth?" Councilor Lux asked.

"Oh yes, I'm used to it now," Aria replied.

"Do you understand the importance of signs?" Councilor Pedor asked. "They need to be used wisely to remind your human form of the correct path to take."

Aria nodded. "Yes, Councilor."

"Are you accepting this challenge?" Councilor Creek asked. "You know that you need to prove that your soul group is capable of growth. Some members have fallen behind."

"Yes, Councilor."

Aria left the meeting confident that she could turn the group around; however, after performing some preliminary analysis, she realized that it was going to be a struggle. Aria waited until all the members of her soul group returned and then gathered them around. She'd been thinking about her strategy to get the group to work more efficiently together on Earth.

Aria had been quicker to recognize her signs during her lives on Earth and was more adept at being compassionate. She knew that if the group members applied themselves, they too could develop these skills. But they didn't seem to believe her. They were all still tired and disappointed from their previous lives in Provincetown.

She told them her plan for their next lives and said that she would participate and that they would be monitored. At that announcement, they showed their excitement and became more positive. They all knew Aria's strengths, and a chance to be watched over was an exciting prospect.

"Who?" Soul Julya asked. "Who is going to watch over us?"

"Even though I have my doubts, the Council told me that I'm ready for this responsibility."

This news caused a great flow of positive energy, and Aria took advantage of it. She had everyone researching and studying, planning signs, and meditating.

All the while, Teacher reminded Aria of the basics. "There's a balance in all energy—a harmony of 'cause and effect' or 'action and reaction.' Signs must be given throughout the lives that you're arranging to remind your soul mates of the optimal path to take. Clues can take the form of an object or may simply be a set of words that are spoken by one of your soul mates. These clues are extremely important, Aria."

When it came time to incarnate, they were confident that they were prepared. As they disembarked, one by one, Aria called out their signs for the last time: "Vanity! Green Hat! Telescope! Necklace! Sunset! Gravity!" Each sign had its own special meaning.

The East River Bridge

Stranded

WAITING WAS NOT AN ACCEPTABLE PASTIME. Mr. Roebling's experience of remaining stranded on a ferry with no control over the situation was unknown, foreign, and intolerable. It was 1853, and Mr. Roebling was traveling from Brooklyn to Manhattan with his twelve-year-old son, Washington Roebling. It was during that journey that he started to think about a bridge that would free people from being at the mercy of winter's fury. The thought nagged at him for years until 1857, when he formally suggested that it was feasible to build a bridge across the East River.

The idea of the bridge was put aside until December of 1866, when a group of enthusiastic citizens, led by Brooklyn's most prominent businessman, William Kingsley, inspired the resurrection of the plan. The weather in January 1867 was particularly severe; the East River was clogged with great masses of ice, keeping the ferries from running in a timely fashion. Continuous sheets of ice had formed from shore to shore, and thousands of people attempted to cross the river on foot rather than wait for a ferry that might end up getting trapped. When the tide turned, the ice immediately cracked apart, leaving many stranded on floating pieces of ice.

After a lengthy debate at the Senator Henry Case Murphy's home, William Kingsley convinced the senator that the project was feasible. The senator submitted an incorporating charter to the state legislature, which passed on April 16th. One month later, John Roebling was named chief engineer. Sadly, neither John Roebling nor Senator Murphy would see the completion of the bridge.

Victoria

June 1867: Victoria's Journey

EVEN THOUGH VICTORIA COMPLETED her journey to America some ten years before, just thinking about it made her soul run cold with fear. She usually suppressed her memories of the time before she stepped onto American soil, but her recollections kept creeping up on her during every quiet moment of the past few weeks, encroaching on her serenity in a most uncontrollable fashion. Her life, which was made up of her mistress Flora's habitual patterns, had been disturbed. The sudden death of Flora's father, Mr. Edward Pearl, had shaken the façade of stability that Victoria had grown accustomed to but had never trusted. Suddenly, she couldn't overcome the feeling that her time with Flora was coming to an end.

Victoria stood behind Flora and peered at her through the vanity mirror, picked up a hairbrush, and gently started to brush Flora's long brown, wavy hair. Flora sat very still, perched on the small chair in front of the vanity. She appeared to be deep in thought—her large brown eyes looking down at her hands, her face relaxed. There was no use in attempting to figure out what Flora was thinking. She didn't wear her emotions on her sleeve but kept them close to her chest, only letting one know what one needed to know and nothing more, always in control of herself as well as her surroundings. There was no idle chitchat with Flora. Her conversation, always accurate, was worthwhile and needed a purpose.

Yet the silence was too overwhelming for Victoria, and she wished that Flora would say something to keep her mind from its nonstop thinking—about the uncomfortable present, the uncertain future, and the past. Inevitably, her thoughts kept returning to a time and place where it all started with Flora, her mistress, friend, sister, and captor.

Victoria was nine years old the day her parents died. She wasn't even sure how they died but remembered them being ill with a fever. They were on their way to America, but it wasn't really a journey. It was an escape. They had fled their home in the middle of the night and embarked on a ship early the next morning. Her father said that they had borrowed money and would never be able to pay it back. Their choice was to take what they had left and to start anew or be forever in debt.

During the journey, her mother and father seemed so optimistic. All three of them took walks on the deck, breathing in the fresh ocean air. Her father spoke of the land he would purchase and the crops they would grow. Mother's eyes shone bright when she talked about the horses, vast forests, and rich soil in America—things they would never see or touch. Instead, they both died just a few days before reaching land.

As Victoria stood on the ship's deck, next to her deceased parents, she felt the cold ocean air on her face and listened to the sounds of the sails leaping in the wind. The continuous sound of the ocean lapping, falling, and splashing against the sides of the ship seemed louder than usual, and the urge to place her hands over her ears was powerful. With her feet firmly planted on the ship's deck, she stood as motionless as possible, with her stomach in a painful knot. She took deep breaths to try to loosen her constricted neck muscles but could only muster short, uneven intervals. Finally, Victoria succumbed and bowed her head to look at the blurry, filthy deck. She absentmindedly stepped on the spot where her tears had landed and smeared them into the wood, leaving a tiny, dirty streak.

When the captain nodded at her, Victoria walked to the banister to look over the edge while her parents' bodies slipped off the boards and into the ocean. They quickly disappeared from view and were replaced with green waves that were now her parents' eternal grave.

A few days later, she bravely disembarked at Castle Garden. Here she had to register and give an officer her name, age, and where she had come from. When asked where her parents were, she explained her situation and begged the officer not to send her back to Ireland.

As brave as she thought she was, she felt her lower lip tremble and tears well up in her hazel-colored eyes. The thin strips of leather that protected her feet from the ground were practically worthless, leaving them cold and wet. Pitifully, she looked down at herself and found that her frock was threadbare; the green color of the fabric had turned to brown, from being constantly filthy throughout the trip. Her hair was an awful mess of dirty, itchy curls. Even as she hugged her overcoat around herself as tightly as possible, she started to shiver uncontrollably.

"Go down to the labor exchange," said the officer. "You could get-chaself a job as a housemaid. Out this door to da right. Make sure you see Mr. Samuel. Da ya hear me, girlie? Ask for Mr. Samuel."

She quickly glanced up into his eyes, and they locked just briefly before she mumbled thanks and ran off into the direction he pointed. He must have known that Mr. Pearl had listed a job with the exchange and that he'd specifically requested a young, orphaned girl for his daughter's personal companion.

When Victoria found Mr. Samuel, he told her that she was perfect for a particular job and to go wait in the corner. She must have stood there for over an hour, tired and starving, getting more and more nervous. Finally, she saw a well-dressed man confer with Mr. Samuel. The gentleman turned and took a good long look at Victoria, from head to toe, through a haze of cigar smoke. With one hand in his pocket and the other holding his cigar, he walked slowly over to her without moving his gaze.

"Miss Victoria?" the tall, distinguished man said.

"Yes, sir?" she said tentatively, looking down at the floor. "Are you the one Mr. Samuel called for?"

"Yes, my name is Mr. Pearl."

"How do you do, sir?" Victoria replied, looking up at her future benefactor. Mr. Pearl stood up straight and looked down upon her as her father used to do. He had soothing blue-gray eyes and gray, wavy hair. She never saw someone dressed in such finery before: a double-breasted waistcoat, dark-blue trousers, coat, and a top hat—all of them made of high-quality fabrics.

"Now, dear, do you have any family here or in Ireland?" he asked, leaning over her.

"Sir, I don't," Victoria said, looking down at the ground. "None here and none in Ireland. My parents died during the trip, and I have no interest in returning to Ireland."

This seemed to please Mr. Pearl very much. He proceeded to ask her if she would like to work as a companion for his nine-year-old daughter, Flora. She would be paid, have her own room, and would participate in lessons with Flora. She would be Flora's friend and ally. Even though she didn't understand half the words that Mr. Pearl had said, Victoria instantly liked him and readily agreed. After speaking with Mr. Samuel, Victoria followed Mr. Pearl out the door and into a waiting cab.

Flora

June 1867: What Am I to Do?

FLORA COULD NOT STOP REPEATING the same phrase over and over again in her mind—*what am I to do? What am I to do?* The fear of having so much responsibility over her father's assets outweighed the sorrow that she felt over his death.

Anxious, she wanted to grasp onto something familiar and safe. Flora's gaze moved from the top of the vanity to the top drawer where she had a secret childhood necklace hidden. It wasn't clear why she felt compelled to reach inside to find and hold it, but she couldn't. Not right at that moment, with Victoria hovering around. The beaded necklace was only taken out in private. Late at night, when there was ample time to hold and examine it, Flora would try to remember the significance of the object.

Flora was told that her mother died during childbirth, but this didn't make sense. If that were true, then why could she picture her mother holding the necklace? The curve of her mother's face, the dark eyes, and the long black hair were vivid. Whenever Flora spoke about these memories, her father would casually wave it off as a childish desire for a long-deceased mother.

Finally, she gave up and decided to think about both her father's assets and the necklace later. She looked up at Victoria through the mirror and wondered where the girl's mind was. She was obviously absorbed in her own thoughts while mechanically brushing. Maybe she was thinking about the store. *Yes, that's what I'll think about: the impending opening of my boutique, The Pearl.*

"Victoria?"

"Yes, Flora."

"Can you put my hair up? And what were you thinking about? You seemed so far away."

"I was thinking about the first time we met."

"Oh," Flora said.

"I was thinking about how your father picked me up from Castle Garden and got me something to eat. Fried oysters and boiled potatoes. I thought it was so generous. Then, when I saw your house, I thought there was some mistake. Your bedroom was so ornate with all your paintings and beautiful bedspreads." Victoria motioned to the walls, which were covered with oil paintings of farms, sheep, and cows grazing in fields.

"Do you remember what you said to me when we first met?"

Flora examined Victoria's face and saw that she looked concerned. "No, I don't remember."

"You said that you would take care of me like I was your sister."

"Now why are you thinking about that? I said that ten years ago, and you remember?" Flora never understood why Victoria was so reminiscent.

"Yes, I do. Tell me—is that still true?"

Annoyed, Flora decided to ignore the question. She took a fleeting look at herself in the mirror but pulled away after just a moment. She could never look at herself in the mirror for long periods of time, as she saw Victoria or Annette, their cook, do whenever they had the chance. To think that Annette would peer in the mirror for extended periods of time made Flora shake her head in wonderment.

Victoria opened a small vanity drawer in order to retrieve some hairpins and asked Flora, "Why don't we give these dressers away and purchase different ones? You don't even like them. Remember you said that the mirrors were too large?"

"Nonsense. We're keeping them," Flora replied, squirming a little in her seat. "I thought you liked yours."

"Yes. I do. But don't they remind you of your father's passing, since they were delivered and day before his death?"

"Please don't speak of that," Flora replied quickly and firmly.

"Speak of what? Your father's passing?"

Flora said nothing but gazed down at the brushes and combs that sat on top of the dresser. The vanities were a gift from Father. He told them months ago that he ordered a present for each of them, and derived great pleasure in making them wait. They had several small drawers as well as a large, round mirror. The deliverymen used crowbars to open the crates and carefully extracted the pieces, laying out each section on the walk in front of the house before hauling them up to their bedrooms to be assembled. But when Flora gazed upon each piece in the bright sunshine, she muttered very softly under her breath that the mirrors were too large.

Victoria obviously heard and commented that Flora looked frightened of the mirrors, but Flora quickly replied, "Nonsense; I'm not afraid of anything."

"I just think that . . . that these dressers seem like they have a bad omen about them, and they should be removed," said Victoria.

"That's absurd," Flora said, shaking her head in disapproval. "You obviously have had too much idle time around here, causing your thoughts to run wild. What we need to do is get back to our store. We haven't been there in days, and I'm afraid that we might not be ready to open next month," Flora said as she gazed towards the window and sighed.

"Could you pick out a dress for me?" she asked, looking at Victoria through the mirror.

"Well, I'd like to get back to the shop too. I miss Olivia and Mum."

Yes. We need to get back to see how Olivia's doing. Flora had been sending her lists of tasks to accomplish while Flora and Victoria were absent. *Thank goodness I hired Olivia. She is such a cleaver girl.*

As Flora gazed out the window, she thought back to the time she first met Olivia.

***

They had met Ms. Olivia Belka by happenstance when the store's sewing machines were being delivered in late fall the previous year. Olivia told Flora that she was walking by and was so overcome with awe over the machines that she struck up a conversation with Flora. Olivia had never encountered a woman that actually owned a sewing machine.

Olivia claimed that she was extremely familiar with the mechanism and boldly asked Flora what she was doing and if a seamstress was needed. Even though Flora had her reservations about Olivia's demeanor, she was in desperate need of a seamstress.

"Ms. Belka, how much do you earn currently?" Flora asked, sitting across from her at the round table, which stood in the corner of the empty store.

"Please, call me Olivia. I make on average seventy-five cents a week. However, I know of many tailors who make much more."

"Are you as talented as a tailor? They can turn out a good suit in no time, and generally speaking, men get paid more than women."

Surprisingly, Olivia didn't hesitate in her response and showed no anger at Flora's comment. Flora was impressed. *Maybe my first impression was incorrect.* Olivia claimed that she wasn't just a seamstress who did finishing work. She could design and create any type of clothing that was described to her.

"Have you ever worked for a tailor?"

"No," Olivia said quite firmly. "I work at Rivers and Sons doing piecework. I've never been asked, and don't think I would like the arrangements. Being in a tailor's apartment seems very uncomfortable to me. You see, many of them don't have storefronts. They do their work in their apartments. It's extremely uncomfortable working in such close quarters with the tailor as well as with the person doing the pressing, who is usually also a man."

"The seamstress and the pressman, who is stationed at a hot stove all day, practically live with the tailor's family. There aren't many moments when you're away from his or his wife's scrutiny and gaze. Then, there are some who are known to take liberties. I've heard the stories."

Flora couldn't keep herself from smiling at the brashness of Olivia's statements. Olivia would be perfect. The store would finally have the seamstress it so desperately needed.

"Olivia, could you sew something for me now? Do you have time?" Flora asked.

"Of course."

After Olivia set up one of the newly delivered machines, Flora handed her a pattern and some material. Olivia then set to work, and within a couple hours, she handed Flora a beautifully sewn hat with embellishments that weren't even part of the original pattern. It was a standard hat made into something special.

"Olivia, how did you learn how to sew like this?"

"My ma taught me how to sew, but I've always been able to figure out how to put things together. I didn't even know that it was a talent until my ma pointed it out. She said that it wasn't something that could be learned."

In order to assist Olivia, Flora also hired Olivia's mother, Melanie, who everyone called "Mum," and insisted that they live in one of the apartments above the shop. Their wages were renegotiated in order to cover their rent, and they immediately moved in.

Startled out of her reverie, Flora said, "Yes, Victoria, we should get back to a more normal routine. There's nothing productive about sitting in this house, mourning all day."

Victoria walked over to the wardrobe, picked out a dress, and brought it over to Flora, who quickly stepped into it and turned around so Victoria could button up the back.

After finishing the buttons, Victoria said, "I'm going to get my wrap from my room."

As Victoria made her way across the room to the adjoining door, Flora said, "I'd like you to never discuss my father's death. I'll think of him as being away on a long trip."

Victoria

June 1867: The Vanity

VICTORIA STOPPED IN HER TRACKS. She was shocked when she heard the words spoken so delicately but with such confidence—the confidence of a woman who wouldn't be argued with. Victoria turned around to see that Flora was rummaging in her wardrobe, looking for something.

Victoria understood that, regardless of what Flora said when they were nine, Victoria was the maid and Flora her employer. Victoria was smart enough to know that the arrangement could always change. Flora, on the other hand, was impervious to life's fragile circumstances.

You never saw Flora crying over a loss; she simply pretended it had never happened. Flora had strength and sensibility and was brutally honest. She could cut you to shreds with words that were spoken quite easily and smoothly. You'd walk away and only realize later how wounded you were from her harsh statements. If you were caught unawares, the undercurrent of her conversation would drag you down and drown you before you knew it.

"Flora, you shouldn't think that way. You . . . you must see him as dead. You should accept this, not hide from it." When Flora didn't respond, Victoria felt compelled to go on. "He wasn't even my father, and I seem more upset than you. How can you be so, so, *cold?*"

Flora found what she was looking for—a parasol. She slowly stood up with the parasol firmly in hand. When their eyes met, Victoria saw that Flora's ears were pink, and her eyebrows were furrowed. Victoria instinctively took a few steps backwards to place more distance between them, but Flora quickly crossed the room. Victoria thought of pushing Flora aside to reach the door but instead stumbled backwards and bumped right into Flora's vanity. She could feel the edge of the vanity cutting into her backside and heard the items on top of the vanity jostling about and falling over, but Flora didn't seem to take notice. Staring right into Victoria's eyes, Flora said softly, "Cold? I'm not cold. I refuse to believe for one moment that he's gone, and I suggest you do the same."

Victoria closed her eyes for a moment and prepared herself to be physically hurt, but thankfully, Flora turned around and walked back over to the wardrobe.

Victoria felt her neck and face become hot. It was important for Flora to face up to the reality of her loss. Flora was only a baby when she lost her mother, so of course she wouldn't remember that. Victoria searched her memory for one occurrence when Flora cried over losing a toy, a friend, a loved one, anything. No, nothing came to mind. She always had this ability to turn away and pretend nothing was wrong. Then, it occurred to Victoria: Flora had never really loved. Victoria turned around and saw the reflection of her red face in the large vanity mirror. She placed her hands on the vanity and fought the urge to push everything off the damn thing, turn it over on its side.

"Flora, everyone knows your father is dead! You didn't even shed a tear at his funeral! What will people think when you start pretending that he's on a trip?"

Flora turned around to face Victoria again and sighed. "You'll do as I wish," she said sweetly and elegantly. "I'd hate to see you work tables at one of those German beer gardens, although they're full of life, and a good salary may be made there. You may even find a husband and have several ill-behaved children. Wouldn't that be lovely?"

With that said, Flora returned her attention to the wardrobe, as if no harsh words were spoken.

Victoria knew the question didn't need an answer. It was one of those statements that mothers made to their mischievous children. A threat that everyone knew would never be carried out but was effective all the same. Flora obviously had complete confidence that Victoria would do as she wished.

"Flora, this isn't right!"

"I don't care to discuss this anymore. I'll simply not think of it at all; it just makes me. . . ." Flora paused for a moment and looked down at the floor. Softly, she said, "It makes me very angry, and I don't like to get angry."

Victoria saw in the mirror's reflection that Flora was out the bedroom door, going down the stairs, and calling out for Victoria to hurry along. Slowly, Victoria retrieved her wrap and met Flora at the bottom of the stairs.

Flora flung the door open and hailed a cab. Uncharacteristically, she opened the cab door and motioned for Victoria to climb in first. *Yes, this woman has complete control over me.*

As soon as they stepped through the doorway into the shop, Victoria could hear Olivia exclaim, "Flora, you're back!"

"Flora, child, how are you?" Mum said, rushing in from the back room. She reached out and hugged Flora as a mother would.

"I'm doing well," Flora said flatly. "Victoria and Annette have been doting over me for weeks now, but this morning, I felt that it was time to come back to work. My father worked as hard as I have during the past year in preparing for the opening of the store, and I don't want to disappoint him."

"Well, ladies," Flora said, "I will be in my office."

As she left for her office, both Olivia and Mum looked at Victoria.

"Victoria, how is Flora really doing?" asked Olivia.

"Flora doesn't want to speak about her father being dead. She's going to pretend that he's on a trip. I'm afraid for her. To what extent will she carry out this façade and for how long?"

"Oh, the poor dear," said Mum, shaking her head. "I know how she feels. It took me a while to accept my husband's death. I'm sure she'll be fine. Just give her some time."

Towards the end of the day, the group busied themselves, doing mundane tasks together at the round table that stood in the corner of the store. Flora started talking about current events from the newspaper. This was something of a tradition while they were all concentrating on their work. She liked to recount interesting stories and seemed to like to listen to the thoughts and opinions of the group. Olivia had to admit that she learned a great deal from these conversations, especially about how Victoria and Flora's perceptions about the city differed from hers and Ma's. Right now, it was the perfect diversion.

"I read in the newspaper today that the city may be building a bridge across the East River from Manhattan to Brooklyn. How could a bridge possibly be built over that river, with its swift current? How deep is the river? Has a bridge so long ever been built? Listen to this quote, ladies," Flora said as she pulled a clipping from her pocket. " 'Let this bridge be accomplished; then this whole section of country would be beautiful and improved, almost by magic.' "

"A bridge—how magnificent. Have you ever been to Brooklyn on the ferry? It's a very quick trip in good weather but not so much when the river is clogged with ice. Remember when people got stuck on the ice!" Ma exclaimed, her eyes as bright as a child's.

"The magic would be in actually building the bridge," Olivia said. "It's taken the city years to build the county courthouse on Chambers Street. It's just a simple three-story building, for goodness' sake."

"I believe the politicians and their friends are excited over the fact that property values in Brooklyn will surely rise if this bridge is built," chimed in Flora.

Victoria added, "It would certainly employ many people. I wonder where it will be built."

"Probably up near the Greenpoint ferry. It will be interesting to see how boats will continue to traverse up and down the river with a bridge in the way," Flora said.

After a long and productive day, Flora and Victoria took a cab home, where Annette had laid out a wonderful dinner. After they finished their meals, Victoria was finally able to relax in the privacy of her own room. There, she lay in bed and thought about how much she missed Mr. Pearl.

The boutique had originally been his idea. Mr. Pearl assessed their skills and determined long ago that both she and Flora had an aptitude for style. In addition, he told Flora and Victoria that he wanted them to be independent and that they needed to have a business to rely on for income instead of relying upon husbands.

He had thought Flora would have a thirst for real estate, as he did, but she didn't. Therefore, Mr. Pearl sold all of his tenements so Flora wouldn't have to manage *"those types"* of establishments. The five-story apartment building was purchased because the clientele uptown would be much easier to manage than those in Five Points.

Victoria had heard from other maids that Mr. Pearl and Mr. Foley, his property manager, were ruthless lords of their slums, which made Victoria uneasy. She never saw this side of her benefactor but didn't discount anything that she heard. When he sold the tenements, it made her wonder if he sensed that his life was nearing its end.

She remembered staying up late at night in front of the fireplace, drinking nightcaps with Flora and her father. Mr. Pearl had interesting thoughts on women in the city.

He said, "Income means power and independence, ladies. Please, don't forget that. Consider the women who have lost their husbands through death or abandonment, like your seamstress, Mrs. Belka. She had mistakenly believed that having a good man to depend on and having babies was a godsend; however, she was immediately impoverished once her husband died. And women are held to a different standard than their male counterparts. Just think: a woman is found the guilty party if a man has forced his way upon her."

Mr. Pearl always spoke with a brash quality that some found unpalatable. He had admitted on occasion that this was a weakness and very un-English. He sometimes pondered if he had some Irish blood in him, which made the girls laugh, especially if he attempted to speak in an Irish brogue.

"I . . . ," Mr. Pearl said with a sigh. "I've everything in order now so you girls will be financially secure upon my death. You needn't find and rely on a husband in order to survive."

They had to agree with their father's assessment about marriage. Flora, of course, was adverse to the idea of being reliant on someone else or of asking permission to do anything. Flora was always so confident, even when she was lying to herself and to others. Victoria could never be so assured. With Mr. Pearl gone, Victoria worried that Flora would decide to send Victoria away. She always felt that Flora was a little jealous of her father's attention being bestowed upon both of them instead of on her alone. But Flora seemed to never be troubled or worried. Perhaps nothing had ever given her reason to doubt her success or her security in life. Even the death of her father left her confidence unaffected.

Victoria, on the other hand, always had the feeling that she had no control over her destiny, like one of the commuters trapped on the East River's floating ice—and praying to reach land on either side.

Aria
(Earth names, Anna and Olivia)

The Soul World: The Intervention

ARIA WAS WORRIED. She saw from her projection room that Victoria had neglected her task of overturning the vanity. Instead, she accepted Flora's inability to face up to her father's death, causing Flora's life to take on a different direction.

Since Aria was given some teacher-level powers, she was able to not only replay any Earthly occurrence, but to manipulate events and view their effect on any human life.

Aria played the scene back several times and then re-played the same scene as if Victoria had accomplished her task of breaking the vanity mirror. Then she played out the entire soul group's lives with and without the mistake. After reviewing all angles, directions, current and potential future mistakes, Aria came up with a plan. An intervention.

She conferred with Teacher, who told Aria that interventions needed the Council's permission. Aria didn't know that and wasn't too happy about having to tell the Council about—what she considered to be—her mistake. In addition, she knew that the Council would have to be persuaded to agree. Teacher had said that the Council preferred not to interfere with a soul's choice, and it was going to be difficult to convince them that an intervention was necessary. However, Aria had to try, so she arranged the meeting.

"Why, Aria?" Councilor Creek asked.

"Council, I believe that this missed sign is jeopardizing the entire group's progress."

"Oh, I see," Councilor Aer said. "Do you think it was wise to hinge the entire group's success on one clue? Did you plan for a backup?"

Aria was devastated. She bobbed around within her own energy for a few seconds but then realized that she had to stop thinking of herself. It was a mistake to think that Victoria could successfully perform this task after being controlled by Flora during their entire childhood.

"I now realize that my plan has faults. However, I believe that this intervention could help."

"You've requested this illness and follow-up dream very late in Flora's life," Councilor Pedor said. "It occurs right before her husband's crisis. Will there be enough time for Flora to adjust? You're also assuming that her husband will be able to adjust in a short period of time."

"I don't know," Aria said. "But is it possible to try?"

After a few moments, the Council members all nodded in agreement. "Your request is granted, as long as Mela agrees."

Aria gave thanks to the Council and set out to find Mela, who needed to agree to be present in Flora's dream. Mela had been Flora's father, Mr. Pearl.

As she traveled, Aria thought about the dynamics between Mr. Pearl, Victoria, and Flora. Their incarnation together in Manhattan was based upon their previous incarnation together, which took place in Provincetown, Massachusetts. Mela was their father in both incarnations.

Aria's personal notes on the Bristol family (Andrew, Isabella, and Jillian) during their life in Massachusetts:

Andrew Bristol was ill, critically ill. He was also a failure as a father. He never paid attention to his children because he had been so busy working for the largest shipbuilder in Boston. In fact, his only interaction with his children was at the dinner table or accompanying them on rare shopping outings. The rearing of his children was essentially left to a paid staff of nannies, housekeepers, cooks, and tutors.

Andrew had never really wanted to get married and have children. His mother had insisted that he have a wife, and she arranged his marriage.

His wife had one child and then passed away shortly after having the second. But he wasn't affected. He considered his wife's death only a blip in the timeline of his life, and his children only an obligation.

All of his interests revolved around the ships and the money they made him. This was his only love. His family was just there to fill small spaces of time in the evening. For him, they only functioned to prove his own self-worth and to assure his social standing in the community.

With the newly acquired knowledge of his illness, everything seemed so meaningless. There were problems to solve, customers to meet, and suppliers with whom to negotiate. But something was now amiss. He wanted to confide in someone about his malady but found that there was no one—none of the people at his office would care, just as he never cared for anyone.

While drinking whiskey in front of the fireplace in his home later that night, he had the stark realization that he was totally alone. Looking down at the drink in his glass, he pondered what he'd been doing all those years. He was now unsure of his ultimate goal in life and didn't know what to do next. He was part of an effort to force many smaller shipbuilders out of business. But suddenly, he couldn't look back on this with pride nor could he think of an instance where he was kind to anyone.

He never cared when anyone got killed, hurt, or maimed while working for him. The ruthless manner in which he treated the company's workers pleased him. But now he wasn't happy with any of his actions. To ask for anyone's sympathy now would be ludicrous.

Andrew simply wanted to escape, so he quickly arranged for a house to be built in Provincetown, Massachusetts, and moved his daughters there. It was their summer home, he told them. Then he went back to Boston and had the contents packed up. He arranged his financial affairs and resigned without any explanation.

When settled in his new home, he found that, to his dismay, his eldest daughter, Isabella, was as controlling and selfish as he was. But he realized this too late and was too ill to do anything about it. She hated Provincetown and longed to return to Boston. Jillian, his younger daughter, was a sweet child who loved the town and had no interest in ever returning to Boston. She enjoyed the quiet atmosphere and often walked along the docks and the bay.

When Isabella was eighteen years old, he died. His will had stipulated that both daughters would inherit his assets at age eighteen, but since Jillian was still a minor, Isabella gained control of everything and arranged it so she would keep control. When Jillian turned eighteen, she received some of what was entitled to her, but not everything. Instead, Isabella gave her a per diem amount, holding her inheritance hostage.

Aria had also carefully read the Council notes as well as Mela's summary notes while planning her soul group's lives in Manhattan. Mela claimed no responsibility in his daughters' volatile relationship. It was a problem between them and had nothing to do with his parenting skills. However, the Council made its recommendation to Teacher: he should be their father again. He would need a spouse that would die young in his next life, leaving him to, once again, raise his daughters by himself.

Since Aria was responsible for their lives in New York, she decided to be that wife. It was convenient for everyone and gave Aria a chance to try to curb Mela's greedy ways. She could be Mela's wife during his earthbound life as Mr. Pearl. After dying, she would immediately reincarnate to join the entire group again.

Aria recalled reading Mela's Council review notes about his life as Andrew Bristol. The Council actually postponed the review until after his daughters, Isabella and Jillian, had passed away. They obviously wanted to see the full effect of Andrew's parenting skills before meeting with him.

Mela's notes on his Council review as Andrew Bristol (Father of Isabella and Jillian):

The Council review was difficult but productive. I've written down some details of our conversations for future reference and reflection:

"Why do I have to be their father again?" I asked the Council.

"Do you think you could have done a better job?" Councilor Creek asked.

"A better job? I gave them everything they could possibly want. They didn't have to worry about their financial health upon my death. They should have been grateful to me."

"Do you think they were grateful for the money?" Councilor Pedor asked.

"Of course!"

"Then why was there so much hatred between the two?" Councilor Aer prodded.

I was silent since I didn't know how to answer this question.

"Do you think that your strategy of simply leaving them money worked?" Councilor Ustrina asked.

"No, but it's not my fault."

"How did you feel about your wealth?" Councilor Pedor asked.

"How did I feel about it? I didn't feel anything about it. I just needed it, craved it."

The Council kept prodding me about this until Councilor Aer asked, "Do you think the money actually caused Jillian's death?"

"Of course not," I replied.

"Let's not pursue this topic any further," Councilor Creek said. "It's not the right time. But I would like you to think about how you could have better prepared your children for a life without you. You need to review your life in Boston and specifically study what alternative paths your daughter's lives would have taken if you had a more active role in their upbringing. Once you learn what the optimal path would've been, meditate deeply about what characteristics you needed to take that path. This will benefit you during your next life."

"Yes, Council. I will."

Mela's notes after his life in New York as Mr. Edward Pearl (Father of Flora and Victoria):

I've looked back at both lives. Raising my daughters without a wife seemed daunting at times. However, I was wealthy in both lives. In my life in Cape Cod, I simply left my wealth to Jillian and Isabella and didn't think twice about it. In my New York life, I put a little more thought into what would be best for Flora and Victoria so that the extra work I spent studying and meditating before being sent back to Earth caused improvement.

Aria was instrumental in assisting me with these plans, and I'm grateful to her that everything came together as planned. The Council said that I don't have to be their parent again, which is extremely satisfying. This will allow me to move on to other aspects of my character that need work.

The East River Bridge

Opposing Forces

ROEBLING DESIGNED HIS BRIDGE to be the greatest architectural accomplishment on the continent. The bridge's two towers would be landmarks in Manhattan for decades to come; they would be instantly recognizable symbols of the greatest city in the world.

The granite towers, strong enough to bear the weight of four huge steel cables, would be 268 feet high and 1600 feet apart with twin Gothic arches in each tower. Each arch would allow a roadway to pass through it and would be high enough so that river traffic could pass unimpeded below. The bridge was built in such a way that even if the cables were to fail, the main span wouldn't collapse.

Roebling considered the quest: ordinary people being able to bring goods into the city from Brooklyn, as well as the desire of city people to make the crossing on foot in pursuit of fresh air and exercise. What did it matter what the bridge was named—the Great Bridge, East River Bridge, Brooklyn, New York, Empire, or even the Roebling Bridge. It would be magnificent.

To describe it simply, Roebling said that the enormous structure was to be "a grand harmony of opposing forces."

Nathan

September 1867: The Graduate

NATHAN COULD OVERHEAR A COUPLE OF locals, who were sitting at a table next to the bar, drone on and on about the color combinations and the effects that rain and heat had on their precious little fall leaves. This conversation was typical during autumn, but the cynicism that Nathan had inherited from his life in the city prevented him from joining in the conversation. *If I hear one more "intellectual" conversation about leaf color or the weather, I might have to punch someone.* Instead of verbalizing his thoughts, he ordered another beer to take the edge off his critical tongue. He knew that he should be appreciating the beauty of the oak trees around town and should take advantage of the fresh breezes that had rarely wafted over his hometown, Manhattan. However, even after more than four years of being in Troy, New York, and studying engineering at Rensselaer, he still couldn't appreciate the natural splendors around him. In fact, the wide-open spaces made him uncomfortable.

The sky in Troy seemed too large, and he frequently heard the sounds of the owls and coyotes. Nathan was told that bears also made their homes in the area, but, thankfully, he had never run into one.

Even as he sat, waiting for his train to Manhattan, festering in the dark pub, and clutching less-than-robust ale, a small smile ran across his face and caused his dark eyes to squint. The one thing he did appreciate, secretly, was walking along the Hudson River, especially in the fall. The river was his respite. Here in Troy, the Erie Canal, Champlain Canal, and the Hudson River met, making an easy route to Manhattan from any city around the Great Lakes or from Lake Champlain. He had walked along the Hudson in New York City hundreds of times without ever realizing how important the river was to the growth of Manhattan.

Even while in Troy, he didn't realize the significance of the locks as an engineering marvel until he actually walked down to see them during his freshman year. Sitting on the riverbank not far from the locks, he watched the barges float past him. Perhaps he should flag one down and jump on—abandon his studies and disappear for good. He could ride the barge up to Vermont and find work at some small pub.

Nathan shook his head, his dark hair falling over his brow, almost blocking his view. *That would never work. How would I find a job? I don't know anyone there.* All of his plans for escape abruptly ended when he applied logic to the situation.

Logic seemed to be his curse but was his best asset. However, the students around him had many more assets that he lacked. He could sense their disdain. Unlike his fellow classmates, he was raised in an environment that had honed his instincts. Growing up in the streets of Five Points, the worse slum in Manhattan, taught you how to read people's motives and assess someone's character pretty quickly.

The other students couldn't hide their dislike for him behind their fake smiles and counterfeit offers; they humored him and had no respect for him. He wasn't the well-rounded student that only a wealthy family could produce. Even during a seemingly innocuous conversation, his classmates seemed able to insert some comment that made their inherited status in life clear.

I can't wait to get home to be with my real friends.

"Da ya want another ale?" asked the barkeep, bringing Nathan's thoughts back to the present. He contemplated ordering another and drinking it down quickly, but then decided against it.

"No, thanks. My train will be leaving soon," Nathan replied as he put on his overcoat.

At the train station, he looked down the track. *Most people would feel happy graduating from college.* Yet, he only felt powerless—always having to do what his father, Kyle, expected. *I would've been happy working in Kyle's Pub for the rest of my life.* He felt he owed it to his father to go to school and "be successful," whatever that meant. But Nathan knew from the start that it was a trap, a trap that had completely ensnared him. Now he had to figure out how to escape Kyle's illusion that he would actually be an engineer.

Why Kyle had so much faith in him—he didn't know. He wasn't even Kyle's real son. Kyle saved him from a life on the streets as a homeless orphan. He found Nathan in an alley near Gotham Court being bitten up by rats.

Nathan didn't recall passing out in the alley but did remember stealing ale with his friends, which, he chuckled, was usually easier to steal than food. After drinking too much, his friends probably staggered home to sleep, but he, on the other hand, must have curled up in a pile of garbage and passed out. When he awoke, a plump Irish woman with red, frizzy hair hovered over him with sweetened tea and demanded that he drink it immediately, before he "caught his death." Even though Nathan had no idea where he was or why he was there, it seemed a lot better than an alley, the police homeless shelter, or the nickel boardinghouse.

"What's your name, dear?" the woman asked.

"Nathan," he replied suspiciously.

"My name is Erin, Erin Laury, and Kyle is my husband. He found you in the alley and brought you here, to our home."

Erin sat down on the edge of the bed and looked intensely at Nathan while he was drinking the tea. Her bright-green eyes closely inspected his dark hair and the faint freckles on his cheeks. Finally, she asked, "Where are your parents?"

"I don't have any."

"Why? What happened?" she cried, suddenly alarmed.

"I don't know," Nathan said with a shrug.

Erin looked down at her faded dress for a moment and then asked, "But where do you live now? Do you live with relatives?"

"No. I mostly live on the streets or in abandoned buildings."

"That's horrible. What do you do for food?" the plump woman asked, shaking her head.

"Well, I mostly steal my food or beg for handouts," Nathan replied while wiping his nose on his sleeve.

"My son died of cholera last year," Erin said with a heavy sigh. "He was only four."

Erin slowly rose from the side of the bed, looked outside the window as if something interesting was happening out there, and straightened the curtains. Then he saw her wipe her eyes and slowly shake her head.

"Would you like some oysters?" she asked, abruptly turning away from the window.

"How much are they?"

Erin just smiled, walked over to the bed, arranged the blankets, and told him to finish his tea before it got cold. She would be back soon with something to eat. Even though she was smiling as she closed the door, Nathan felt very uncomfortable.

"Where am I?" he whispered.

He got out of bed and leaned over to look out the window, careful not to disturb the curtains that were fussed over a few moments ago. All he could see was the brick wall of the building next door and could only tell that he was on the second floor. When he turned around to get back into bed, he saw that the room was sparsely furnished with just a bed, a trunk, and a chest of drawers. But the bed was soft, and the bedding smelled so clean that Nathan felt he was spoiling them just by lying in them.

A few minutes later, Erin brought the plate of food, as promised—oysters and boiled potatoes. They were the best oysters he ever had, but anything was better than what he had to scrape together on a daily basis. After she took the empty plates downstairs, she returned with a piece of apple pie. He looked down at it tentatively. It seemed so extravagant that he felt that it was a mistake to be given such a dish.

"Well, go ahead. Eat it. Or are you too full?"

With that, Nathan dug in and enjoyed every bite. He never tasted an apple pie before, although he had seen them many times. He just was never able to get his hands on a piece; it was soft and sweet, with a flaky but fleshy crust.

"What's that—that taste in the apples? I've never tasted anything like it."

"It's my secret ingredient," Erin said, smiling at him.

After his recovery from the night in the alley, Kyle convinced Nathan to stay with them. The next several years with Kyle and Erin went by quickly. The couple made it their sole duty to make sure that Nathan went to school, where he quickly outpaced the other students.

Even though Nathan was a good student, he still couldn't keep away from his friends at Five Points. He smuggled food to them whenever he could, and later, he spent a fair amount of the money he earned working at Kyle's Pub on ladies, drinks, and occasionally, opium.

Bee, his best friend, had warned Nathan time and again that taking the drug could drown him and that he had gotten involved in a lifelong addiction. But Nathan never heeded her warnings. He always believed he had control over the drug, but sometimes, it just got the better of him.

On three occasions, Kyle had to scoop him out of an opium den and sneak him back into his room. Bee was obviously telling Kyle where he was, even though she would never admit to it. There were also times when Nathan would come down to breakfast with a black eye or scrapes on his body. Erin wouldn't say anything, but Kyle would lead him outside and place an arm around his shoulder.

Kyle was taller than Nathan by a good six inches. Kyle was extremely trim, but his presence was commanding. His face was angular and rugged looking, and when he smiled, fine lines wrinkled across his forehead and around the corners of his eyes.

Standing outside, behind the pub, Kyle put his large, calloused hands into his pockets and looked down at the dirt.

"Nathan, who are these boys that you sneak out to hang around with?" Kyle asked, squinting his eyes at Nathan.

"They're just friends," Nathan replied with a shrug.

"Did your friends give ya those bruises, or did your friends cause them?"

Nathan looked into Kyle's blue eyes and then took a longer look down the road.

"Kyle, I belong down there. I have fun with those guys. They accept me for who I am."

"Nathan, m'boy, I understand ya better than you think. But, ya see, Son, I don't have to prove anything in this life. I've a wife that I love and a business that I started with the two hands ya see here."

Kyle held out his strong hands, palms up, and looked down at them.

Putting his hands back in his pockets, he said, "You have to think about what ya need to prove to yourself. Acceptance from the boys down at the Points doesn't mean too much when that acceptance comes from you being just like them. How do ya see yourself? Do ya see a confident and independent young man, or are you satisfied just being part of that group of boys?"

"Well, I really don't feel like I'm part of their group."

Kyle didn't say anything but seemed to wait for Nathan to proceed. When Nathan didn't say anything more, Kyle said, "Then why do ya continue to be with them? If you're saying that ya don't feel any loyalty to them, I'm glad but am confused about why ya still go down there and participate in their nonsense."

"I don't know. Maybe it's just like I said—that it's enough that they accept me."

"How do you present yourself when you're with them?"

"What do you mean—'present?' Do you mean represent?"

"Well, I mean you change your clothes, ya change your demeanor. Do ya tell them that you're going to college?"

Nathan slowly shook his head and looked back down at the ground.

"Then they have only accepted what you've presented to them. Now, boy, I'm not going to tell ya what to do, but I will say that those people that ya fraternize with down in the tenements don't care about you one lick. You know, they have nothing to lose in life."

"Nothing to lose?"

"That's correct. They can do whatever they want and not worry about losing anything."

"Well, I don't have anything either."

"I'm not talking about money, Son. I'm talking about your future. They have no future. They will be doing the same thing day after day. They will gradually get involved with the gangs and most likely end up dead. They have no interest and no chance of changing the course of their lives. You have the tools to build a future that will be different than your past."

"It's hard for me to imagine the life that you're talking about." Nathan ran his hands through his hair and stared up at Kyle.

"I know, boy. But it's there. It will take time, but just remember that you have to adapt."

"Adapt? What does that mean?" Nathan was always amazed by Kyle's English vocabulary.

"It means that other people have a different way of life. A different—well, let me see . . . a different way of handling situations. You have to be open to changing and accepting that different way of life."

"I don't think I can."

"You will, Son. I have faith."

When Nathan first arrived at Rensselaer College, he remembered that conversation with Kyle often. Most boys had a "circle of acquaintances," while he had none. While the majority of the students had money for decent accommodations, he rented a small room located in a basement. During classes, he would inevitably hear his fellow classmates brag about the distinguished careers they would have—always competing with each other. He noticed the snickers and sideways glances. The steady, heavy load of pressure was endured year after year. But he studied hard, kept out of trouble, and graduated. This was accomplished out of the respect he had for Kyle, the man who had faith in him. But he never adapted. He didn't know how.

He climbed off of the train in New York and immediately into a cab that would take him to the pub. *Now that I'm "educated," what will I do?* He had to escape from this situation. If he knew that it would come to this, he would've run away from the both of them long before.

The cab slowly made its way through the city and pulled up in front of Kyle's Pub. He paid the driver and bounded into the Irish eatery, slamming the door open with such force that everyone standing at the bar turned to see what had happened. All at once, everyone cheered and yelled for Erin, who had gone to the cellar. The place seemed exactly the same as the last time he was here, about a year earlier. This place was special to Nathan and to the neighborhood.

"Nathan!" Erin cried as she ascended the ladder from the cellar. Nathan helped her up and gave her a huge hug.

"You must be starving and thirsty! How was your trip, dear? I'm so proud of your finishing school, and Kyle is just beside himself with pride." All the while, as Erin rambled on, she was looking him over from head to toe. She led him to the bar and sat him down, poured him a beer, and got those oysters rolling around in breadcrumbs. Her hair was now a duller shade of red, perpetually frizzy from the heat of the stove. Erin looked a little plumper and maybe a little shorter, but not by much. As she spoke, her back was towards him, and her hands were busy cooking. She pushed stray hairs from her face and finally rested her hands on her hips as she looked over the status of everything on the stove.

Nathan looked towards the end of the bar to see if there was any pie available.

"Ya know, Nathan, some people come clear across town to get one of my pies," Erin said, with her back still towards him.

"You don't say? They must be pretty darn good. Do you have a slice for me? Uh, when I finish my supper, of course." Nathan smiled. She could always read his mind.

"Oh, you can have all the pie you want until the next time you get on my bad side!"

In minutes, Nathan was looking down at a plate of oysters, potatoes, a steamed quarter-cabbage, and a large, fluffy biscuit.

"Nathan, my boy!"

Nathan looked up and saw Kyle coming through the door with his arms open to bestow a hug. Nathan felt his eyes well up with tears at the sight of Kyle. He reached out and let Kyle envelope him in his large, strong arms.

"Kyle, how are you?"

Kyle released Nathan from the bear hug but kept a grip on Nathan's arms and looked down at him with watery eyes.

"Very good, very good, Son. I'm so proud of you. I know how difficult this was for you, but education is the only way out of these slums."

"But Kyle, you know how fond I am of the slums."

Kyle looked at Nathan with some seriousness in his eyes, but then they both started laughing.

"Oh, you know how to get my blood boiling, don't you, boy? Here—look, Son, I kept this article that I saw in the paper. The city is going to build a bridge to Brooklyn. It says here that it will start on Fulton Street in Brooklyn and end near city hall. I think it might pass right by us! Just think of all the hungry workers that will be in the area needing supper and beer."

When he spoke of hungry workers, Kyle stared at the pub's ceiling with a faraway look in his eyes. It was the same dreamy expression he had when he reminisced about his days as a firefighter—before New York had a professional, paid fire department. Kyle caught the bug during the great fire of 1835, which destroyed over five hundred buildings in the heart of New York's financial district. Kyle was very young when he witnessed the inferno, which could be seen as far as Philadelphia.

"Kyle, why is it that you don't go back to firefighting?"

"What made you think of that all of a sudden?" Kyle said.

"Well, my mind works in mysterious ways."

"Obviously. Well, you know, it just hasn't been the same since they started getting paid. And it just wasn't for me anymore."

Kyle rubbed his chin while he talked.

"They liked to fight a lot and started competing over who would get to a fire first. Then Erin begged me to stop shortly after we lost our little one. It was right after a fire that killed ten firemen, so I promised her that I would quit."

"I didn't know that."

"Well, a man doesn't like to admit how much power his wife can have over them," Kyle said with a big grin. He started to laugh, causing Nathan to join him. Kyle had such a unique combination of humility and strength. Nathan could almost picture Kyle's strong hands pumping water or holding the heavy hose as he emerged from a burning building.

"And, just between me and you," Kyle whispered—he turned around to see if anyone was standing close by before continuing, "I think she was a little jealous."

"Erin?"

"Yes. The ladies like the firemen."

"You know, Kyle, Erin always used to tell me that you could get any woman you wanted. She used to look over at you while you were tending the books in the corner of the pub. She would be wiping down the bar and would look over at you and sigh. I'd ask her what was wrong, and she'd confide in me."

Nathan paused.

"Well, what did she say?" Kyle looked like a young boy who wanted to know if the girl he loved liked him back.

"She would say, 'Look, Nathan, at how handsome he is. He could get any woman he wants. Why would he want me?'"

Kyle stood up tall and looked over at Erin, who tended the bar.

"She doesn't have a thing to worry about. That woman has a grip on my heart and soul like you wouldn't believe."

Just then, Erin looked up and returned his gaze, which shifted from neutral to smiling to questioning.

He looked at Nathan and said, "I hope to God that you'll find a woman that does the same for you. It's the best and *most maddening* thing in the world."

"Kyle, what are you two whispering about over there?"

Both Kyle and Nathan jumped to attention when they heard Erin's voice, and they started laughing.

"How does she do it?" Nathan laughed.

"I don't know. She can just look at me and know what I'm thinking. Now, getting back to you, Son, this bridge seems like something that will need many engineers. How long do you think it would take to build a bridge? I would think that something like this would keep a man employed for what—four or five years?"

Nathan looked down at his feet while Kyle was talking about engineering. He didn't feel as if he was really an engineer and didn't like the idea of real, highly pressured, having-to-follow-directions type of working. *What a horrible person I am. But I didn't ask to be placed in this position. On the other hand, I never said that I didn't want to be in this position.* At that moment, Nathan felt like an ungrateful person.

"What do you think?" Kyle asked, excited.

"I think it's great. Does the article say anything about where to report for an interview?"

"Ah, no," Kyle said, looking down at the article again.

"Kyle, do you mind if I work at the pub for a couple months while I look for work?"

Kyle gave a long, hard look at Nathan, as if he was sizing him up for a fistfight, but his eyes were soft.

"Mind? I was going to suggest this myself!"

Nathan couldn't remember a time when Kyle looked as happy. He felt a guilty twinge in his gut again, but it did make him feel better that Kyle was happy to have him work here for a while. This would only be temporary. Eventually, Kyle's expectations would encroach upon him again. It was as if they were opposing forces standing back-to-back, each pressing on the other but going nowhere.

Later that night, Nathan snuck out of the house and walked down to Five Points. He could hear the sounds of the boats in the harbor, and for a fleeting moment, he planned to escape by slipping onto a boat bound for the East Indies. His hands toyed with the coins in his pockets, which he was about to spend on some fun.

A smile crept onto his face. *Me on a boat? I know nothing about boats! Instead, I'll purchase a horse and ride out west. Imagine camping on the plains, or wait, I don't even know how to handle a gun. There are Indians and animals out on the prairie. How would I defend myself? There must be some safer way to escape.*

Nathan's plans continued as he walked towards the most dangerous neighborhood in the country.

Aria

(Earth names, Anna and Olivia)

The Soul World: As Planned

ARIA WATCHED NATHAN GO INTO A BAR in the heart of Five Points, where he would meet with his old friends. He didn't have the ability to make his own decisions yet, but Aria was confident that everything in his life was currently in its proper place.

Kyle's statement about Erin having a "grip on his heart" would stick with Nathan for years to come. Aria knew that Nathan would often reflect upon the differences between both sets of his parents. The first set, his biological ones, enabled each other's unfavorable habits and the second set strengthened each other. He hadn't met Flora yet, but when he did, Aria hoped that he would think of Kyle's words about love often.

Aria also hoped that the residuals of Nathan and Flora's misunderstood relationship in Provincetown wouldn't carry through to their life together in New York.

She projected Nathan's last Council meeting as Soul Aiden. During that meeting, Aiden and the Council reviewed his previous life in Provincetown as Kelvin Massey. His wife was Jillian Bristol.

Aiden's Council notes from his life as Kelvin Massey:

During our life together in the 1700s, I was a sailor named Kelvin, Kelvin Massey. My wife's name was Jillian Bristol. Early in our marriage, my wife's face was disfigured from an accident. Her sister, Isabella, took care of her. During that time period, I became angry that I had married Jillian. I believed that I should be married to her sister, Isabella. This was stupid for me to even consider. What made me think that I had a chance with Isabella? Isabella must have sensed that I was still thinking about pursuing her. So Isabella confronted me when I came to see Jillian, who was lying ill at Isabella's home.

"Never think for one moment that you and I could even be friends," Isabella told me, standing in her parlor with her hands on her hips. Her blue dress floated around her. Her exposed chest was pink from anger.

"You're a beast. If I didn't make myself clear when you began to pursue me, I'll make it crystal clear to you now. I find you to be an ugly man and one full of anger. You're a sailor! The only reason Jillian married you is because I manipulated her into doing so. I love my sister but am tired of taking care of her all of the time. She was a mousy woman to begin with, so her face now," she said, waving her hand in the air, "should be of little consequence to you."

I stood with my hands in my pockets and felt completely disappointed.

"Do you think she has grown to love you?" she asked while walking around me. "Ha!" she said when she stood in front of me once again. "Little chance of that! How can this arrangement involve love when I gave her no choice but to marry you? So put any thoughts of me out of your head, as well as any thought that your own wife even loves you. But she's been an obedient wife, no?"

"Yes, Jillian is a good wife," I said, hanging my head. In fact, she was a wonderful, giving wife. However, I became angry upon learning how Jillian had supposedly manipulated me.

I thought back to that fateful afternoon when I had drunkenly pounded on Isabella Bristol's door, hoping that she would answer and not her skinny sister. But alas, the scraggly thing opened the door and invited me in. She poured me a glass of whiskey, sat down across the table, and stared at me with her big hazel eyes.

"Wat are you lookin at?"

"Do you think we could get married?" Jillian said.

"Wah? You an I get married? Why woul I do that for?"

"Because I have money," Jillian replied with ease.

"Ahh, ya do? Does ya sis have money?"

"Yes, but she's getting married, remember?"

"Ah, yes."

That set the wheels in motion for our marriage. It wasn't that I was a greedy person. It was just that a little more money would be nice to have, and I was imprudent enough to think that being married to Jillian would get me closer to her sister.

Suddenly, I shouted to Isabella, "But she asked me to marry her! Begged me! Why would she do that? How could you have, as you say, manipulated her into this marriage?"

"Because I know her weaknesses," Isabella hissed. "She needs to feel needed, and I told her I didn't want her around anymore. I told her that if she didn't get you to marry her, I would send her away. She loves this stupid, small town," Isabella said smugly, "You see, Kelvin, dear Brother-in-Law, I've complete control over her. Oh, and then I sweetened the pot by telling her that she would finally get her inheritance if she married you. So—I accomplished two things: getting her out of my house and getting you out of my hair. In two days, she will be well enough to move back in with you. You should be thanking me for taking care of her, and you weren't even at sea."

The Council members were pleased that my rendition of the story was accurate. Some souls fresh from Earth needed a little assistance remembering details of their lives.

"Tell us, Aiden. Why did you let Isabella take care of your wife?" Councilor Creek asked.

"I didn't care about Jillian. I felt no need to take care of her."

"What did Jillian think of this behavior?" Councilor Aer asked. "Was she angry when she returned home with you?"

"Angry? No. She acted as though she was at fault. She was ashamed about how she looked and made me take down the one mirror we had in the parlor."

"What changed your relationship? Why, if you didn't love her, were you so angry and heartbroken when she died?"

I had to think that over for a moment before responding, "In that life, I was born into a volatile family where my father beat my mother whenever he liked. It was a horrible, heartbreaking experience for me, and when I married, I could actually feel that urge to hit Jillian. It would've been easy, since she was so small and vulnerable. But I fought the urge, and she . . . she was so sweet and soft-spoken. She always thought of what I needed. Cooked what I liked. Never held any of my bad behavior against me."

"Did you ever raise a hand to her?" Councilor Pedor asked.

"No, never. I started to really love our time together. It seemed as though, from the first day of our marriage, she wanted, and almost needed, it to work. She put her whole heart into making me happy. And . . . and I. . . . Well, I had just started to realize and enjoy her love when she was taken. I would be on the ship, looking across the sea, and I would actually miss her. It wasn't as if I woke up one day and loved her, but when I found she had passed away, my heart totally broke. I came to the sudden realization that I took her love for granted. It was love that I had never earned, a love that I probably didn't even deserve at all."

"What happened when you came home to learn that she had died?" Councilor Gens prodded.

"It was too much to bear, but I reacted with anger rather than sorrow. I wanted to kill Isabella."

"Why?"

"Because if I'd never got mixed up with her, I wouldn't have been going through this incredible pain. But instead of killing Isabella, I turned to alcohol as an escape. I thought about retribution all the time. I sometimes followed Isabella, but I didn't have the courage."

"Courage? Is that really true?" Councilor Inbur inquired.

"No, that's not correct. I couldn't hurt anyone. I didn't have the heart to. Her love, my Jillian's love, had softened it. It had nothing to do with courage."

After reviewing the notes Aiden wrote after his Council meeting, Aria felt confident that Aiden was still on track as Nathan. Kyle and

Erin's love for each other had created a foundation, which Nathan could build upon with Flora—when the time was right.

She watched Nathan enjoy catching up with his friends and knew that his whole world was about to be changed. In fact, soon, she was going to meet with Nathan's parents, Kyle and Erin. They weren't part of Aria's soul group, and she wanted to thank them for their works.

Kyle and Erin incarnated together, sharing dozens of lives. They also had a long history of starting fires together. They didn't just start fires in one life, but did it again and again, life after life. Aria wasn't sure exactly when this obsession had started or why, but they had found it extremely difficult to break the behavior pattern. The last fire they started had killed many people, but, as usual, they didn't care. When they had both died and had come back to the Soul World, they were shown how this fire had adversely affected so many families.

For some reason that Aria didn't know, this one fire had finally caused them to make more of an effort to change. Their teacher suggested that they spend the next several lives enduring the same pain that they had caused; therefore, they worked as husband and wife, losing children and suffering much heartache together. Between each life, they assessed whether or not their capacity for compassion had increased. After many lives together, their relationship as husband and wife strengthened, and, in their most recent lives, they always chose to die together.

The East River Bridge

Man of Science

EVEN A MAN OF SCIENCE GETS HIS STRENGTH from his soul. When his body was old, Roebling still poured energy into his work with the same heightened passion as he had when he was twenty-five years old. The inhumanity of slavery tugged at his loving heart, which motivated his eldest son to join the Civil War. More, a man of science can be moved by nature's beauty and by philosophy, poetry, and music. Roebling's soul was deep and his philosophy of life, wide. He profoundly felt that he successfully communicated with his deceased wife and that he could "convince" his body not to fall to the ravages of a cholera epidemic in Niagara Falls.

But fate wouldn't be kind. Maybe it was predetermined that when he stood upon a cluster of wooden piles at the end of the Fulton Ferry dock, a ferryboat would hit the side of the slip and crush his foot. And even though the pain must have been excruciating, Roebling continued to work and deny his fate until, finally, he lost consciousness and collapsed.

Upon waking at his son's house on Hicks Street in Brooklyn, he consented to have his toes amputated without anesthesia. Being a devout believer in hydrotherapy, he poured water over his foot day and night; however, within a week, tetanus was detected. Twenty-four days after his accident, and several days of suffering with lockjaw, fevers, seizures, and terrible pain, John Roebling died.

The New York Bridge Company decided that Roebling's son, Washington Roebling, would be the only man that could take John Roebling's place on the bridge project. The elder Roebling made

Washington an expert on the engineering of the *caissons* that would be the foundation of the two bridge towers. Upon his father's orders, Washington and his wife, Emily, had traveled extensively through Europe, learning everything there was to know about *caissons* and the new material the cables would be made of—steel.

Elizabeth

July 1869: Reunion

ELIZABETH "BEE" SHANNON, WHO WAS hosting a party at her inn, journeyed from the heights of joy to the depths of sorrow within seconds of hearing of the deaths of Kyle and Erin. One of Nathan's old acquaintances seemed to derive immense pleasure in telling Bee the horrible news in great detail. She never understood why some people enjoyed spreading bad news.

The man's smiling face quickly turned to a frown when Bee sternly asked him to leave. Vince, Bee's guardian, appeared out of nowhere and fiercely glared down at the man, so he took it upon himself to find the door as quickly and as quietly as possible. She then asked Vince to politely tell anyone who asked about her to say she felt ill and had to leave the party.

Vince was her protector and the sentinel of her establishment, Bee's Inn. He had the ability to handle any situation, whether performing the most violent task or gently guiding an old man out to the street and assisting him into a cab. With Vince in charge, Bee hastily returned to her private apartment next door.

Her immediate reaction to Kyle and Erin's death took her a little by surprise. She had seen neither of them since Nathan left for college some years ago. She sighed. Those two were so close—it seemed just natural that they should die together.

Oh, Nathan! What would he do without them? She was so worried for him that she started to pace around her parlor. After straightening a few paintings that were tilted, and dusting off a few figurines that sat on the end tables, she sat down on the sofa. For her, cleaning was a

Elizabeth

by-product of deep thinking and nervousness. What a horrible coincidence for them to die in a fire, just as Nathan's real parents did.

She had just lit the lamps when she heard a soft knock on the door. Reluctantly, she crossed the parlor into the foyer to answer the door, expecting that it was Vince. Instead, she saw Nathan. Immediately, she opened the door, and he stepped in without saying a word. Softly, Bee closed the door and brushed past him to lead him to her parlor. He quickly sat down and put his head in his hands.

She quietly poured him a generous glass of whiskey while staring at his crown. All that could be heard was her dress rustling as she walked. She placed his drink on the chair's end table and stood in front of Nathan until he finally looked up at her. Kneeling, she gently took his face into her hands and kissed it. He reached out, and they embraced.

"Bee, you're my only real friend. You know who I am."

Bee did know Nathan better than anyone. They had grown up together in Five Points. Bee lived in Gotham Court on Cherry Street, one of the most horrible tenement houses in New York. Nathan also lived in squalor until Kyle and Erin took him in. But he would still come back to the neighborhood to find her, and then the two of them would explore with zeal.

Most of the time, Bee ended up at the pub where Erin fed them. Erin taught her how to make her famous pies and fried oysters. Bee actually loved to cook and became friends with many of the regular patrons. She even pretended that she was part of the family. Erin was generous with her hugs, and Kyle had an infectious smile that would linger in her mind for hours.

Sweet Erin. She actually thought that one day Nathan and Bee would marry—spoke about how attractive their children would be.

Bee was a striking young lady of five feet six, with curly, auburn hair and green eyes. She had high cheekbones, smooth and unblemished skin, a slim waist, robust hips, and ample breasts.

Nathan was tall and lean, with deep dark eyes, black, wavy hair, and a slightly crooked—but handsome—nose. He was sensitive and easy to talk to. Not easily shaken into fits of temper, like so many other boys Bee knew. Nathan had a cool confidence. But, as she learned, if you did shake him, there would be hell to pay.

He showed his temper only once while fending off some boys. They were pretty harmless but working their way up the ladder of juvenile delinquency.

One day, she and Nathan were walking down an alley. They encountered the boys standing firmly in their path. Bee remembered feeling the hair on the back of her neck stand on end, her senses warning her of the danger ahead.

"Let's turn around, Nathan," Bee whispered.

"No, they won't get me on the run."

They were standing toe-to-toe with the boys when one of them looked Bee up and down and said that after they beat up Nathan, one would hold her down and the other would have his way with her.

Snap. Bee saw that something in Nathan's facial expression immediately changed, and at the same time, he viciously attacked. The boy had been looking at Bee's face smugly when Nathan's unanticipated blow smashed into him so hard that it broke his nose, causing him to fall unconscious to the dirt. When the other boy, a little shocked, made a move towards Nathan, Nathan quickly grabbed the boy's coat with both hands, whipped him around, and threw him right into a wall, cracking the side of his skull.

Bee just stood. She couldn't believe what she saw. Nathan then walked over to the boy with the broken nose and stood there for a moment and looked down at him. He seemed to be thinking; then he aimed a swift kick to the boy's mouth.

Bee gasped at the sound of the boy's teeth cracking and suddenly felt faint. Nathan appeared at her side and led her away from the scene.

They never spoke about that altercation. Most boys would've loved to brag about how they beat someone up, but not Nathan. Bee suspected he felt bad about breaking the boy's teeth. Now it made sense that no one really bothered him. She was sure that he had a reputation for this sort of behavior. Nathan was a difficult person to understand. On the one hand, he liked being part of a group when sitting at a bar. But Nathan was truly a loner, and, though he seemed to fit in perfectly with his friends, he stood out as different. Nathan was a bundle of contradictions—it was the only way to describe him.

Then, that fateful day came. They were walking in silence down Market Street towards the East River when Nathan slowed his pace.

"Bee, I'm going away to school soon."

"I know."

"Come with me."

Bee stopped walking and looked up at Nathan's serious face. Going to college with Nathan would be unacceptable. She had other plans.

Those plans didn't involve Five Points or the Tenderloin, the places to go for men interested in the cheapest form of prostitution. But Bee had her sights on a more upscale position. It didn't take long before Miss Asa, owner of the Asa House, agreed to take her in. Asa was thrilled to find out that Bee was still a virgin, and she knew just the man that would be interested. Asa would be able to charge a very high price and get Bee's career off to a great start.

"No, Nathan, I won't go with you. What would people think? Or perhaps you'd want me to pose as your wife?"

"No, I guess that won't work out. Why don't you work at the pub?"

"I decided to join the Asa House."

That's when he became angry. He leaned over her as a father would to reprimand his daughter.

"Nathan, this is what I've chosen," Bee said, while looking straight into his dark eyes. "You can't change my choice, and it's already done. I do love you and Kyle and Erin, but this is what I want to do."

"Are you doing this because I'm leaving you? There's no need to be afraid. I'll always be your friend."

"Afraid? I've never been afraid of anything! You're the one who is fearful of facing life by yourself, afraid of having to make your own decisions. You're scared to leave this horrid cesspool where you don't have to live up to anyone's expectations."

"I don't understand."

"Every time you come back to the old neighborhood, you shake off responsibilities like you shake off your wool coat. You feel superior—no, no, that's not right. You feel comfortable here. How will you feel when you're in college? Will you find the trashiest neighborhood and secretly escape there every weekend? Who will fetch you out of the opium den when the pressure of life gets to you? Or will you face your own fears, your fear of failure, and pull yourself out of the gutter? Look at Kyle and Erin and how much they have given you. This is your opportunity to actually work for something."

"But what does that have to do with you? Bee, please reconsider working at the pub. You're a great cook, and everyone loves you there! There's no reason for you to be a prostitute when there are others here to help."

Bee quickly dismissed the thought of working at the pub. She couldn't possibly make enough money working there to leave the slums. It would barely sustain her.

"Are you too good to work an honest job like—like your mother! The person that thinks they're too good to work, too smart to take advice, and too stubborn to ask for help!"

With that, Bee became furious. How dare he say something like that! Her whole body became rigid when she spit out her response, "I've already made my choice." She spun around and walked away, never to see him again until this very night.

Nathan

July 1869: Nathan's Loss

NATHAN PULLED AWAY AND HELPED BEE onto the small sofa next to his chair. He picked up the glass, took a good pull of whiskey, and stared into the cold fireplace. Nathan played with his glass, observing the way the light hit the crystal at different angles. He moved his intense gaze from his drink to the window and, finally, to Bee's eyes. Quietly, he started talking.

"Bee, you were right."

"Right about what, Nathan?"

"Being around my friends at the Points was comfortable. But always being surrounded by smart, gifted people was pretty damn humbling."

Nathan took a sip from his drink.

"I kept thinking about how to escape. I knew where every pub was within walking distance. But I had to work twice as hard as everyone else, so entire weekends were spent just studying."

Nathan looked up into Bee's eyes.

"Now that I'm home, the temptation to be with my old friends is hard to resist. Being with them is a great ego boost, and I fear that I've learned nothing from my college experience. I've been working at the pub, but a couple times a month, I go a little crazy and have to go out drinking. No opium, but the urge is still there."

Nathan's eyes welled up with tears. He took a handkerchief out of his pocket and buried his face in it. After a few moments, he wiped his eyes and took a gulp of his whiskey.

"I was down at Five Points, having a good time with my old friends. Near dawn, I started to walk home and was planning on quietly slipping into my room. But suddenly, the air became heavy. I realized that there were too many people around for that late hour, and then I started to realize that something bad had happened."

Nathan paused and took another sip from his drink.

"As I picked up my pace, I realized that there had been a fire, but it didn't even occur to me that the pub had caught fire. The closer I got, the more the feeling of dread and panic hit my heart. As I approached our street, I realized that there were no buildings on the block at all. It was totally burned out. Suddenly, patrons of the pub surrounded me, and with a combination of pity and amazement, they asked if I was OK. 'Where's Kyle and Erin?' I asked. But no matter how many times I asked, no one would answer. Finally, the fire chief approached me and confirmed my most horrible fears: they were dead."

Nathan stopped and took a gulp of whiskey from his glass. Tears welled up in his eyes again as he carefully placed his glass on the table and put his head in his hands, his fingers hidden within his dark hair.

"I'm alone again," he whispered. "I spent the last several months working in the pub and drinking at the Points, accomplishing nothing, lying to them about how I was pursuing a job at an engineering firm in Boston. What kind of person behaves like that?"

"Nathan, I'm so sorry."

Nathan lifted his head.

"And why a fire? It's so ironic that Kyle died in a fire, because he had been a fireman. I know he wasn't an active fireman, but once you're a fireman, you're one for life." Nathan looked down and shook his head.

"You know that Kyle made me promise just last week to use my education in order to better myself. He said that it would take time, but I would find my way. He really understood that I was having a hard time adjusting. That it was difficult for me in school and difficult to live on the straight and narrow. It seems as if I just heard what he said a few days ago. He was giving me time and space to let me come to my own decisions. He never once confronted me about how much money he spent educating me, never voiced any disapproval or, worse, disappointment. He mentioned that he saw ads in the newspaper that they were looking for engineers to work on the bridge. But I readily ignored him, pretending that I didn't hear. What a coward I am and what a patient, loving parent he has been to me. Or . . . had been to me."

"And Bee," Nathan said, looking up at her, "I'm sorry for how I acted those many years ago. I had no right to be so judgmental. God, I should be the last person to judge any person. I can go for days at a time justifying my bad behavior, but even now, as I speak, I'm afraid that I'll continue to slide into this same routine."

"Why are you so afraid?"

"I don't know."

"Are you afraid of being successful, afraid of telling the truth, afraid of taking a chance on yourself, or that others may think you aren't smart enough?"

"I. . . . When I look in the mirror, I see a . . . a fraud . . . someone who conned his way into the hearts of two decent people."

"That's not true! Do you mean to tell me that you cheated on all of your exams? That you didn't love Erin? That you had no respect for Kyle?"

"No, no. But . . . I don't feel genuine. I feel like . . . like a boy from the streets that put on nice clothes and found himself in Delmonico's and . . . and doesn't know which fork to use!"

Bee couldn't help but laugh, which made Nathan laugh through his tears. It was so wonderful to see Bee's bright, and yes, genuine smile—the smile of a true friend.

"What makes me think that you do know which fork to use?"

"I confess—I do. I had a professor that taught us etiquette and, worst of all, dancing."

"No!" Bee exclaimed.

"Yes. He used to say, 'What would your future employer think if he took his college-educated employee to a restaurant with important customers, only to find that you didn't know how to read a wine menu, use your napkin, or which utensil to use!'"

"Nathan, seriously, you'll be a great engineer if you only give it a chance. You simply lack confidence. You're a person who believes that there's only one outcome to each situation. Sometimes you force fit that outcome, but this kind of thinking will most likely be to your advantage when you're an engineer. However, when you make decisions that are based on emotion, you tend to leap to a decision, and you never waiver, no matter what the cost."

"When have I done that?"

"I bet you did it when you said your farewells to that bunch of guttersnipes before leaving for school. You told them that you would always be their friend, no matter what, didn't you?"

"Yes, but so what if I did?"

"Do you really want to keep that commitment? And if so, why?"

"Well, why not? I can still be their friend."

"I don't think that's a very good idea. Their influence is bad. They have no interest in your well-being."

"Of course they care."

"Did you tell them you went to engineering school?"

"No. I told them that I was working in Boston at a large beer hall."

"Why would you lie?"

"Because I didn't want them to know. They wouldn't understand."

"How do you think they would feel if you showed up dressed in a nice suit and you told them that you were a successful engineer?"

"I don't think they would care."

"Then why haven't you told them about your education?"

Nathan was silent.

"I'll tell you why. It would make them feel very uncomfortable about you. They wouldn't like it that someone they knew actually improved his life. It wouldn't make them happy at all. In fact, they want to see you fail and maybe even assist in causing you to fail."

"That's silly."

"The reality of your success would be too much for them. They would push you until you lost everything. They're not worried because they have nothing to lose."

Nathan's face suddenly turned pale, and he sat back in his chair.

"Nathan, what's wrong? Are you all right?"

"Yes, yes, I'm fine. It's just that Kyle said the same words a long time ago. He said that they had nothing to lose."

Nathan took another sip of his whiskey, deep in thought. Bee got up and topped off their drinks.

"Bee, should I try to get a job as an engineer on the bridge?"

"Of course. Why wouldn't you? But did you hear about the bridge engineer—what's his name?"

"Roebling?"

"Yes. He refused all medical care and decided he knew best how to cure his foot. I would say that's an emotional decision for a man of science."

"It's his belief."

"Is he a doctor?"

"No."

"Are all extremely smart people so stubborn? Do they all have confidence that they know everything and are smarter than everyone else?"

"Oh, yes. There were many of those types at the university. There were times when I just wanted to punch someone in the face to teach him a lesson in humility."

Nathan got up and made his way over to Bee's fireplace. He examined a row of several small world globes. Each globe had a simple base and was impaled on a piece of metal, acting as an axis, which allowed the globe to spin. One caught his fancy, and he picked it up and started spinning it on its axis.

"I'm afraid of the engineering job because I would only be doing it for Kyle. Everything I've done has been for him and I..." Nathan stopped midsentence but continued to spin the globe.

"You what?"

"I don't know what I expect of myself. I've no goals, no purpose."

Nathan continued spinning the globe, lost in thought.

"What are you thinking?"

"I was thinking about how angry I am at my parents."

"Kyle and Erin?"

"No, my real parents. I think they taught me to have low expectations for myself at a very young age. I was also thinking about how they died."

"I was worried about how you would feel about that."

"Well, one was accidental, and one was not."

"You don't know that for sure," Bee replied.

"Yes, I do."

"You're not thinking of retribution again, are you?"

Nathan said nothing.

"Nathan, I'm telling you that the fire that killed your real parents wasn't set on purpose. Why would Mr. Pearl do that? He owned the building."

"Because *he* was a greedy, self-righteous ass. *He* could collect insurance from the building and pocket it at our expense. When I dropped off our rent at Mr. McGuire's office, it was always right before *he* showed up. Remember how he used to saunter into the office as they lit their cigars and laughed at us?"

"They didn't laugh at us."

"Yes, they did. Then those two girls were always in tow. The little brats."

"What does that have to do with anything?"

"Nothing, except they benefited from his actions. That day, I swear I heard him say that the building was worth more if it was burned to the ground."

"Maybe you hang on to this scenario because it makes you feel better."

"Feel better?"

"Yes, to ease your guilt for not being there when it happened."

Nathan paused and looked at Bee.

"I. . . . I'm sorry, Nathan. I shouldn't have said that," Bee said.

"Yes, I've escaped death twice now by not being there."

Bee got up and took the globe from Nathan's hands and placed it back on the mantel.

"I wasn't there for either fire. Both times I was out drinking." Nathan turned to face Bee.

"So are you admitting that you feel guilty about that?"

"Yes."

"Do you know what I think?"

"What?"

"I think that the second fire is a message."

Nathan laughed. "An entire block has been wiped out and several people have died all in order for a message to be sent to me? Are you crazy?"

"Don't laugh at me, Nathan! Yes, this fire is a sign. It's a message."

"Well, tell me—what's the message?"

"I don't know. That's for you to figure out. Instead of asking yourself why this has happened as a way to feel sorry for yourself, start asking yourself why it happened at all. And why has it happened twice?"

Bee went over to the window and looked out. After a few moments of silence, she said, "He was a patron."

"Who?"

"You know, Mr. Pearl, the supposed arsonist."

"He was?" Nathan said, incredulously. "At the Asa House?"

"Yes. No, no, my inn. Not with me. I would never have agreed to have him. He used to be with Rachel."

"Rachel? Is she one of your girls?"

"Yes. But she's more than that. She's my friend. I've been very close to her since she showed up at my doorstep, practically starved to death."

Bee gazed upon the expression on Nathan's face and said, "I didn't force her into this life. Her father did by molesting her from an early age."

Nathan said nothing in response, so Bee continued. "She lives here with me, in my apartment, and is a wonderful person. But he, Mr. Pearl, was very rough with her. Rachel has a high tolerance for this. Many men like to be rough, but he went too far one night."

"What did you do about it?"

"I sent Vince out to inform him not to come back. Vince is my. . . . Well, he's my protector. I instructed him to tell Mr. Pearl that my house doesn't provide that kind of service and asked Vince to recommend another house."

"Recommend?"

"Oh, yes. He has never come back, so I think he took the advice."

"This Vince guy must be very persuasive."

"Yes." Elizabeth let her voice trail off.

"It seems as if you have more to say on the subject. What's on your mind?" Nathan asked.

"Well, there were rumors." Elizabeth paused.

"Yes. Come now—speak up," Nathan urged.

"I had been told on more than one occasion that Mr. Pearl owned the women on Bayberry Street."

"The Bayberry Street prostitutes!"

"Yes, the most wretched bunch of all in my profession. I believe that he was used to treating his women 'like that.' Vince told me it was true and suggested to Mr. Pearl that he use own women next time."

"That's astonishing. I had never heard about Mr. Pearl's association with the Bayberry women."

"Oh, Vince was quite sure of it."

"Does Vince stay with you also, in your apartment? Or is this his?"

"This is my apartment. Vince is my lover and a well-paid employee."

"It sounds complicated," Nathan said skeptically.

Bee sat back down and took a sip of her drink.

"What happened to your friend Rachel and what you just told me are just more reasons to hate the greedy bastard," said Nathan, shaking his head. "Bee, any ideas on where I can stay tonight?"

"You're going to stay here. We'll look for an apartment for you this week, and you'll look for a decent job. And Nathan?"

"Yes?"

"Don't spin my globes."

The East River Bridge

Purpose Driven

BOTH JOHN AND WASHINGTON ROEBLING were purpose-driven men with foresight. While John lay on his deathbed, he confidently assigned his son the task of taking over the East River Bridge project. Not that the senior Roebling had control over this decision, but letting his son know that his father had faith in his abilities would give Washington the confidence to accept the task.

Not that Colonel Washington A. Roebling himself lacked confidence. He had served beside the elder Roebling during the twelve months before his father's death. Before that, his father had sent him to Europe to study *caissons* and steel. John Roebling provided his son the best engineering education at Rensselaer Polytechnic Institute in Troy, New York. They had both worked together on the Pittsburgh-Allegheny Bridge and the bridge in Cincinnati. Washington had also designed and built bridges during the Civil War under extreme and dangerous conditions.

However, when Washington walked into a room, he didn't think himself better than others. He was unassuming and humble, unlike his father, who had some of the earmarks of genius: commanding presence, extreme formality, vision, and impatience. Yet what Washington did inherit from his father was that one-track, absolute conviction that he knew the answers to everything, without the need of counsel.

Olivia

August 1869: Olivia Wanders

IF THE WEATHER SEEMED AGREEABLE, Olivia would often wander about the city. She would get on an omnibus or a horsecar and hop off when something interested her. Many times, like today, she would make her way to Castle Garden. The building seemed to hold some kind of magnetic quality for her.

Olivia knew that it was more than just an attraction. She was looking for something more there, something that she might never find. Maybe she just wanted to relive the first few moments of her life in America—when she walked out of that building with her family intact, excited at the prospect of starting a new life together. Her father looked so proud, and Ma, trying to be brave, followed closely behind him, too timid to take her eyes off the back of his boots. As Olivia stood in the grass and looked up at the imposing structure, she knew that a great mass of immigrants would again be passing through those doors, just as they did every day.

Olivia remembered the many times she observed their faces; they had such hopeful looks, yet, by far, the vast majority seemed scared. The reunions she witnessed always made her feel positive and happy. If she was lucky, she could sometimes watch a family wandering aimlessly in front of the building, each member looking concerned. Olivia would follow them through the crowd, their dirty and tired children in tow, struggling to keep their belongings from being stolen. Then she would see them, meet whomever they were seeking. That transformation from apprehension to worry to high anxiety and, finally, to joy and tears was touching. Someone was there to meet them, to take care of them.

Olivia stood in the middle of the lawn in front of Castle Garden with her head down, thoughtfully kicking a stone. Some days, she just got plain tired of having to worry about Ma by herself. No, that wasn't right. It wasn't the responsibility of taking care of her mother; it was the loneliness. Even a brother or sister would be of comfort. When she finally turned to leave, she came to the decision that she would no longer visit Castle Garden. There was nothing to be gained here. She felt as if she was just dwelling in the past.

After one last glance, She hopped onto another omnibus and got off near the Alms House. The Alms, an old and rather large building, served the community of Five Points. When she entered the building, she knew that this was where she really belonged. The Alms was a place that anyone could visit. The building served many purposes: it allowed the homeless to stay the night, and it provided such basic services as reading classes and religious services. Many children in the neighborhood didn't attend school; their families were simply too busy trying to find work, food, and warmth. The homes that they lived in were usually single rooms shared by many, with only dirty straw to lie upon and vermin lurking in the shadows. Olivia assumed that she had lived in an environment beyond reproach during her stay near Five Points. But their small room was always clean; after all, it didn't take much effort to draw water into a bucket from the public spigot and bring it up the stairs.

However, her job wasn't to pass judgment on people's living conditions. Olivia had many opportunities to practice humility when making house calls with the ladies of the Alms House. In their calls to check on the ill or to deliver food and fresh water to the elderly, they needed to face many smells, scenes, and behaviors without showing their abhorrence. The sisters and the ladies had taught her to be immune to these scenes and to only concentrate on what she could do to help. It was difficult to refrain from yelping at the sight of a rodent—or worse, insects that crawled up a wall or across a table. It was disturbing to witness the leisurely way the tenants would flick a roach away with their fingers and gaze upon it as it hit the wall and fell to the floor. She learned to keep away from rails and doorjambs and lifted the hems of her dresses so they would be off the ground. Not that her clothing was fancy. Olivia liked to wear simple dresses, which were made from the finest material she could find.

She was a scavenger when it came to fabrics, and she searched the city for old fabric that no one else wanted. Her favorite fabric importer was Rene Marchand, who was always ready to negotiate a deal to get rid of fabrics that wouldn't sell. Under Olivia's care, these almost-discarded bits and pieces were used to make clothes for needy children.

The children at the Alms House ranged from those who only stayed the day or afternoon, usually for a meal, to those who lived there permanently. At least once a week, a child would ask if one of the ladies could check in on their parents. In the majority of cases, their mothers or fathers were simply drunk, but once in a while, they confirmed the worst for the child—their parent had expired.

Sometimes, the children were better off after their parents had died. It was a heartbreaking revelation, but Olivia had seen many orphans adopted by fine people. These selfless folks nurtured poor and broken children back to emotional stability. Sometimes, the ladies of the Alms House would intervene in family situations. For instance, a young girl about five or six years old was often left out in the cold while her mother prostituted herself in their room. Finally, the ladies confronted the mother and threatened to take the child away if she didn't stop. Olivia was there to witness the mother looking at the child as if she were baggage that needed to be disposed of.

"Take her away!" the woman said in a husky voice and slammed the door in their faces. Olivia was astonished. She reached down and picked up the little dark-haired girl and held her close.

"Don't you worry, darling; we won't abandon you," she whispered in the girl's ear.

That little girl, Lucia, was brought to the Alms House, as were hundreds of other children. Olivia saw her every week and witnessed the progress that was made in nursing her back to health, providing her some basic education, and placing hope back into her heart. Lucia was at the Alms House for only six weeks before she was adopted, and once she was, Olivia never saw the sweet girl again. Olivia sighed, thinking that Lucia was only the first in a long line of children that had made her way into her heart.

She walked down the hall to the childcare room, which was reserved for children who had come in from the streets just for the day. As she approached the room, she saw Sister Britta walking towards her.

"Olivia! I'm so glad you're here. There's a distraught woman here who only speaks Polish. Could you talk to her for me?"

"Of course," Olivia replied.

She followed Sister Britta to one of the private rooms, where a mother sat with her four-year-old child on her lap. The woman seemed older than what she probably was. She was very tall and slim and wore an old housecoat; her faded hair was tied in a skimpy bun. Her complexion was pale, and her eyes were dark and solemn. She was fussing over a tear in the child's blue calico dress with her delicate, thin fingers until she sensed that they were approaching. When Olivia looked into her eyes, she could feel the intense sadness reflected there.

After introducing herself and listening to the woman, Olivia said to the sister, "She says that her husband passed away about a year ago and that she has become very ill. She cannot stand for long periods, due to weakness. She has no family to care for the child, and she knows that she won't be able to work or to take care of the child anymore."

The woman interrupted Olivia to tell her more. Olivia was amazed that the woman could keep her composure. Her story was heartrending.

"She says that it would be better to give the child away now rather than later. She doesn't want to wait until the winter and is terrified that she might pass away in her sleep and leave the child alone. The child is young enough to make the transition easier. But she doesn't know how to do it. Do you just take her, right now?"

"Tell her," said Sister Britta, in a quiet, soothing voice, "that she can bring the child to us during the day. We can keep her occupied, playing with the other children and getting used to being away from her. After several days of this routine, the length of time spent here can be extended. Whenever she feels ready to leave the child, she can. And do tell her how we'll try to find parents for her child. Let her also know that we can help her in her time of need. You know what to say, Olivia dear."

Olivia communicated this to the woman, who quietly started to cry, her tears dripping onto her daughter's head. These situations were hard for Olivia to witness. She would always start to cry herself, in sympathy for the women's distress. This was no different. By the end of her translation, Olivia was crying and comforting the woman, assuring her that, since she was ill, she was doing the right thing. She was making sure that her daughter would be safe and cared for before it was too late.

Afterwards, Olivia went back to assist with supper, but she suddenly felt exhausted and couldn't stop thinking about the poor child. She wanted to take all of these children and bring them home with her, but she knew she couldn't take care of them. Flora wouldn't react well to a child running around the shop.

She'd been telling Flora about her trips to the Alms House in hopes that Flora would take an interest. She worried about Flora and her lack of exposure to people who had a different life than hers. Flora's life wasn't balanced on a thread, as were Olivia and Ma's. At any time, Flora could decide to close the shop or get new seamstresses. She had no idea how much Olivia and her Ma relied on her.

As Olivia wearily walked down the hall to leave the Alms, Sister Britta appeared out of nowhere.

"Olivia."

"Yes, Sister?" Olivia said, pausing at the door.

"I wanted to tell you how much I appreciate you being here. You have a gentle and patient disposition that's unique. Have you ever considered entering the sisterhood?"

Olivia was taken by surprise. She never thought about religion in a serious way. Her family was Roman Catholic, but her parents never practiced.

"I. . . . Well, I've never given it any consideration. But no, I don't think I've had that kind of calling." Olivia was almost embarrassed and felt her neck start to turn red. "I'm sorry, Sister, but I have no attraction towards any religion. Does that make you disappointed in me?"

Sister Britta didn't look upset, but Olivia knew that the sister never showed much emotion.

"No, I'm not, but I just felt compelled to ask. You see, I understand. I believe that you have an old soul, and old souls usually have no interest in or attraction to organized religion." Before Olivia could respond, Sister Britta abruptly turned away and left Olivia standing alone in the doorway, totally perplexed.

She could do nothing but think of the sister's words until she got home and found Ma making pierogi, Olivia's favorite dish. She could smell them before she even entered the apartment, and her stomach grumbled with pleasure.

"Mama, oh, how I love you!"

"Oh, yes, I know, my darling. You love me and my pierogis!"

"Only if they're stuffed with potatoes!"

Olivia walked over and gave her mother a great big hug. But Olivia wanted to be hugged a little longer than usual. She felt so safe in her mother's arms.

"What's wrong, Olivia?" Ma asked as Olivia finally pulled away.

"Oh, Ma, it was horrible today. I translated for a woman who needed to give her child up for adoption."

"You're such a sensitive person," Ma said, shaking her head and flipping over a pierogi. "I know how much this upsets you. I'm worried about you, Daughter. You go to that Alms House and have sympathy with everyone there until you've been worn down."

"I wanted to take the child myself," Olivia said softly, looking down at the floor.

"You know we can't care for a baby," she said, briefly looking sideways at Olivia. "We can't just leave a child alone in our apartment while we go to work, can we? In addition, you aren't married. They don't give children to single women."

"I know, Ma, but I still want to."

"Did she say where she was from?"

"Yes, but I didn't know the place, and now I can't remember what she said. Ma, I'm so glad that I was old enough to help you when Da died."

"Me too. I don't know what I would've done if you weren't. Well, I would've eventually packed up to go home. Ah, could you imagine having to go back to those sisters of mine?"

"Oh, no! My head is aching just thinking about it!" Olivia said.

Ma sighed. "It's such a shame that they were so nasty. If they were nicer, we would still be home."

Olivia reached over and put her hand on Ma's arm. "Do you want to go home, Ma?" Olivia said sincerely. "I don't want you living with regrets."

"No. I don't. I was only saying that they were the reasons that I left."

"Ma, Sister Britta told me today that I've an old soul. Do you know what she meant? Is it something from the Bible?"

She took the frying pan off of the flame, sat down, and sighed again. "I always knew that you had gold in your fingertips and a caring heart. There are some that can understand people and why they act the way they do. There are others that quietly and positively affect the lives of those around them. They know what to say and how to say it. They use the passage of time and take advantage of small, inconsequential moments to influence the behaviors of others. Others may see the empathy that you have as a weakness, but to observe this compassion and to see you take action upon it is like being a witness to pure strength of heart. This is the passion an old soul has; this is the passion that you have."

Olivia sat down at the table in silence as her ma finished frying the pierogi in butter. They didn't say another word until they had eaten every last one of them. The heavy dumplings sat in their stomachs as bricks as they climbed into bed, and even the next morning, they weren't hungry. Both of them laughed at how much they had eaten the night before but enjoyed the luxury of having done so.

"Mumsie?" Olivia asked while they tidied up their room and made coffee. "I had another strange dream last night."

"Tell me."

"I was sitting in a chair. There was nothing else around except for whiteness, like whitewashed walls. Out of nowhere, scaring me to death, a bolt of fabric was thrown . . . no, dropped . . . squarely at my feet, making a loud noise and waking me with a jolt out of a sound sleep!"

"Was there anything about the fabric that you remember?"

"Um, I think fabric had a pattern of small—small, red apples."

"Do you think you know who threw the fabric?"

"No," Olivia replied.

"You answered too quickly. I think you do know."

"You won't interpret it to my liking if I told you."

"That's silly; tell me."

"OK, OK. I think it was that Mr. Marchand, the fabric importer."

"Who?"

"Oh, you don't know him. He's that skinny Frenchman that I buy fabric from down at the piers."

"I see," Ma said. "When he threw the fabric, it made a loud noise, so it was done to shock you. So you wouldn't forget. A reminder of sorts. The apples are interesting."

"Why . . . what?" Olivia said impatiently.

"It represents being a teacher. And this Mr. Marchand—he has thrown something at you that's valuable to him. Yes, it's clear." Ma nodded.

"Well? How long will you keep me in suspense?"

"You're bound to marry him!" Ma proclaimed, with a serious look on her face.

"Ma! No! That's plain ridiculous!" Olivia yelled back.

Ma tried to conceal the huge grin she had on her face by sipping her coffee, but Olivia glared at her from across the table and wouldn't speak to her until she left for the store. "Ma, I'll meet you downstairs."

"Don't forget to bring down the coffee."

Olivia took the coffee pot and made her way down the stairs and into the back entrance, which Flora had already unlocked. She put the coffee down on the stove in the store's kitchen and got the fire going. Then she walked around to Flora's office.

"Good morning, Flora. Good morning, Victoria."

"Good morning, Olivia," they both said, practically in unison.

"I brought you down some of Ma's coffee. It's in the kitchen. Do you want some? I can bring it here for you."

"No, we'll come back."

Olivia already poured herself a new cup and brought it over to the small table in the corner of the store.

"Do you want an apple dumpling?" Victoria said with a box in her hands.

"Well, sure, even though I'm still full from Ma's pierogis last night."

"What's a pierogi?"

"You've never had one?"

"No," Victoria said.

"It's like a dumpling stuffed with potatoes or cabbage and fried in butter."

"It sounds delicious," Victoria said, sitting down next to Olivia.

Flora soon joined them and asked Olivia what she did on her day off. Olivia didn't tell the ladies about the orphaned child but did talk about the rest of her visit at the Alms House. She told Flora about how much was needed there, but Flora took no active interest. However, Olivia was a patient person. She worked for the long term and knew that sooner or later, she would get through to Flora. Victoria was much more empathetic. But Victoria needed Flora's approval before doing anything on her own.

Olivia didn't think Flora wielded this power over Victoria on purpose. Flora just didn't realize how oppressive this was to Victoria. But there was one time that Olivia saw Victoria stand up for herself.

One of Victoria's jobs was to find any sundry item that women would find interesting. She often went down to the piers with Flora to see new items that were being imported from different countries. Victoria had a good sense of what women needed and what they didn't even know they needed until it was on their shelves. Almost everything she picked was successful.

Olivia happened to be there when Victoria made one of her first purchases: a gross of small music boxes. Flora made it clear that they weren't sensible. They actually argued about them in the importer's warehouse. The argument caused the salesman, Mr. Rene Marchand, to lower the price. He was mainly an importer of fabrics, but once in a while, he had other items that he thought would sell.

"Victoria, these boxes will never sell," Flora said.

"I think they will. They're so adorable."

"What would you put into a box so small? It would only fit, maybe, a small necklace."

"What does it matter? They're so darling and look—when you open it, it plays music!" Victoria said, staring at the trinket in her hands.

"So?"

Mr. Marchand looked extremely nervous. He glanced over at Olivia, with whom he usually dealt with for fabric negotiations. When he realized that Olivia wasn't going to help, the small Frenchman simply stood by, wringing his hands and looking about the warehouse to see if anyone else was witnessing the exchange. Then he finally intervened. "Ladies, ladies, I give you good price, no?"

Flora and Victoria turned, their hands on their hips, and looked at the Frenchman with blank stares. Mr. Marchand said nothing more and looked down at his feet as the women turned towards each other again to continue their conversation.

"Listen—we can place these on the tables; they'll catch the eye of the young ladies waiting for their mothers. They'll be cheap enough so the mother will agree to get the music box, if they're patient. We'll sell dozens of these. They can be planted throughout the store and placed in the window."

Victoria picked up another variety of the box. "Look—they come in different shapes, sizes, and with different music. They're adorable!"

Olivia was completely enthralled by the debate and was surprised when Flora relented and turned to Mr. Marchand. Flora usually didn't let Victoria win any discussion, which made Olivia suspect that she just wanted to teach Victoria a lesson.

"All right, Mr. Marchand; what's your best prices for these little music boxes?"

Sure enough, Victoria was correct. She was dubbed a genius at merchandising, and to Olivia's knowledge, Flora never argued with Victoria again about sundry purchases.

"Olivia," Flora said. "You and Mum need to come for dinner this Sunday. It's so quiet without you. Can you come after you visit the Alms? Should I send a cab for Mum?"

That was the first time that Flora ever spoke a word about the Alms. Olivia considered this a success.

"Yes, I can be there at four o'clock. A cab would be perfect for Mum."

"Can Mum make those pierogi things for dinner?" Victoria asked like a child would.

"Oh, yes. That's a great idea. You had better pick her up at noon then. They're a lot of work to make, but she would love to show Annette and to spread the joy of eating them!"

The East River Bridge

Brooklyn Foundation

THE FOUNDATION OF THE BROOKLYN TOWER was built upon a three thousand ton *caisson*, which is French for "inverted chest." It measured 102 feet by 168 feet, with eight-foot thick walls and a fifteen-foot thick ceiling made of layers of yellow pine. In May of 1870, the *caisson* was launched into the East River and moved into place at the Fulton Ferry slip.

On the evening of December 1, 1870, the interior ceiling of the *caisson* caught fire. When the fire was discovered, a panic ensued, and all eighty workers ran for the ladders, seeking exit. Quickly, the foreman took control. He informed Roebling of the fire and ordered the men to attempt to put it out. However, nothing they tried worked; the flames continued to burn deep within the layers of yellow pine. Five hours later, at 3:00 a.m., the fire was extinguished. Roebling made his way home and suffered from the ill effects of being in compressed air for great lengths of time. At 8:00 a.m., he was informed that the fire was still burning. With this news, Roebling had no choice but to flood the *caisson*, risking the integrity of the structure. The anxiety-stricken engineers waited for five hours before the water finally reached the ceiling.

Two days later, the *caisson* was pumped free of water. With the inspection concluded, engineers found that the *caisson* was sound, and the fire damage could be successfully repaired. Finally, by March 1871, the interior of the *caisson* was filled with bricks and concrete and sealed off for good, completing the base of the first tower. However, the chief engineer's life was changed forever.

Flora

March 1871: The Piers

FLORA DECIDED TO TAKE ADVANTAGE of a temperate March day, so she took a cab to Market Street, home to one of her favorite bakeries. Afterwards, she walked towards the piers, where she could look across the river towards Brooklyn. There, she had read, the Brooklyn *caisson* lay deep beneath the water.

Some days the water appeared to be calm, but if she looked a bit more closely, she could see that the currents ran deep and strong. She had never taken the ferry across the river because boats simply scared her, but she hoped to one day walk across the bridge and look down at the water. Even though she read whatever was written in the newspapers about the bridge, it was still difficult to imagine how large the bridge was going to be.

Her preoccupation with the bridge grew even greater after she read a newspaper story about the structure of the *caissons*. She could hardly imagine how any person would agree to go under the water into a chamber that held both extremely hot air and freezing water. No matter how many times she read about the decompression chamber, she couldn't fathom why it was needed. Then the *caisson* fire had occurred in December. Again, there was an account of the contraption in which the men could hardly stand up straight. After reading the description over and over again, Flora felt faint with fear.

She couldn't comprehend how the dirt and stones were removed. She had read that it was done by way of a pool of water—inside the *caisson*. How can all the water be kept out except for this pool? Oh yes, something called *air compression*. Oh drat, some of these ideas are too complicated to understand.

As Flora walked along the river, deep in thought, she noticed a man approaching her. He was staring right at her. *Do I know this man?* She'd been to many social gatherings, and this man was dressed in fine clothing. It was possible that she had met him but just couldn't recall. As they approached one another, he started to slow his pace. *Oh dear, who is he?* His smile was bright, and his eyes were as dark as his hair. He walked like a man who was confident and at ease. Flora was certain that she didn't know this man because she would've definitely remembered him and his slightly crooked nose.

"Good morning, ma'am." He took off his hat. "I noticed that you were looking over at Brooklyn to where the bridge is being built."

The man turned slightly to look towards Brooklyn, giving Flora a full view of his handsome—and somewhat rugged—profile.

"In fact, I've seen you here on other occasions, but you seemed to, to . . . um . . . be too preoccupied to strike up a conversation."

Flora stared up at this man; her initial reaction was to tell him to move along. She wasn't so sheltered that she didn't understand the dangers of walking in the city by herself. However, listening to his tentative and shy conversation and seeing the way he toyed with the hat in his hands put her at ease. At the same time, she continued to search her memory for a previous introduction.

"Do I know you, sir?" Flora said as she held on to her parasol tightly in one hand and her package of pastries in the other. How foolish to think that she could defend herself with either one of these articles. She should have a knife in her pocket, as Victoria had always told her.

"No. I like to walk on this road and couldn't help noticing that you also favored this route. It seemed to me that there was no other way to meet you other than taking a bold move and striking up a conversation with you. Why do you walk this way by yourself here, surrounded by some of the worst neighborhoods in the city?"

"You're correct. It's an unsavory area, but I've found no problems during the day on the main roadways. I also like a pastry shop not far from here, and I frequent a nearby market. In fact, I find the community to be full of life."

"So you like the excitement of the city?"

This man was being quite bold in asking such personal questions. Yet Flora couldn't move, as if he had some sort of control over her. She found that she couldn't resist answering his questions. *How maddening that I have to stand here, looking into the face of this tall stranger.*

"What's your name?"

"Nathan Gibson. And yours?"

"Flora. Flora Pearl."

"Miss Pearl," he said with a grin. "It's grand that we've finally been officially introduced."

"I wouldn't call this a formal introduction. In fact, it's not proper at all."

"So tell me, Miss Pearl—what's your interest in the scene across the river? Let's try to find some common ground so we can hold our relationship in some kind of 'proper' context."

"I won't tell you anything more, Mr. Gibson. There's no relationship here. I should call for the police."

"Here," he said, grinning from ear to ear. "Before you leave or start screaming for the authorities, take my telescope so you'll be able to see the other side in more detail. As time progresses, the view will become more and more interesting."

Flora tucked her parasol under her arm, held out her hand, and took up the telescope. She had never seen one like this. It was a small, retractable telescope, with a circular mother-of-pearl eyepiece. She couldn't help but bring the telescope up to her eye to see across the water. *I never thought of getting one of these!* It seemed that this Mr. Gibson was a clever being.

"I often wonder how it will look and how it will change the city when it's complete," Flora said, gazing across the river.

Flora removed the telescope from her eye and turned to look up at Mr. Gibson. He was a few inches taller than she was. From the way he spoke, he seemed educated—but a bit brash. His shoes and clothing were extremely well made.

"Oh, the entire feel of the city will be different after the bridge is completed. People will be able to cross the bridge and get a breath of fresh air. Imagine watching the boats float up the river and being able to gaze down at their decks."

While he spoke, he looked across the water. This gave Flora the opportunity to notice how his eyes squinted a little as he talked and how he grinned when he was done speaking. When he looked back down at Flora, she immediately looked away and tried to think of something to say.

"Yes, it would be nice to breathe in some fresh air," she said as she turned and looked into his eyes. Flora had some potential suitors but had found them all quite boring and their conversation meaningless; however, the feeling that came over her when her eyes locked with this Mr. Gibson was, on the contrary, quite meaningful. She suddenly wondered how he would look lying next to her in bed. Those lovely lips, hard chest, and body. . . . The images in her imagination were shockingly clear.

"I was wondering what you're thinking," Nathan said, amused.

"Excuse me? I . . . I must be on my way. I've an engagement and am afraid I may be late."

Flora took a few steps backwards and then turned and quickly departed. She was grateful that the day was crisp, since she was suddenly extremely warm and uncomfortable. "Is that man laughing at me?" Flora muttered, half turning to see his amused face. The nerve!

Flora made her way back up Market Street and hailed a cab. Something had been taken from her or, at the very least, had infiltrated her and was working its way deep into her soul. While gazing into those dark eyes, she'd experienced a jolting human connection. How dare this man just walk right up to her and cause something so mysterious to pass between them!

When she arrived home, she quickly hung her coat, brought the pastries into the kitchen, and asked Annette if she could bring some tea up to her room. In the safety of her room, she sat down at her vanity and gazed through her window.

From there, she could look right over the street and into Washington Park. Her father used to tell her stories about the park. "In the old days," he would tell her, "they buried people there when no one else claimed their bodies. Many people died from yellow fever a long time ago, and they're all buried there as well, one on top of another." Flora used to ask him if they were still there, and her father would scare her into thinking that there were ghosts roaming around, still outraged that they were buried in unmarked graves.

He would say, "Be careful, Flora dear. When it rains outside, don't leave the front door open too long. Ghosts like to find shelter from the elements in the nearest home."

Sometimes he would go too far and scare her to death. On such occasions, poor Victoria had to sit next to her bed at night until she fell asleep.

She smiled as she let down her long, brown, wavy hair and brushed it with little enthusiasm. Her father sent her the brush-and-comb set while he was in Paris. Lovely mother-of-pearl handles and stiff bristles made for excellent brushing. *Mother-of-pearl?* Oh my, Flora didn't remember handing Mr. Gibson's telescope back to him. Running back down stairs, Flora rummaged through the pockets of her wrap and reluctantly retrieved the item. The memory of his face swiftly returned. The way he looked so deeply into her eyes made her feel as if he actually stole a piece of her and took it with him. *A rude beast—with those dark eyes and the smile of a mischievous boy—and his chuckle. . . . It was adorable.*

Flora wearily made her way back to her room and stared at her oval face and dark eyes, but she pulled away after just a moment. She heard the front door slam, a sure indication that Victoria was home.

"Victoria, I'm upstairs!"

A few moments later, Victoria burst into Flora's room with a tray of tea and finger sandwiches, as well as some pastries.

"Oh Flora, I'm so exhausted from spending the afternoon with that more-energy-than-she-knows-to-do-with Rachel! We went all the way up to Hendricks in an attempt to find her mistress a gift. She says that she must do all her talking while she's out because the men don't like women who talk. You know, they tell her secrets."

"Victoria, please don't descend into talking about the details of her vocation. I don't know how you even became friends with her."

"I met her at the shop, of course."

"Does she buy anything?"

"Only small items. Oh, she buys our perfume, but that's all. I don't think she can afford anything else from our shop," Victoria said as she helped herself to tea and a small cream puff.

She peered at Flora while eating her pastry. Then she got up and walked around Flora, set her tea down on the vanity, picked up the brush, and continued to smooth out her long hair. After a minute or two, Victoria said, "Well, you seem to be deep in your own thoughts. What did you do today?"

Without looking up, Flora replied, "I went down to the bakery on Market Street and then walked down to the piers to see about the progress of the bridge."

"Oh, that darn bridge! What *is* your obsession with that thing? And *why* do you look so far away? I asked you what you did, but I really want to know what happened! You look almost flushed. Are you getting the flu?"

Flora debated with herself about whether to tell Victoria about the few moments, out of the many hours of her day, that she spent with that dark-haired-beast person. Then she decided to let Victoria suffer in anticipation of her story. Good stories should always be withheld as long as possible, and she needed to ponder over this story before speaking it out loud.

"I had the most dreadful feeling come over me today."

"What?" Victoria interrupted. "I knew I should have gone with you today. Did you wear your wrap?"

"Of course I did. Annette wouldn't let me out the door without it."

Due to Victoria's interruption, Flora had to mentally prepare herself all over again to tell her story. The sun was getting lower in the sky, which made Flora's room glow. Flora liked to look at Victoria's face in the mirror. She seemed to be concentrating on brushing, but in actuality, she was probably trying to hold her tongue.

After all the years Flora and Victoria spent together, Flora was always amazed at how difficult it was for Victoria to stop verbalizing every little thought she had in her head. She found it uncomfortable to accept any pause in a conversation, which Flora felt should be given to quiet contemplation.

Victoria's face was pleasant to look at, and Flora wondered why she had no suitors. She had great quantities of the most glorious red-blond hair, which she found difficult to keep under control. By the end of the day, small curls would pop up from the bun at the back of her head.

"I was gazing over the river towards Brooklyn when I saw a man approach me."

Flora paused, knowing that it was taking all of Victoria's power to keep her mouth shut.

"I observed that he was an educated man by the way he was dressed and actually thought I might know him. However, it turns out that I didn't."

"You spoke to him?"

"Yes. He was very charming but rude for striking up a conversation the way he did with me. What kind of man stops a woman in the street, one he hadn't been introduced to, and starts a conversation?"

"Sounds like an extremely confident, rebellious sort of man."

"Yes, he did seem rebellious, as you say. He was—what's the word I'm looking for? He was . . . *smug*."

"What's his name? Are you sure we don't know his family?"

"I'm sure that I don't remember his name and probably wouldn't even recognize him again if I passed him in the street tomorrow. The only problem is that he let me use this telescope." Flora motioned to the item that was sitting on the vanity. "And I accidentally ran off with it."

"Ran off? Why would you run off?"

"Well," Flora said, fidgeting in her seat and looking at the ceiling. Her lower lip protruded slightly while she pondered whether or not she should answer Victoria's question. "Well, I got angry at his impertinence and feigned an appointment."

"Lied? Oh dear, I sincerely hope you don't see this man again. He has put a flush into your cheeks! I think there's more to your encounter than you're telling me."

"Flush in my cheeks? My cheeks are only flushed from being angry about forgetting to return his telescope. It's as if he's in this room right now." Flora stopped and let her voice, as well as her gaze, drift. "He looked at me as if he knew me. As if I was familiar. I had a fleeting thought that I knew him and—well, I don't know. Then I was angry because he was able to read my face."

"What do you mean—read your face?"

"For a moment, when I looked at him, I felt—well, I felt a distinct familiarity."

Victoria put the brush down and sat in the chair next to the vanity. She nibbled on a miniature cream puff and said, "I've never heard you speak on such a personal level about your feelings."

Flora started to arrange the items on her vanity—except for the newest addition to the collection, the telescope. She didn't even want to touch it.

"Do you want to talk more about it?"

"No. I'm sure that this feeling will pass."

With that said, Victoria got up and freshened her tea. She picked up another pastry and said that she was going to bathe and get to bed early.

Flora knew that Victoria was correct about her inability to express her most personal feelings. As she started to undress, Flora fretted a little about why she never seemed to have an emotional connection with anyone. Her father was detached, which was expected of English fathers. He often spoke about how her mother was very lovable, always hugging him and becoming upset when she heard of any bad things happening to anyone. This made him a bit uncomfortable at times, but he also admired her empathy. He often used to say, "You, my Flora, are like me. A godsend, since your mother is not here."

Other than her father's passing remarks, he didn't speak of her in great detail. Sometimes, Flora saw wistfulness in his eyes while they were enjoying each other's company in front of the fireplace, but Flora could never bring herself to prod her father. She'd been taught not to. At least Victoria knew her mother before she passed.

Victoria didn't speak of her mother often but did say that she was very artistic, a trait that Victoria inherited. But Flora often wondered what traits were passed down from her own mother. Flora started to regret not pressing her father for more information about her mother. But what good would it do? She wasn't one to dwell on the past or think about mistakes; she just moved forwards, objectively reviewing her options and choosing the most logical one.

Flora pulled open her drawer and unwrapped her necklace. She felt that if she peered at it enough, some memory would come back to her. As she let the beads slip through her fingers, she felt an urge to do something. Something that would be meaningful. At once, she thought of Olivia.

Olivia once said that Flora should spend some time at the Alms House in order to feel more connected with people. She was always talking about how she helped the women and children there. But Flora wasn't listening to sweet Olivia. Flora seemed immune to Olivia's passive powers of persuasion. She saw how Olivia's influence worked on other people but didn't think it would ever work on her. Yet this was starting to make sense now.

Flora felt more and more uncomfortable about the wealth that she had. Every month, she went to her stockbroker, the dreaded Mr. Adams, to discuss her finances. This was something that she and her father did together religiously. She needed to keep an eye on her finances, but she didn't like dealing with that man. Her father and the broker were such greedy people. They felt such joy from the large numbers written upon pieces of paper. How absolutely silly it seemed to look at mere numbers and feel joy.

Flora, on the other hand, didn't feel pleasure at all about that money. She felt more and more anxious as the numbers rose. Deep in her heart, she knew that she didn't deserve this money. The nest egg started by her grandfather grew with her father. Their quest for money overrode everything else in their lives. Her guilt over how this money was earned overwhelmed her.

When she asked Mr. Adams about creating a foundation, he looked at her with disdain.

"Why would you want to do such a thing?"

The tone of his voice made Flora feel like a stupid child, and she got mad at herself for continually subjecting herself to the demeaning way he treated her.

"Because I want to do some good with this money."

"Good? Do you mean to give it away?"

"Yes, in a responsible manner. In a way that directly helps people."

"I cannot agree to that," Mr. Adams responded dryly.

"You don't have to. It's my money."

"Look, Miss Pearl. Why don't you have dinner with me tonight? We can discuss this further."

"You've no intention of discussing this with me. You already stated that."

"Then just have dinner with me."

"No."

"Why not?" said the toothpick of a man.

"Because I know that you're only interested in getting your hands on my account."

"That's not true. You're a beautiful woman."

With that, Flora got up to leave. "I suggest that you keep your personal opinions to yourself."

"Or what? Are you going to move your money somewhere else?"

She didn't feel the need to answer and simply turned around and left. She couldn't bear the thought of having to see him again next month.

Flora asked herself why she would even discuss anything with a man she disliked so much. She'd let this situation continue for too long, and every month that she tolerated this behavior, the more aggressive he became.

Flora placed her necklace back in its hiding spot and took out a pencil and a piece of paper. Starting to calculate what she would need to withdraw from her account to start a foundation, she immediately saw that she would need to examine all of her expenses before determining what to put aside. *This will take some time and consideration.* She didn't like to make rash decisions but wanted to think things through completely. Maybe she should consult with Olivia.

The East River Bridge

New York Caisson

IN MAY 1871, THE SEVEN THOUSAND TON NEW YORK *caisson* was launched with a splash from the shipbuilders' yard at Greenpoint. It was estimated that the depth of this *caisson* would need to be eighty feet below the water level, two times the depth of the Brooklyn *caisson*.

The *caisson* itself was made with a twenty-two-foot thick ceiling, seven more than was made for Brooklyn's, so as to withstand the heavier masonry load. To make it less vulnerable to fires, this *caisson* was lined with a thin layer of iron, and it even contained a rudimentary sprinkler system. Every precaution was used to build the *caisson*, since the entire bridge hinged on the integrity of the two structures. The uncertainties and risks in building this foundation weren't considered by the average citizen, but they were certainly life-and-death matters to the bridge builders.

Flora

June 1871: Elizabeth's Dress

FLORA NOTICED A WOMAN WITH wavy, auburn hair waiting at the shop's door as they approached. She was wearing a dress of lead-blue bison cloth under a short-waisted jacket that was trimmed with large buttons. She was standing on her tiptoes with her nose practically pressed to the window. When the woman noticed Flora and Victoria approaching, she took two steps away from the window.

The day was bright and sunny but unseasonably cool. This was a relief to Flora, who didn't like the heat of summer. If it was deemed too hot, Flora wouldn't even open the store.

"Has something caught your fancy?" Victoria asked.

"Oh yes, that dark-green hat on the right side of your window. It's stunning."

"Do come in," Victoria said.

"What a lively shop this is. Is the proprietor here? I'm in need of a new dress," the woman said as she looked over the various hats and scarves that were on display.

"We're the proprietors of this shop. My name is Flora Pearl, and this is my sister, Victoria."

Flora saw a reaction in the woman's eyes when she said her name but thought nothing of it. She was probably just surprised to meet a female shop owner, as so many of her patrons were at first.

"How do you do? My name is Elizabeth Shannon."

"How do you do? My assistant, Olivia, can aid you in creating a dress. What kind do you need?"

"A formal gown, but I have simple tastes. Do you know when she will be available to assist me?"

"Let me check." Flora walked over to Olivia's appointment book and looked it over with care.

"She has an appointment available on Wednesday afternoon at four o'clock. Is that suitable?"

"Yes, that's perfect."

"Would you like to see that hat now?"

"Oh, yes, thank you."

As Victoria laid out the pastries that they had always made available for customers and their children, Flora busied herself by taking the hat down from its window display. Elizabeth took the hat and looked it over carefully, from the top to the inside stitches. She was obviously a woman who had particular tastes.

"This is just beautiful. Do you do all the assembly?"

"We did make this particular hat here at the store. It's the creation of the woman who will be helping you on Wednesday. You won't find another like it anywhere else.

Elizabeth walked over to their full-length mirror and carefully removed her hat. Flora then positioned the new hat on top of her head and arranged the lace ties under her chin.

"I have a dress that this hat will go perfectly with," Elizabeth said as she fussed with the lace around the edges. "How long has this shop been open?"

"It's been open for about four years."

"It's so refreshing to see women that own their own businesses and who take control of their lives. In fact, I frequent women-owned businesses as much as I can."

"Thank you. That's very kind. Some women don't like that I own this boutique."

"Why so?" Elizabeth asked, turning to face Flora.

"Victoria, what did that rather large woman say to me the other day—do you remember? I don't want to mention her name."

"Ah, yes; she said, 'You should be home tending to babies. What kind of husband allows you to spend all this time alone in this store?'"

"Oh, dear; what did you say?" Elizabeth asked.

"I told her that I had no interest in marriage," Flora replied.

"Tell our new friend what you said after that!" Victoria said.

"Well, I told her that I had no intention of marrying and that she should run along back to her jail cell before the warden got back home."

Elizabeth stared at Flora with merriment in her eyes and started to laugh.

"Well, good for you, Miss Pearl. She must have left in a huff. I guess she won't be coming back."

"Oh, I don't mind. She'd been here several times and never purchased a thing—but she had no problem in helping herself to several pastries."

Elizabeth wandered around the shop while Flora was talking. She picked up a bottle of perfume and gave it a quizzical sniff. "Oh, very nice. This smells familiar." She placed the bottle down and turned her attention to a display of hatpins and brooches.

"Oh, these hatpins are so unusual. May I?"

"Of course. Here, let me get them for you. Flora walked over and brought the pins down to the counter for Elizabeth to see."

"It's so refreshing to be around successful women. I've become quite disillusioned by seeing so many women in this city who are destitute. They have no skills and are left with children to care for by themselves because their husbands have abandoned them either by death or by flight."

"You sound like my father. My dear father is very much opposed to me being dependent upon a man," Flora said.

Elizabeth stopped her inspection of pins and looked up at Flora's face. "Dear, I hope you don't let your own father bully you into living the life of a spinster."

"Oh, no. I've nothing against marriage, as long as I find a man as progressive as I am about women's issues. Do you think there's a man out there who is?"

"Hmm, men can be manipulative. They may court you and tell you all sorts of things to trap you into marriage and then retract everything once the deed is done. I'll take these three pins, please."

"Yes, these are lovely." Flora called out, "Victoria, could you wrap these for me? I forgot to start the stove. Please excuse me for just a moment, Miss Shannon."

When Flora returned, she saw that Victoria had wrapped Elizabeth's purchases and that the two of them were deep in a conversation. As Flora approached, Elizabeth looked at her and said, "Victoria was just telling me how you usually don't arrive at the store this early on Mondays. Usually you stop at the Alms House to assist with breakfast."

"Yes. We couldn't go this morning because we have too much to do here today."

"What else do you do at the Alms House?"

"We—that is, everyone that works at this store is involved in some way. We meet with the women, give them advice and guidance, and provide them with any assistance that we can. Victoria just ordered several washtubs to distribute to some of the women next month. The lives of the women there seem so bleak. I don't know how they can live in those buildings."

As Elizabeth was listening, her face took on a different look.

"Miss Pearl, that's so generous of you. What would possess you to hand over your hard-earned money to these women?"

"Well, we just started this endeavor. And we don't just hand money over to them. The washtubs will be our first actual donation, but we're meeting with the people who run the mission next week to review what's needed and where we can offer assistance. We've decided that Olivia will be our main liaison, since she's more familiar with the institution."

"When I was a child," Elizabeth said, while looking at her package, "I visited the Alms House quite often and listened to the sisters' sermons. They were inspirational."

Flora was taken aback to hear this. This obviously successful woman had come from Five Points?

"But I'm shocked," continued Elizabeth, "that you would give your money to people that may not deserve it. What good does it do? Do you really believe that you'll make a difference?"

Elizabeth's tone of voice wasn't confrontational; she honestly sounded perplexed. This made Flora want to answer her as honestly as she could.

"I believe that I've been given every opportunity to succeed, mainly with an education and money. Small things, such as a new washer, can do some good to make a woman's life just a little easier. I haven't had to struggle as they have, and this endeavor is of little financial risk."

"But isn't opening a store a risk? It may not have been successful."

"It would be a risk if I poured all the money I had into it, but the money that was used to start the store is of little consequence to me. Losing that money wouldn't change my standard of living at all. Therefore, my risk is small. But let me answer your question about making a difference. When I was a child, my father started a reading program at the Alms House with the sincere desire to help the children of the neighborhood."

"He did?" Elizabeth said with zeal, interrupting Flora.

"Yes. Of course, he did so anonymously. The fund will probably last at least ten more years without needing replenishment. I believe that it's made a difference."

Elizabeth seemed completely speechless and was a bit pale.

"Are you well?"

"Yes, yes, of course. I was just surprised. I know of that program. It just never occurred to me that someone was responsible for starting it and that it needed money to sustain itself."

"Yes, the reading program is good, but I feel there's so much more that can be done. One of my shortcomings is that it's very difficult for me to relate to some of these women. From what Olivia tells me, most turn to prostitution or become alcoholics, or worse. I'm reminded not to judge others, since I cannot even begin to understand their day-to-day hardships." Flora suddenly stopped. "Oh, I'm sorry; I didn't mean to go on."

The front door opened, and a woman with two young girls walked into the shop.

"Not at all, Miss Pearl." All three women looked over at the woman as she reprimanded her daughters in a soft voice. "You have other customers now, so I should be on my way. I'll be back on Wednesday to meet with Miss Olivia."

After Elizabeth took her leave, Flora went to her office, but she could overhear Victoria talking to the woman and her daughters. They wished to purchase parasols but didn't find one they liked in the store and quickly departed.

"Do you know what that woman, Elizabeth, is?" Victoria said, her voice just above a whisper in the office doorway. From there, she could see the front door.

"No, should I?"

"She's a madam. *That* was Rachel's mistress."

"Nonsense! Her dress wasn't one of a madam's. Regardless, how would you know? I thought you had never met the woman."

"Because everyone knows who Elizabeth Shannon is. You don't have to actually meet her to know who she is. She's mistress of the most expensive house in the city. These women are refined. Rich gentlemen don't go to the slums for this type of service. And they don't just perform the . . . well, you know . . . They also accompany their clients out to dine, to the theater, and to parties."

"Is this what you and Rachel talk about during your outings?"

When Elizabeth returned for her appointment, Flora simply closed the shop so they could pick out fabric and patterns and continue their previous week's discussion uninterrupted.

After Elizabeth was introduced to Olivia, Flora brought out a very nice bottle of port for them to sip.

"Elizabeth, do you drink port, or would you prefer tea?"

"Why, port, of course; I love port!"

As Flora poured the sweet drink, Olivia asked Elizabeth a series of questions about the new dress that was to be constructed. It was to be suitable for an evening out at a cultural event. She'd been using a tailor uptown, but Elizabeth felt that his designs were no longer stylish.

Olivia was a genius when it came to patterns, fabric, and adornments, and soon she had Elizabeth sold on an off-the-shoulder dress made of a cream-colored silk fabric and tulle. She was so excited and confessed that she never had the opportunity to make such a luxurious piece before. Flora was once again surprised at the depth of Olivia's skills and had no doubt that she would be able to make this garment.

"Well, Olivia, I can't wait to see if the dress you make is as comfortable and as elegant as you say. I'm in need of many dresses a year. So if your work is good, you'll be my seamstress of choice."

"Oh, my, that would be lovely! Your husband must be a very important man to be attending so many social events."

"Oh, I'm not married, and I don't think I ever will be," Elizabeth said with some sadness in her voice, looking down at the glass of port in her hands.

"Why not? You're a very beautiful woman," Flora said.

"Hmm, that's kind, but I won't marry because of my—well, because of my profession."

Elizabeth looked up at Flora and placed her glass on the table.

"Ladies, I don't have any friends outside of my profession, and I'm being silly in thinking that I could. Why would women like you be friends with someone like me?"

Elizabeth stood up and started to walk towards her wrap.

"Elizabeth, please come back and sit down," said Flora, getting out of her seat.

"We don't want you to leave," Olivia added. "We've seen many women take this path. Please, come sit back down with us."

Elizabeth looked around the table and saw that no facial expression had changed in the least, so she put her wrap down and took her seat.

"But, Elizabeth," Olivia continued, "do you honestly think that was your only choice?"

"At the time, yes, of course."

"Does that mean you're contemplating leaving the profession?" Flora asked. She saw nothing intrinsically wrong with being a prostitute but didn't think it was healthy for the heart and soul.

"I'm seeking something else to do but have found that I've no other skills. To be honest, the other ladies that work in my house cannot see any further than the present."

Suddenly, a stranger appeared at the door.

"Oh, that's my friend, Vince," Elizabeth said.

Flora got up, opened the door, and invited him in. He was tall, with dark hair and a mustache. As he approached the table, Elizabeth stood up and took her place by his side. With her hand on his arm, she introduced him to everyone around the table. Flora saw that Vince's gaze weighed heavily on Victoria and caused her to blush.

After the pleasantries, Vince looked at Elizabeth and said, "We must be leaving soon for your engagement." His voice was smooth and his accent definitely Italian. Flora discerned that this man's elegance was only a façade.

Flora went to retrieve Elizabeth's wrap while Vince made small talk with Victoria and Olivia. But Flora observed that Victoria, who was usually so chatty, now seemed to have nothing to say. She didn't realize that Victoria was shy, or perhaps she was just shy in front of handsome men!

Aria

(Earth names, Anna and Olivia)

The Soul World: Corin's Free Will

ARIA KNEW THAT ELIZABETH—or Corin, as she's known in the Soul World—had exercised her free will to choose which path to take in her various lives. Aria and Corin both understood that there was only a slim chance that Elizabeth would resist her urge to become a prostitute during her life in New York. She'd been struggling with the problem for several lives but was getting closer to her goal: avoiding self-exploitation.

Corin was once a male Indian of the Iroquois nation, and she had a short, but productive, life as a tradesman. The Council noted:

> *Even though the trading routes he developed benefited the entire tribe, he stole some of the goods for his own use, and on several occasions, he stole the virginity from some of the young Indian women from neighboring tribes.*

And then there was the life she had lived as a private tutor in Britain. The Council noted:

> *Corin was less interested in teaching young students than in seducing and extorting money from her well-meaning employers. Even when placed in a situation where she was to teach manners, dancing, and the art of entertaining to aristocratic pupils, she degraded herself by remaining a greedy and sexual being. She was quite successful in this life; she always had steady work by procuring excellent references by extorting them.*

About her incarnation as the wife of a salt tradesman, the Council noted:

Corin traveled everywhere with her husband, who was a tradesman dealing in salt. They didn't travel alone but in large groups. In this life, Corin was a co-conspirator with her husband. They stole at every opportunity, even though they made a good living from his profession. She also agreed to have sex with other men in the group, as long as the price was to her liking. Unfortunately, her husband grew weary of her. He killed her and buried her body in the sand. The other men of the group had grown fond of Corin because she did have a kind heart. The men appreciated her, and she made every man feel special and loved, even though she was being paid for her service. If Corin had refrained from exchanging sex for money, she would've made the group stronger.

The type of death Elizabeth would experience in her Manhattan life was dependent upon which occupation she chose. Because she chose to be a prostitute, her death was fated to be painful. The group believed that this would bring Corin closer to reaching a tipping point, and, hopefully, she might find it easier to resist prostitution in subsequent lives.

Aria was saddened when Elizabeth made her choice known to Nathan early in their lives together. Nathan couldn't persuade Elizabeth to change her mind. However, choosing to become a prostitute instead of working at Kyle's Pub would ultimately serve its purpose in lives to come.

The East River Bridge

Derrick Accident

AS AN EIGHT-TON BLOCK OF GRANITE was being lifted to the top of the seventy-foot high Brooklyn tower, two derricks broke off from its top, plunging the derricks and granite back to earth and killing three men and injuring five. This incident caused confidence to wane in the management of the New York Bridge Company. An investigation ensued, and the company was exonerated of any wrongdoing.

However, there was skepticism over the integrity of the city's government, which many thought required additional oversight. The New York Bridge Company was carefully scrutinized in the quest to uncover fraud, corruption, and misuse of funds in the construction of the bridge.

Victoria

October 1871: Move Out

"FLORA, I WANT TO MOVE OUT of the house and into the vacant apartment above the shop."

Victoria and Flora were both seated at the dining-room table, drinking their coffees and reading the newspaper. The morning sun shone brightly on the china and the silver and caused them to gleam.

Flora's eyes didn't even leave the newspaper when she said, "No."

"Why not? I'm not a prisoner here, am I?" Victoria asked.

"No, you're not. But I need you here."

"No, you don't. You can get along fine without me. You can stop paying me as your companion. Just pay me for the work I do at the shop."

"You can easily be replaced at the shop. Where I need you is here. Who else would take care of me and my personal tasks?"

"Replaced at the shop? Why would you say such a—such a horrible thing to me?"

Flora sat back in her chair and looked at Victoria's face but said nothing.

"Well, Flora, if I'm so dispensable, why don't you just let me leave? Or am I just here to remind you about your daily schedule?"

"No, don't be silly. You assist me every day. You help me run this household, make sure the cleaning people keep up with their duties, and help Annette plan meals. There are many things you do."

"Then when will I be able to move out on my own?"

"I don't know. Let me think about it."

"Rachel says that you just want to control me," Victoria replied, even though Rachel had never said any such thing about Flora. It was really Olivia who urged Victoria to talk to Flora about moving out. Olivia also said that perhaps Flora really needed Victoria near her. With her father gone, Flora would be left totally alone. This was something that Victoria hadn't even considered.

"Rachel? What does she know of anything? I don't like you being friends with her."

"Why not?"

"Because she's a bad influence on you. She's always trying to get you to flirt with men, and she tells you that you should be courting."

"But I should be. Do you want me to be alone like . . .?" Victoria stopped short.

"What? Be alone like what?" Flora demanded, but she kept her voice neutral.

"Like an old spinster," Victoria said slowly. Victoria wanted to add the words "like you" to the end of the sentence but had the good sense to realize it would be a mistake.

"Oh, Victoria, you won't be a spinster. You just needn't go out and flirt and make a spectacle of yourself. The right man may just walk right into the shop one day, and you'll fall madly in love."

"Oh, Flora, what are the chances that a man will walk into our shop?"

"You never know."

Victoria was tired of playing this game and just wanted to lash out at her. For a moment, Victoria inwardly debated about whether she should tell Flora some details of her father's life. Details that her "sister" didn't know about. Rachel had told Victoria that Mr. Pearl used to visit Elizabeth's house but was told never to return. Rachel wouldn't tell her why. Victoria knew that Mr. Pearl loved his money, so perhaps there was a disagreement about how much he was charged. *Does Vince know the details of Mr. Pearl's history?* But nothing would be gained by knowing the sordid details or by telling Flora.

Victoria believed that it was bad enough that her benefactor frequented the establishment, but to be banned from it was even worse. From what Rachel had told her, Mr. Pearl was permanently ejected from Elizabeth's house about a year before his death. At about the same time, Victoria had noticed a sudden change in Mr. Pearl's demeanor. She had noticed a faraway look in his eyes in the evenings while they enjoyed after-dinner drinks in the parlor.

One night, he said something completely out of character. He confided that Flora was like her mother in one way. Victoria paid full attention—he never talked about Flora's mother. No one even knew her name, not even Annette.

"Flora's mother," said Mr. Pearl, with heaviness in his voice, "didn't see the value in accumulating wealth. I'm afraid that Flora has the same problem. I'm worried about her. She may not be able to handle the strain of being responsible for so much money after I pass."

Victoria thought that was the oddest thing she had ever heard: a strain from having too much money?

"When you were both very young—you may remember this, Victoria—she made me give money to the Alms House."

"Why, yes, I remember. But she didn't suggest the donation. I believe you did, Father."

"Yes, yes, you're correct. Regardless, I remember the day distinctly. She was fine one moment and then was greatly disturbed the next. As we left Mr. McGuire's office—you know, our old property manager before Mr. Foley."

"Yes, I remember him."

"Well, we were leaving the office, and she pointed at some children across the street and asked me why they didn't have shoes. She said, 'Look, Father—I have many pairs of shoes, but most of the children here aren't even wearing shoes.' "

Mr. Pearl's voice seemed far off, as if he was reliving the moment.

"I asked her why she cared, and she said that it made her uncomfortable having to go to Mr. McGuire's office. The children there always stared at her when she got out of the cab. She noticed how the other children were dressed and how they seemed hungry. She was actually upset and asked me why we needed so much. Well, you know my Flora, and you know that she isn't the most compassionate person; however, it was clear to me that it was her wealth that made her uncomfortable, not necessarily their plight."

"I don't understand the difference."

Mr. Pearl looked directly at Victoria with his piercing gray-blue eyes, which gave her an eerie feeling in the pit of her stomach.

"She wasn't concerned about people lacking money or not having enough food to eat. No, no. She's not that empathetic. She was concerned that we had too much, more than what we needed. Her exact words were, 'Why do we need so much?'"

Mr. Pearl leaned over to retrieve his glass of whiskey and took a gulp.

"It unnerved me. These were the exact words her mother had used on more than one occasion."

Mr. Pearl leaned close to Victoria and whispered, "Do you believe in spirits, Victoria?"

"Yes, I do." Victoria's hair stood on end when she answered him.

He leaned back in his chair and looked at the ceiling. "I had a dream the night before Flora voiced her concern. It was an extremely vivid dream about Flora's mother. In the dream she said to me, 'How much do you need?' That's all she said and I. . . ." Mr. Pearl paused. "I immediately woke up and had to light a lamp because I thought she was in the room with me. So . . . when Flora used these same words, I felt—well, damn it; I felt nearly faint! Why would she communicate her feelings in the exact words her mother used?"

Mr. Pearl took several puffs of his cigar and let the smoke slowly escape from his lips so it circled his face. He took one more puff and quickly exhaled the smoke. "So . . . I told her that I would give a large sum of money to the Alms House. She asked why, and I said I wanted to help the children who needed shoes. She looked perplexed and said that she needed to talk to you about the situation. You know, she depends on you, Victoria, for balance in her life. It was you who suggested that the children needed to learn how to read. You thought that it was the most important gift that you had been given."

Mr. Pearl's gaze returned to his drink. "That was a very mature suggestion on your part."

"Thank you, Father."

"Then last night. I had another dream about her."

"Your wife?" Victoria was almost afraid of what Mr. Pearl would say next.

"Yes. She said the same thing to me."

The hairs on the back of Victoria's neck stood up all over again, but the conversation abruptly ended because Flora entered the room. It almost made Victoria feel that this information was a secret, not to be talked about freely—almost as if Mr. Pearl was ashamed of himself. Then Victoria remembered something that she had previously forgotten. At one point during their conversation, before Flora had entered the room, he asked Victoria to "watch over her and take care of her." Victoria could picture Mr. Pearl's face. He hadn't shaved in a couple of days, and his eyes looked more blue than gray at that very moment.

"Victoria, look at me, girl. You have to make a promise to me."

"What, Father?"

"You need to watch over her for me. She needs someone to . . . to help her."

"Help her do what? I've never seen her need assistance."

Mr. Pearl started shaking his head very quickly. "With this, she does. She needs help. Well, how can I say this? You know Flora. She's too self-centered. No, that's not right. She needs help putting her feelings into words. Yes, she's a cold person. That's fine for a man, but not for a woman. She's missing the softer side of being a woman. Do you know what I mean?"

"Yes, I do. She likes to control the people around her more than she wishes to be a part of their lives."

"Yes! That's it!" Mr. Pearl exclaimed.

You were so right, Father. Flora does need help.

The sound of Flora's voice caused Victoria to snap back to the present. Flora had been talking to her while buttering her toast, but Victoria didn't hear a word of it.

"Did you hear me?"

"Ah, no, Flora, I'm sorry. What did you say?"

"Oh, never mind."

Victoria owed Mr. Pearl a few more years of taking care of Flora. She wasn't being treated poorly, and she did love Flora very much, but knew that sooner or later she would need to find her own life. She was patient and would wait.

"I've decided that we're moving out of this house anyway," Flora said flippantly.

"What? When were you going to tell me?"

"I just did."

"But . . . I mean . . . don't you think I should have been asked what I thought?"

"No. Why should I ask you?"

"Because it affects me!"

"Oh, Victoria, sometimes you're so dramatic. What does it matter where you live?"

Once again, it never ceased to amaze Victoria how easily Flora could push her down and, at the same time, tell her that they were equals.

"The renovations on the top floor have been completed. It has been converted to one large apartment for us. There are three bedrooms. Annette will occupy a one-bedroom apartment on the third floor. Now, we won't have to waste time commuting to work."

"I have to admit that I like the idea of moving up there, even if it has to be with you. The neighborhood here is getting a little worrisome."

"Yes, and now the weather won't be such a factor. It's so difficult to go outside when it's so cold—or hot, for that matter."

Victoria was glad that Flora chose to ignore her sarcastic remark about having to stay with her. She was so good at ignoring things she didn't want to hear. Nevertheless, Victoria was excited about the prospect of moving uptown.

"When are we moving?"

"I've arranged to have several men and carriages at our home in two weeks. Tomorrow they will drop off the moving crates. I want to make sure that certain items are packed properly, like our paintings and china. This will actually give us an opportunity to rid ourselves of unwanted items. We'll sell pieces that we don't want anymore."

Flora sipped her coffee. "So, you see, there's no need for you to move out at all. We're going to move into that building anyway."

"You know that isn't the same as having my own place."

"Why do you want to live by yourself? I would think it would be dreadful."

"You're right, Flora; I don't know what I was thinking."

Victoria knew it was fruitless to attempt to convince Flora how free she would feel living on her own. Then she could do anything she wanted without Flora looking over her shoulder.

"It isn't right for a young woman to live by herself. Oh, come. Look at the hour. We should get going."

During the cab ride, Victoria contemplated the move. It would be nice not to take this cab ride every day back and forth from the store. She also noticed that Flora hadn't mentioned her father in a long time. Maybe she had come to terms with his passing. Selling her home seemed like a good sign.

"Flora?"

"Yes?" Flora turned a little in her seat so she could see Victoria's face better.

"What did you think of that man, Vince?"

"Who?"

"Elizabeth's friend, Vince, her driver."

"Oh yes, but we only met him briefly. How can one make a judgment about someone with whom they hardly exchanged a dozen words?"

Victoria looked down at her dress and contemplated how to proceed.

"Why are you so interested in my thoughts about him?"

"Because I've met him on several occasions. He's suddenly begun to escort Rachel to some of our outings together. For instance, Rachel and I had planned on taking a cab to Central Park to visit the zoo last week, and when the cab pulled up to the house, Vince was there."

Victoria stopped to see if Flora would say anything, but she didn't.

"He said that he always wanted to see the zoo but never had a chance."

"Did you enjoy his company?"

"Why, yes, I did. He was a gentleman to both Rachel and me. He insisted on treating us to apple dumplings."

Again, Victoria waited for a response from Flora, but there was only silence.

"He keeps showing up with Rachel. Well, not every time, but it seems that he's there any time he can think of a plausible excuse." It was time to be direct with Flora. "What do you think?"

"I think you should proceed with caution. Remember who he's friends with."

"What does that mean?"

"I believe that Vince is Elizabeth's establishment head. He probably protects her."

"Hmm, you're probably correct. I feel so secure when I'm with him."

"Is this why you want to move out? To be with him?"

"No! That's absurd."

"Is it? Why would you talk about moving out on your own and talk about Vince right afterwards? I think that you want the freedom to see Vince without me knowing, but let me make this clear, Victoria.

I'm responsible for your well-being, and that includes finding you a suitable husband."

As soon as Flora finished her sentence, the cab stopped in front of the store. Flora paid the driver, and Victoria obediently followed her into the store. Victoria wasn't angry about Flora's outburst. She'd purposely instigated the conversation to see how Flora would react. Victoria knew that there was nothing serious about Vince's presence. She knew that he protected the girls who worked at Elizabeth's house and wasn't trying to pursue her. Victoria did like Vince but had no illusions of them falling in love with each other. Being with him was far from a priority in Victoria's life. However, it was nice to be around a man for a change.

Flora knew nothing about love or how to evaluate the qualities a man needed to make him a good husband. She sincerely doubted that Flora would marry, which meant that Victoria wouldn't marry. Flora's manipulation of people ensured that her life was tidy, controlled, and in place.

Aria
(Earth names, Anna and Olivia)

The Soul World: Victoria Doing Well

"**V**ERY GOOD, VICTORIA!" ARIA SAID. Victoria, known as Vesta in the Soul World, didn't feel victimized by Flora's control. Instead, she resolved to understand the behavior and see Flora's frailties as a human being. Aria was proud, since this was an area that the two had spent a lot of time studying before incarnating. It was important for Victoria to see why Flora was trying to control her. Victoria showed Flora understanding and patience instead of lashing out in anger.

Vesta and Aria had reviewed Vesta's Council session concerning her life as Isabella Bristol many, many times together. During that life, Vesta, as Isabella, had mastered her sister Jillian into complete submission. As a team, they came up with this technique of "understanding" as a way to stop the power struggle between the two of them. Vesta, as Victoria, had to instill a feeling of hope, inner peace, and strength in her human form. If all went according to their plans, Victoria would show Flora that it wasn't necessary to control Victoria in order to be loved by her.

Vesta's Council session after her life as Isabella Bristol in Provincetown:

"How was your life with Julya in Provincetown? Did you and Julya love each other during your life on Earth?" Councilor Creek asked.

"No. I wielded control over Julya when we lived in Provincetown. Her name was Jillian—Jillian Bristol."

"Yes, that's correct. And your name was Isabella Bristol. Why did you like to control your sister, Jillian?" Councilor Aer asked.

Vesta had to think for a moment. "She was my younger sister," she said. "Yes, it was because I hated her."

"How could you hate her?" Councilor Creek asked. "You were so much more attractive than she was. You received all of the attention and admiration from your family and friends."

"She was smarter than I was. She was independent, kinder, and purer in character. It made me feel inferior. I wanted her to need me. Therefore, I fully exerted my control over her, bending her to my will. It made me feel powerful. She resisted, of course. Told me how much she hated me and tried to convince me to go back to Boston and leave her alone at the Cape. But I was marrying a man that owned a great deal of property, so it wasn't possible to leave."

"Please elaborate on how you controlled her."

"Well. . . . Oh, one evening after we had finished dinner, I laid out her choices. Either marry an unsavory man or be sent away."

"Why would you do that?" Councilor Aer asked.

"I thought he would be suitable for my sister. I was her guardian, and it was my job to find her a husband."

"That doesn't seem correct. Let's view this scene for a moment so we can review it with accuracy," Councilor Lux said.

Councilor Lux pointed at the wall where a projection of their life in Provincetown would display.

Vesta looked up and saw her house amid Provincetown. It rivaled any captain's house, with a broad porch on the main level and a small deck upon the third. Numerous times she made her way up the narrow, winding steps and through the dormered attic to stand upon the deck. The gentle, faraway echoes of seagulls, bells, and boats rocking in their slips blew in from the bay. But she longed for the sounds of horses on cobblestone boulevards and the clamor of peddlers selling their wares on the streets of Boston. Inside, Isabella and Jillian were seated in the dining area, across from each other at the table. Jillian seemed distressed.

"Please don't make me marry that heathen," Jillian pleaded.

"You'll do as I wish." Bella sighed, seemingly bored with the whole situation. "You've been a nuisance to me since our father passed. You have your choices—now choose. You must marry that man in one month. If you don't, then I'm sending you back to Boston."

"But why him? Can't I marry someone else—anyone else!"

"No! It has to be him!" Isabella shrieked, leaning across the table.

"But he's a wicked man." Jillian sobbed.

"No, no," Isabella said soothingly, smoothing down her dress. "He just needs a good woman to settle him down."

"But how can I get a man to marry me? Look at me, Bella—I'm an ugly duckling!"

Isabella sighed. "Well, that's a problem, but it's your problem now, isn't it?"

Councilor Lux paused the scene and looked at Vesta.

Vesta faced the Council members. "I now feel ashamed about how I treated Jillian."

"Go on."

"Over time, I trained my sister to be an obedient person. I weakened her spirit, weakened her confidence. By the time I sat her down at that table, she felt she had no choice in any matter. I created a person who didn't have the strength to make any of her own decisions or weather any kind of stress or illness."

"But Vesta, why this man?" Councilor Creek asked.

"Because he was the most despicable one that I knew of. He was also lurking about, trying to get my attention. I wanted my sister to suffer and never to experience one shred of happiness. He was known to be violent and—" Vesta paused.

"And what? Please, continue."

Very softly, Vesta said, "I was hoping that he would kill her so I wouldn't have to give her any more of my inheritance. I mean, our inheritance."

"What happened when she became ill? What did you do?" Councilor Lux asked.

"Do you mean when she fell off the wagon and cut her face and hands?"

"No, when she was ill with a fever."

"Um, I did nothing." Confused, Vesta asked herself, "But why didn't I help her?"

"What you just said is not correct. You didn't do 'nothing.' You're forgetting what you did," Councilor Pedor said gently. "Teacher, help Vesta remember the details."

Teacher reached out and touched Vesta in order to assist her in remembering.

"Oh, no. How hateful!" Vesta was visibly disturbed by what she was remembering.

"Please tell us what you did."

"Jillian was married for a few years to Kelvin, the despicable sailor. The one I forced her to marry. He was on a long trip, and I had received word that the boat he was on would most likely be delayed from making berth by about a month. It would be the perfect opportunity to test her."

"What do you mean by test?" Councilor Aer asked.

"I needed to know if they were really in love or not. I hated the idea that she might be happy. So . . . I . . . I. . . . One night, I changed my dress and went down to the pier with a pocketful of gold coins. I waited in the shadows until this man I knew of, a sailor, appeared. His ship had just made berth that morning, and I knew he would be leaving the ship to go to the saloon for supper. I wanted to intercept him."

Vesta raised her arm in front of her, as if she were stopping the sailor.

"I reached out and touched his arm, and he quickly turned to see who it was. When he recognized me, I asked if he would do a favor for me, one for which he would be well paid. Of course, he agreed when I showed him the coins."

" 'Well, what do you want me to do?' he asked. 'Do you want me to kill someone? If you do, this isn't enough.' "

"I asked him to . . . to . . . tell everyone that would listen that he heard that Kelvin's ship was lost at sea. If he could get Jillian to overhear him talk about it, it would even better."

" 'Oh, that's cruel.' He laughed. 'It's not killing someone, but I'll still need more.' "

"I gladly handed over two more coins, which made him very happy.

"He said, 'You're going to make her very unhappy until his ship returns. It'll be late, but it will return, you know.' "

"I turned to go back home with a huge grin on my face. You see, they had looked too content together. It couldn't be true. How could she be happy with such a beast? Especially one that she had no choice in marrying."

"Tell us what happened to your sister when she heard this news," Councilor Ustrina said.

"To my surprise, she was anguished."

"Surprised. . . . Why were you surprised?" Councilor Ustrina said.

"Because I didn't know that she actually loved him. I was so sure that she wouldn't care. She should have been relieved to be free from him. At first, she denied the news, but over time, she became angry and bitter. Then, when the ship still didn't arrive, she became ill. I wasn't happy that she really did love him. Then I was smug when she started to deteriorate. She's weak. How cruel I was. Even at her funeral, I stood over her grave and smiled, as if I had won something. And then, when her husband came home, I laughed at him and said, 'How ironic that your perceived death caused hers. And don't think it's because she loved you. She was just a weak, needy person.' "

"Why would you lie to Kelvin about your sister not loving him?" Councilor Pedor asked.

Vesta paused for a moment and said, "Oh, just to hurt him. He demanded to know who had spread the false story that his ship had been lost.

I feigned innocence. I told him that everyone in town thought his ship had sunk."

All of the Council members remained silent to give Vesta time to relive her terrible behavior.

"Oh, he was terribly hurt," Vesta murmured.

"How did you feel about his anguish?" Councilor Gens asked.

Vesta paused, as if she was trying to remember her exact emotions at the time. "I felt happy."

"Why?"

"I don't know."

"Was it because you had proved your complete control over two innocent people?" Councilor Creek asked.

"Yes, that's correct," Vesta replied.

The East River Bridge

Caisson Disease

MANY PEOPLE KNEW OF THIS STRANGE illness, but no one knew how to prevent or cure it. An attempt was made by the bridge physician to filter out workers who might be susceptible to the disease, such as men who were older, had other ailments, or drank too much. Even the hours a person worked were decreased, due to the belief that the length of time exposed to pressurized air was the main cause of the disease. However, all these efforts didn't yield a solution nor could doctors prevent the inevitable physical toll the men had endured.

No one knew exactly how many deaths the ailment caused or how many men suffered long-term effects from the disease; however, the number of cases was high enough to cause Washington Roebling to order the sinking of the New York *caisson* to stop at seventy-eight feet and six inches in the following month. Instead of bedrock, the massive structure would sit on sand.

It was during this time that Roebling himself experienced another attack of the disease. He was now the second Roebling to endure injury or illness as a result of this bridge. He lay near death for several days in the same house on Hicks Street where his father had suffered before him. Throughout the early summer, Roebling continued to endure more painful attacks, but work in New York City continued.

Nathan

May 1872: Solitary

SOLITARY. IT WAS A WORD THAT STUCK with Nathan ever since he learned it at school many years ago. He recalled that *solitary* meant "being, living, or going alone without companions; or single, isolated, not part of a group." This word struck a chord in him, since he felt that every description of the word was an accurate portrayal of him. When he was living at the pub, studying at school, drinking with his friends, and now, sitting at his desk at work, he felt solitary. Most of the time, he enjoyed being alone. Yet when he walked home, especially at dusk, he felt a great sense of loneliness. Since he'd lost his lust for revenge against the Pearls, the thought of alcohol and opium seeped into his mind.

On Saturdays, he would usually head out to the pubs. On work nights, he kept up with the discipline from his school days and went home and just read the paper—alone, by himself. He became weary of this way of life—needed to move on. Deep down, he understood what this meant. He couldn't remember a time when he really took control of his actions. There were always others who guided him and told him what to do. But not today; today, as he walked along the East River, he made an epic decision.

The wind that coursed off the river was unusually fresh. Even in May, when spring perfumed the air in other parts of the country, it was an anomaly for New York.

Ah. Nathan stopped short. Watching Flora was the best part of any day, let alone a cloudless spring day. He watched from afar as Flora pulled the telescope out of her coat pocket and peered through it for a long while. She was such a creature of habit. If the weather was nice, he would find her peering at the bridge on a Saturday afternoon, with her pastries in hand and whatever else she picked up on the way. Sometimes, he even sighted her on Market Street, purchasing items from street vendors. Why she was so consumed with the bridge he didn't know, but just seeing her use that telescope made him feel closer to her.

She gazed towards the place where the New York *caisson* had recently been filled with cement. He'd actually been down in that *caisson* a few times when the excavations first started. The garbage that had to be pulled out of the river was shocking. Suddenly, Nathan saw that Flora had either taken off her hat, or it had fallen off, causing her long, wavy-brown hair to fall about her shoulders. As it unwound down her back, Nathan imagined plunging his hands into that wild mass of hair and pulling her close to him.

She just stood there, looking through her telescope with the wind drifting through her hair, her velvet, blue dress pressing against her body. Nathan watched with intensity, wondering what she would do next. From Nathan's perspective, he could see the Brooklyn tower looming in the background and Flora in the foreground. The resplendent scene made approaching her all the more intimidating. He instinctively took a step forwards to get a better view but found that his knees were weak, probably due to his not eating a proper meal that day, so he decided to just stay where he was.

Flora lowered the telescope from her eye and quickly glanced around, as if she felt his gaze. Other people had passed her by without as much as a second glance, but she didn't seem concerned with anyone in particular. Slowly, she placed her hat on the ground and stepped on the edge so it wouldn't fly away in the wind, gathered up her hair back into a knot, and efficiently pinned her hat back into place.

He followed her up to Market Street, where she hailed a cab. As he watched the cab make its way down the street, he promised himself that they would be together. He could feel it in his heart; this solitary heart that had never once felt love instinctively knew that this was his woman. His soul demanded to be united with her.

He strolled back to his apartment, which was in disarray as well as stuffy. His days spent working on the bridge were quite tiring. Inspecting the stonework at the towers, interpreting drafts for other workers, and fielding a multitude of issues throughout the day were all thankless tasks.

Nathan changed his clothes to those better suited for the old neighborhood. He really didn't feel like catching up with his friends, even though they always welcomed him with open arms and shots of whiskey. They really didn't care about Nathan. In the old days, he felt that this was the greatest escape from reality, but right now, all he wanted was reality. He was tired of trying to avoid life. Bee was correct about his friends. They were going nowhere in life.

He sighed as he stood in the middle of his dusty apartment. So much of his time and money were just wasted on these people. The last time he saw them, he felt as though he was paying for them in the same way that he paid for the attention of a woman at Bee's Inn. His lack of integrity grated on his nerves. Vowing to himself that he would lead a more respectable life, he kicked newspapers that lay strewn on the floor into a pile in front of his sagging sofa.

Bee was the only person who would understand. But he was hesitant about telling Bee about Flora. Bee knew about his secret goal of retribution against Mr. Pearl, but vengeance seemed a remote possibility now. He didn't have the heart, the nerve, or the fortitude for such an endeavor anymore.

I'm twenty-four years old, for God's sake, and I've nothing to show for my life except this dump of an apartment. Nathan looked down at the newspapers and started to gather them in his arms but gave up. Giving the mound one last kick, he turned and walked straight out the door.

On his way to Bee's apartment, he purchased the nicest bottle of port that he could find. As he approached her building, he saw Bee getting out of a cab with several packages.

"Nathan! You have perfect timing," Bee said, smiling at him.

Nathan helped her with the parcels, depositing them on the floor in her foyer. The room was lined with several oil paintings, which were all floral in nature. They both proceeded into Bee's parlor, which contained more paintings. The centerpiece of the room was her fireplace, with the delightful globes lined up in a row on the mantel.

"Nathan, what's bothering you so? I know you well enough to know that something's on your mind."

"Where are Rachel and Vince?" Nathan asked as he opened the bottle of port.

"Rachel went on an extended trip to Provincetown with a man. I'm sure they will end up getting married and will never return. I don't know where Vince is at the moment. I told him that I was going to be out shopping all day."

She stood at the window as Nathan poured the drinks. He handed one to Bee and then wandered around the room a bit as a stalling tactic. With a start, he realized that all of Bee's paintings were of flowers. Bee quietly sipped her drink and watched him.

"I think I'm in love," Nathan said quickly.

"You? In love!" Bee gasped. "Which one? You're with different girls all the time."

Bee wearily walked over to one of the chairs and sat down. "Come here and sit next to me."

But Nathan stood firm near the fireplace.

"I . . . I hardly know her. I've only spoken to her briefly once, but I've seen her from afar many times. She dresses so magnificently. Well, she doesn't overdo it, but you can see how confident she is—but without the least bit of vanity. Oh, and she's obsessed with the bridge. Don't you think that's an interesting coincidence?"

Nathan felt he was rambling and realized that he'd started pacing the room. He looked at Bee and saw her concern.

"If you've hardly spoken to her, how do you know that she's obsessed with the bridge?"

Nathan froze in his tracks and then slowly walked around and took his seat next to Bee, looking at her round face. Her hat was still perched on top of her head, and her hair whimsically curled around the edges of it, with tendrils charmingly escaping. When Bee saw that he was looking at her hat, she removed it and placed it aside.

"Because I've been following her around the city for over a year now, maybe two. I introduced myself to her just once as she walked along the East River, looking over at Brooklyn. That's the only time I spoke to her. I gave her a telescope that I see her using all the time. But I don't have the nerve to approach her again."

"Why did you approach her to begin with? Is she that attractive?"

Nathan knew he had to confess everything now. Bee's attention to his every word was evident. Why would he approach her? Nathan knew why, but to confess to Bee would be to admit the truth.

"Nathan, who is this girl?" Bee asked very slowly.

Nathan hesitated. He didn't want to tell her because Bee would know in an instant who Flora was. He was suddenly afraid of what Bee would say. She was always so right in her assessment of people, so he knew that she would respond with a correct appraisal.

"Well, who is this girl—what's her name?" Bee asked again.

Nathan couldn't meet Bee's eyes and looked down at the floor when he said, "Flora Pearl."

Suddenly, there was complete-and-deafening silence. Bee put her glass of port on the small table beside her chair and looked at her gloved hands folded in her lap.

After a while, Nathan finally, and tentatively, asked, "What are you thinking?"

"Why did you seek her out?"

"I didn't seek her out."

"So your paths crossed by coincidence?"

Nathan looked at his shoes as if they were interesting.

"After Kyle and Erin passed away, I went to find Mr. Pearl and discovered that he'd passed away. I was standing across the street outside their house when I saw her enter. Suddenly, I was filled with rage. She . . . she used to sit in the carriage when her father came down to meet with his manager. Do you remember? Sometimes she and her sister would follow Mr. Pearl into the office. After collecting his rent, that was the house they came home to. Oh, it's a huge house, just across from Washington Square Park that was built by taking advantage of poor people who had no choice but to live in his slums!"

Nathan paused and took a sip of his port. He pushed back his hair, knowing that Bee would immediately recognize it as one of his nervous habits. He had heard his voice begin to rise, so he took a moment to compose himself.

In a more controlled voice, Nathan went on, "I stood there for a long time, wondering why I never knew where this man lived before that very moment. Then I walked away and started to plot my revenge. Now that I can't kill Mr. Pearl, should I burn the house down and leave them all homeless? Should I strangle the breath out of his daughter? Drag her to the river and drown her and then throw her body in for the rats to gnaw? There needs to be retribution for what he has done!"

Nathan got out of his seat and started pacing the room again. He stopped at the fireplace and examined the small globes that sat on Bee's fireplace mantel. He couldn't help but pick one up so he could twirl it on its stand, even though he knew that Bee didn't like when he did that.

"I started to follow her." Nathan paused as he put down his drink and picked up one of the globes. He started to twirl it, staring at the small Earth go round and round.

"The more I followed, the more intrigued I became. She owns a boutique not far from here. She, her sister, and another woman go to the Alms House in the morning once or twice a week. That other girl that I referred to as her sister may not be her sister. They don't look alike. She may be a cousin because they seem to be close, as family would be. I think it's the same little girl as when we were young, but I don't know." Twirl, twirl the globe. Nathan felt as if he was under some kind of spell. "I can picture her now, as she walks down Market Street, stopping at carts and talking with the merchants.

"When I regard her face, as she walks through the worst parts of the city, I can see that she's confident, but she doesn't look down on people. When the day is nice, she slowly makes her way from Market Street down to the piers."

Nathan carefully placed the globe back on her mantel and turned away from the fireplace. He picked up his port and sat down in the chair next to Bee's.

"I've come to you for advice about how to proceed."

Bee sat back, took a sip of her drink, and, for a few minutes, seemed to be contemplating all that Nathan had told her.

Finally, she said, "For years, when we were children, you could only speak of getting revenge for what Mr. Pearl had supposedly done to your parents, your real parents. Of course, I believe that your anger is only your guilt that they were dead, and you were alive. Or you were angry that you had been left alone and didn't know how to go on. I never saw you grieve over the death of your parents. You just showed your anger. How have you suddenly come to terms with that? Do you still believe that the fire was set on purpose? By Mr. Pearl?"

Nathan took a sip of his port, considering her question for a moment. It was a good question and brought to light some things that he'd been contemplating but couldn't yet figure out.

"A few weeks after the pub burned down, one of Kyle's best customers asked me why I didn't die in the fire. He asked me why my life was spared."

"Someone asked that? What did you say?"

"Nothing. I was too shocked at the question. And I often think about how you said that the fire at the pub was a sign or a message. Do you remember saying that?"

"Yes, and I felt a little guilty. I was afraid that you were going to think I meant that you deserved it."

Nathan shook his head. "I was so mad for being left alone again."

Nathan paused and then continued, "Kyle didn't want me to run a pub. He had larger aspirations for me. They had patience and faith in my abilities, yet I found every excuse not to be out on my own. The fire forced me to change and to get a job that finally uses my education, even though I just wanted to stay angry at the world and blame someone for the catastrophe. There was no one to blame and no one to tell me what to do anymore. And anger? It seems to have dissipated, and now I can think a little more clearly."

"But what about your feelings towards Mr. Pearl?"

Nathan leaned forwards and placed his head in his hands, his fingers laced in his hair.

"I've wasted so much time and energy thinking about that man. I'm tired of being—being *stuck*. I've forgiven him. I'm relieved to forgive him. You're correct. I've no proof that he started that fire. It doesn't seem to matter anymore. Then, when I started to think about this so-called forgiveness that I've most graciously bestowed on the late Mr. Pearl, I realized that I wasn't really forgiving him. I was actually forgiving myself. Giving myself pardon for being that young boy who was out drinking while my parents were killed. Both times."

"I've never heard you talk like this before."

Nathan looked up at Bee and saw the sincerity in her face.

"Yes, Mr. Pearl may have been a despicable person, but I've found that retribution won't solve anything. My anger has to be resolved by simple forgiveness."

"I know her."

"What?"

"Yes, I know Flora. I buy almost everything in my wardrobe from her little shop."

"Does she—Flora—know what you do?"

"Yes, and she doesn't care. As far as I can tell, she's sensible, honest, and a truly good person. Oh, she has her problems, but who doesn't? She speaks of Mr. Pearl as though he were alive, in Europe, on an extended trip. But I'm not in a position to question her about it. I've also found out about just one positive thing Mr. Pearl did that may surprise you."

"What? Tell me."

"He actually funded the reading program at the Alms House."

"Yes, I forgot that's how you learned to read."

Bee was quiet for a moment, contemplating something.

"You can't let her know that we know each other," Nathan said.

"Well, she has never mentioned you."

"But if I do start to court her, what would she think if she knew that I knew you? Am I offending you?"

"No, you're being realistic, but I have to think it through. I don't like to lie."

"What about her father? Should I tell her that I knew him, that he was my landlord?"

"I don't see how you can now," Bee replied. "You would've told her as soon as you learned her last name. Do you think she would ever find out? If you do tell her, you have to do it at your very next meeting. So you must confess that you knew of her father—the details don't have to be discussed."

"Did you tell her that you knew her father?"

"No, but I didn't live in one of his buildings. So," Bee said, "are you going to ask Flora to have dinner with you?"

"Yes, something like that, or maybe just coffee and pastries. I believe she has a sweet tooth."

"No, no, no. You have to make the first date special. Do I have to teach you everything about normal life?"

"Tell me—what do you think of her? How did you happen to be in her shop?"

"Rachel told me of the shop. When Flora introduced herself, I was quite surprised. The name of her shop is The Pearl, but I just didn't make the connection until she spoke her name. I immediately wondered why she would be working. I'm sure she has enough money to not work and to just find a husband and have children. But she's not that kind of person."

"What kind of person do you think she is? I can only surmise by my having followed her around. How despicable that sounds."

"Well, she's quite a shrewd business person. But—" Bee stopped and paused to think.

"What—but what?"

"She's never been courted by anyone. At least I don't think she has. She's aloof. Sometimes it's difficult to know what she's thinking."

They were silent for a few moments.

"Where are you staying tonight? Rachel's room is unoccupied, if you want to stay. You can actually just move in there while she's gone. Your apartment is dreadful."

"That's kind, but I like my dreary apartment. It keeps me humble."

"You can keep it if you want, but stay with me now. It's lonely without Rachel here."

"What about Vince?"

"Oh, the rooms are far enough away, so you won't bump into each other. I'll be sure to tell him tonight that you're visiting."

"Yes, please do. I don't want him to 'accidentally' beat me to a pulp because he thought I was an intruder."

"Yes, yes. I will. But I'm sure you could hold your own," Bee said in amusement. "Does that mean you're staying?"

"Yes. Let me go back to my apartment to get a few things, and then I'll be back."

"Good. I'll make something for us to eat. It just so happens that I made apple pie yesterday."

Nathan couldn't help but grin from ear to ear as he made his way out her door and onto the street. What would he do without Bee?

Aria

(Earth names, Anna and Olivia)

The Soul World: Nathan Doing Well

ARIA WAS EXCITED THAT NATHAN HAD reached this point in his life. He made the decision to pursue Flora, but Aria knew that Flora wouldn't be an easy conquest. When Nathan and Flora had planned this relationship in the Soul World, Flora warned Nathan that he would probably have to work hard in order to gain her trust. The residual from their past life together as Kelvin and Jillian was bound to spill over into the next. Jillian had spent so much time waiting for Kelvin, while he was away at sea, that she felt bound to reciprocate.

This was a hurdle that Aria felt Nathan would clear. Once cleared, the true test of their relationship would lie in the future. But she didn't want to think about that right now.

"Aria?"

Aria turned to find Teacher approaching.

"Yes, Teacher. Welcome."

"Aria, your updates have been very promising. I felt that you had a little breakthrough just now."

"Nathan forgave Mr. Pearl. By all indications, it seemed sincere. In addition, he's decided that it was time for him to move on in his life. He's spent too much time idle, without any emotional growth."

"What of Flora? Is she progressing towards her goals?"

"She's progressing. Slowly. She's gravitating towards her secret desire to do good works with all of the wealth that she has. She's started to do some volunteer work and has given some small donations."

"Do you think her actions stem from guilt more than compassion?" Teacher asked.

"Does it matter?" Aria asked.

"Yes, it does. Actions that originate from guilt are actions that are meant to pacify one's self. Those that stem from compassion are deemed selfless acts," Teacher said as she made her departure.

Aria was left alone to contemplate Flora's actions. It was some time ago that she first asked her stockbroker to assist her in starting a foundation. *I'll have to go back and review her decision-making process, but I'm sure that Teacher is correct.* Her motivation was probably guilt.

The East River Bridge

New York Caisson Filled

BY JULY OF 1872, THE NEW YORK *CAISSON* was filled with cement and stood at a depth of seventy-eight feet, with the Brooklyn tower standing at a height of one hundred feet above the waterline. In November, work on the Brooklyn tower temporarily stopped, and in December, work on the entire project was delayed due to bad weather. By December, Roebling was no longer able to travel to the bridge site because of the serious condition of his health.

Understanding that his time might be limited, Roebling documented all he could about the completion of the bridge while his wife, Emily, prepared for the worse. For some women, his illness might have been an excuse for hysterics and helplessness, but not for Emily. The situation would be confronted fearlessly and confidently, ignoring any prejudices people might have about women.

Emily was already a bright woman, having studied mathematics and science. With her husband's tutelage, she comprehended the intricacies of bridge construction, allowing her to translate Washington's ideas and transmit them to the head engineers. In addition to making her daily rounds to the bridge site, she took care of her husband, mentally and physically. She was his protector.

Flora

July 1872: The Decision

FLORA FELT A LITTLE NERVOUS when she and Victoria entered the bank's office. This was the first time that she had invited Victoria to come with her to one of these meetings, but it wouldn't be the last. She wanted to protect her decisions, and having Victoria with her made her feel more assured. Victoria was her witness. She scolded herself for not thinking of bringing Victoria with her before.

"Flora, why am I with you?" Victoria breathlessly said, trying to keep up with Flora as she made her way through the bank's airy lobby lined with tellers. "This place makes me feel very uncomfortable. It's a man's place, not a woman's."

"It's a place for people with wealth," Flora said matter-of-factly. "They don't care whether you're a man or a woman, just that you have money to invest or to deposit. The more money you have, the happier they are to assist you in investing it."

"How does investing your money make them happy? I don't understand."

"To put it simply, when you invest money here, they make you pay a fee. The more money, the bigger the fees."

Flora elbowed past several people and entered a hallway. The sign above the door stated, "Financial Affairs".

A few steps down the hall, Flora stopped. "There he is. See that man standing in the hall?"

"The skinny one leaning against the wall?"

"Yes, that's who we're going to see."

Flora turned her attention back to the man just as he exclaimed, "Aaaah, Miss Pearl!"

He appeared a little too happy to suit Flora's current mood. Mr. Adams was abnormally thin, and his clothes, as usual, didn't seem to be tailored properly. This particular double-breasted suit wrapped around his body too tightly, making Flora wonder how he managed to sit comfortably. He had a mop of greasy, curly hair perched on the top of his diminutive head, which, in turn, stood on a long column of a neck. His jacket and pants were as pale as his face, making it appear as if he were a small stick protruding from the earth with some mud stuck at the top.

"How lovely it is to see you. And who is this?" he said, turning to Victoria. "Where have you been hiding this lovely creature?"

Mr. Adams took Victoria's hands and looked her over from head to toe. It made Flora want to kick him in his bony shins. *I would probably snap his leg if I did that.* Then she smiled. The image actually made her feel better.

"This is my sister, Victoria."

"Oh, yes, I've seen your name in the files. Please, come into the office. After you, ladies."

After they were seated, Flora said, "Mr. Adams, I want to make some changes in my portfolio."

"Well, are you buying, selling, or both?" he said with too much enthusiasm.

"I'm buying, selling, and changing."

"All right. Are you sure that you're confident in making these decisions yourself?"

Flora ignored his statement and continued, "I'd like to sell all of my railroad stocks and, with the proceeds, purchase the items that I've outlined in this letter." Flora showed Mr. Adams the piece of paper she retrieved from her handbag. "See here?"

"Yeess. Hmm, but that's quite outrageous. The railroad stock is rapidly rising in value right now. You shouldn't sell one share."

Flora cleared her throat and continued, pointing to the letter, "I'd like you to sell another $50,000 worth of my holdings. Here, see—I've made a list here of what I want you to sell."

"All right. And what do you wish to buy with these proceeds?" Mr. Adams said, with a little smirk on his face. He looked at Flora as if she were a child.

"I would like you to contact my attorney, Mr. West. Send him the proceeds. I've outlined all of that information, also."

"Why do you owe him so much? I'm astounded!" Mr. Adams sat back in his chair and feigned deep displeasure.

"I don't owe him anything. He'll be setting up a special account for me. He'll be reinvesting my money in low-risk bonds, but I'd like this money to be totally separate from my accounts here."

Mr. Adams sat straight up in his chair and stared at Flora over his glasses. "Special account, ha? You want to give your money to those slum dogs, don't you? I don't think it's wise to surrender so much of your portfolio."

"Oh, I've figured it all out. I've determined what I need for expenses, how much my investments return, how much profit I make from the store and apartments, and I've found that $50,000 doesn't pose much risk."

"I don't think your father would approve."

Flora suddenly stood up, which caused Victoria to rise as well. "Mr. Adams, I'll be expecting *my* money to be on *my* attorney's desk by the end of the month. Is that enough time for you to complete the necessary transactions?"

"Well, um, yes," he said in a confused manner, slowly standing up himself.

"And I do want the transactions that are listed on this letter executed immediately. Oh, yes—there's one other thing that you most likely didn't notice on this letter. I would like you to transfer all of my cash accounts to the East River Savings bank."

Flora turned to Victoria. "Victoria dear, would you please sign this document also? It's all in order. Our attorney wrote it for us. Mr. Adams, do provide my sister with a quill."

"Of course." Mr. Adams seemed extremely confused and so agitated that he just did as he was told. But as Victoria was signing, he said, "Miss Pearl, why are you taking money out of this fine institution? Your father would be very displeased. In fact, I should bring the bank manager over to discuss all of these transactions with you in detail. You obviously don't know what you're doing."

"Mr. Adams," Flora said in her firm, confident voice. "You've been intimidating me for too long. I've no interest in seeing the bank manager of this institution. He's not made any effort to meet me or attend to any of my financial needs previously. I've been stuck with you. On the other hand, I've already met with the bank manager of the East River Savings bank, and he hasn't intimidated, scorned, disapproved, or reproached me. If you had given me one ounce of respect, all of my cash accounts would still be here. However, I'll give you a chance to redeem yourself by efficiently handling these transactions that are still in your power. Do you think you can do that? Or should I move those accounts also?"

"No, ma'am. I'll take care of everything."

"Thank you and good day."

Flora turned, and they both exited the office, leaving Mr. Adams looking as though he had just lost his best friend.

"Flora, I don't understand," Victoria said, trying to keep up with Flora. "Well, I think I understand. Although I'm still a bit confused, I'm also very impressed with how you handled that Mr. Adams."

Once Flora was outside, she paused and took a deep breath. Victoria walked to the curb and easily hailed a cab. Once inside, Flora put her head back and closed her eyes. She couldn't believe that she had actually done it. After all this time of being afraid to make a move, she had finally done it! And she felt great about it.

"I didn't know you had so much money."

Flora opened her eyes and looked at her companion's perplexed face.

"I do, and I don't like it."

"But why?" Victoria asked. "And what did he mean by seeing my name in the files?"

"You're listed as my sister in the files. Your name is on every account we own, right alongside mine. You do know that my father legally adopted you. You're my sister. Do you know what this means?"

"No."

"It means that if I die, you'll get all of my assets. That is, unless I'm married. No, that's not right; you still are entitled to half, even if I'm married. Your name is on the accounts. Hmm, I need to clarify this with Mr. West."

Flora could see that Victoria instantly became uncomfortable with this revelation.

"Regardless, let me make this simple. As of right now, you do already own half of my assets."

"What!"

"Well, I'm holding it in trust for you until you're twenty-five years old. I don't have to legally ask your permission to do what I wish with this money, but the money that I've just withdrawn and moved around is half yours."

"Flora, how much money do you—I mean, we—have?"

"Let's not talk about that right now. I want it to be clear to you that with this money comes great responsibility and guilt."

Flora became quiet and looked out the window.

Quietly, she continued, "This money is from the poor people that lived in my father's buildings. These people lived in squalor, scraping together pennies in order to keep a roof over their heads. I heard my father on many occasions talking to his property manager. How they would laugh about the tenants' complaints! They would conspire about how they would squeeze more money out of them." Flora closed her eyes and tried to gain control over herself. She felt uncontrollably angry and didn't like that feeling. "Yes. Our father did horrible things, more than I probably know about."

Flora recalled looking at her father's ledgers. Each entry in the book had a code, which was simply a word without the vowels. It didn't take her long to figure it out. Each tenement building was listed along with others that were harder to figure out. One was WTR. This was some kind of water business that he ran on the side. She knew nothing of it but remembered a supplier at the pier making the offhand, impolite comment, "Oh, you're the water-baron's daughter, humph, the controller of the water." His wife gave him a jab in the side with her elbow, causing him to immediately apologize.

The codes of BYBRRY1, BYBRRY2, numbering up to twelve, were perplexing. She didn't even want to imagine that they stood for the Bayberry prostitutes in Five Points.

"Flora, why are you telling me these dreadful things?"

"Because it's time to do something about it instead of ignoring it. I want to do something meaningful and have been planning this for a long time. I've figured out my finances and how to lighten my financial burden. I'm learning that I can start making a difference in people's lives. I don't want to just go down to the Alms House and let those people tell me what they think should be done. I want to be able to do what I think is important—but I'm getting ahead of myself. I'll tell you more once we get to the shop."

They were at the shop fairly quickly. Since it was still before lunch, there wasn't much traffic. As they rushed through the shop's door, Flora saw that Olivia was assisting a customer while others waited. After Flora dropped her wrap in her office, she hurried back and helped a customer step into her new dress so the alterations could be completed. All the while, her thoughts kept wandering.

Do we need more space? Should I expand and hire another seamstress or keep using the few independent pieceworkers that we have?

Several ladies that lived in the neighborhood assisted Olivia and Mum with finishing work. Even though the work wasn't steady, everyone involved seemed to like the arrangement. Flora decided to consult Olivia about this topic later.

After the long day finally ended, Flora went into her office for some peace and quiet. She was opening mail at her desk when Victoria came in.

"Flora, why the secrecy?"

"What do you mean?" Flora asked.

"Why haven't you ever told me about this before? Why didn't you tell me that our father had left both of us this money and not just you?"

"Does the money mean that much to you?"

"No." Victoria looked surprised. "No, not at all." She looked down at the floor, which made Flora wonder if she were about to cry.

"What is it, Victoria?" Flora said patiently.

"Well, I didn't think . . . didn't think that Father really considered me his daughter. I know that I used to call him 'Father,' which made him very happy. I never really felt comfortable using that term, but it made his face light up, so I used to force myself to use it."

"Oh my! Of course he thought of you as a daughter. He made it clear to me from the very beginning that you were part of the family."

"No, no, that can't be true. Father never treated me that way, and neither do you," Victoria said with tears in her eyes.

Flora was taken aback by Victoria's statement. She took care of Victoria as a sister would. Why would she think otherwise?

"Why would you say that?"

"You're overpowering, Flora. You treat me like a servant, like I'm expendable," Victoria said, tears streaming down her face.

"No, no, I treat you like a little sister. Look, Victoria. . . ." Flora got up from behind her desk and walked over to Victoria. She placed a finger under her chin, almost forcing Victoria to look into her eyes. "I'll always take care of you and will do for you what I think is best. It's not because you're my servant, but because you're my sister. It's my obligation to be tough on you sometimes and to watch over your every move."

Victoria simply nodded.

"Now, compose yourself. We're going to go upstairs and interrupt Olivia and Mum's supper. I need to talk to all of you together. Just give me one minute; I'll be right back."

Flora went to the front of the store just to be sure that the doors were locked. By the time she went back to the office to get Victoria, she looked better. Flora retrieved a bottle of port from her desk. They made sure the back door was locked and then took the stairs to their seamstresses' apartment.

Mum seemed surprised to see them at the door so late and asked if there was something wrong. Mum always thought that anything out of the norm meant that there were drastic problems. After assuring her that all was fine and that she wanted to talk to everyone together, Mum let the women in.

"Hey, are you OK?" Olivia said with a worried look on her face.

"Yes, yes. Is it so unusual that I come over?" Flora asked.

"Yes, it is. Usually you send Victoria if you need to tell us something," Mum explained as she placed food on the table. She didn't even ask if they wanted dinner but assumed they would. It was just so typical of Mum to treat all of them as if they were her family. Flora wished that she could just *be* like that. Just let herself go and be completely giving. Even the small gesture of setting a table place for her and Victoria—without giving it a second thought—was so appreciated at that moment. Flora considered that perhaps she was overthinking this gesture, but she still couldn't get over it. Asking guests to stay for a dinner that Annette had prepared seemed frivolous by comparison.

"What do you have there, Mum?" Victoria asked.

Whatever it was, it smelled delicious, which made Flora's stomach rumble.

"Stuffed cabbage," Mum replied. "I know that Annette has left you a cold dinner tonight."

"How do you know that?" Flora responded in surprise.

"My dear. I know everything that goes on around here!"

Flora just had to ask, "How do you find the energy to cook after such a long day at work?"

Mum stood up and looked into Flora's face. At first, Flora thought she had upset Mum, but she was smiling.

"I'm Polish," Mum said with a laugh and a shrug.

Suddenly everyone was laughing at Mum's proclamation.

"Here, sit down, everyone," Mum said.

The cabbage was stuffed with salty ground beef, cabbage, and diced potatoes. Everyone agreed that Mum should teach Annette how to make the dish. Finally, after they were all done eating and Olivia had finished stacking the dishes in the sink, the women sat with expectant looks on their faces and glasses of port sitting in front of them.

"A toast," Flora said, with her glass held up.

Each woman held up her glass.

"To a new beginning."

They clinked their glasses and took sips of their port. Flora took her seat.

"I want to propose some changes to our little shop and our lives."

Olivia's face turned pale, and Mum's hand went up to her throat.

"No, these aren't bad changes. Don't worry," Flora said. "I'm going to make all of you partners in the store."

Both Olivia and Mum looked at her with astonishment. Finally, Olivia spoke up, "What does that mean, Flora?"

"It means that each of you will own your own percentage of the store. I'll maintain fifty-five percent of the store's ownership. Victoria, Mum, and Olivia, you'll own the rest. This means that you'll each receive fifteen percent of the profits."

"This . . . this doesn't make sense to me. Me—own a store? Will I not get a salary anymore?"

"No, Mum. Nothing will change as far as your salary. You see, your salary is an expense of the store. The building's maintenance, the cleaning people, and the fabric and supplies are all expenses that I pay for using the store's profits. Your salary won't change. What will change is that instead of me getting all of the store's profits, you'll get some. The store's profits are calculated by all of the money we get from the goods that we sell minus all of the expenses."

"But why, Flora? This seems like a trick. Why would I get more money for doing the same work?" Olivia asked.

"It's not a trick. I've come to realize that without the three of you, my store would fail. What if you decided to move? You could find another job as a seamstress for about the same pay. However, if you're a real part of the store and have a stake in it, then you'll stay. Olivia, if you created a new hat that many people wanted to purchase, wouldn't you want to work harder if you knew you would get more money for making that hat? I want you to have the feeling that you have some control over our success and over your future."

Flora looked around the table and saw the excitement in everyone's eyes. The concept was foreign to them, but they looked as if they were just beginning to see the potential of such an arrangement.

"But there's more."

"More? How could that be?" Mum said.

"Yes. I'm starting a little charity group."

Olivia's face beamed. "Oh, Flora, I'm so happy."

"What . . . what does this mean, 'charity group?' " Mum asked.

"You know that we purchased washtubs to distribute and that we all volunteer at the Alms House. This is good, but I want to create a long-term effect on people. I've set aside a large sum of money. It'll be invested to last a long time. This is what my father did when he started the reading program. With this money, I'd like to start doing good works for our community. It doesn't have to be restricted to the Alms House either. I'm giving this responsibility to Olivia."

Olivia gasped. "Oh, Flora."

"I won't be sure for another couple of months what our budget will be, but we'll have one. This will give you time to think about what you want to do with the money."

"Flora, why all of these changes? What happened?" Olivia asked.

Flora looked at everyone, all her friends, around the table. How could they understand the guilt that she felt, knowing that her father had earned much of his money in a dishonorable fashion? They had way too much money for it to be from just the tenement rentals.

"Having this much money is a burden for me. I'm alone and don't need it all."

"Flora, you're young. One day you'll have children and will need to be taken care of."

"Yes, Mum, that's sweet of you, but I've taken that into consideration. Hopefully I'll have a husband who can help support a family when the time comes."

"What if there's another great fire and the whole apartment burns down?" Olivia said.

"Well, I have insurance. I know, however, that many insurance companies go bankrupt after fires, so my money is not all in this building. I haven't considered what would happen if we lost the entire store, but I should. And I want you to come to me with any other questions you have. We're a team now."

Flora looked around the table and saw that every woman was deep into her own thoughts. Now that this problem had been faced and resolved, Flora felt that she stood on firmer ground. She was happy that at least one part of her life felt complete, but knew that more serious work lay ahead.

The East River Bridge

Washington Roebling's Health

WASHINGTON ROEBLING AND HIS WIFE traveled to Wiesbaden, Germany, in an attempt to restore his health. Upon their return to New York City in late 1873, Roebling purchased a house in Columbia Heights, one-half mile from the bridge. The Roeblings then stayed in Trenton during the three years the towers and anchorages were being completed.

During that time, he outlined instructions for finishing the towers and stringing the cables. Roebling devised the logistics of the delivery of material including the various wire ropes that would be needed. He documented each stage of the construction, step-by-step, and thought out every anticipated issue that could occur. For each problem, he wrote his instructions on how each should be handled. His foresight was immense.

Washington Roebling had complete confidence in all his decisions and recommendations to both his engineers and to the board of trustees. There was never a question about where he stood on a particular position, and he plainly communicated what he felt was the right course of action on any and every technical matter. He even kept up-to-date on the endless administrative tasks required of a man who had hundreds of employees to look after, as well as his own personal correspondence. Because of his high level of attention, many may even have thought that he was stationed in New York City and was a completely healthy man.

Elizabeth

August 1873: Group Gathering

IT WAS A BREEZY SUNDAY AFTERNOON, and all four women sat in the middle of the store, working on their own various projects at the round table. A wind blew through the room by way of the open windows, causing dresses to rustle on their hangers. Elizabeth could hear the delicate sound of the wind chimes that Victoria had recently purchased as a new item to sell in the store. She only unpacked one set of the small bells yesterday and hung them in the corner of the room.

"What do you think of the chimes, Elizabeth?" Victoria asked.

"Oh, they're perfect! Not loud, very soothing. I think you have another item that will sell. I may purchase one myself and hang it in my bedroom."

The store had been so busy that week that it was necessary to catch up on some of the more mundane and tedious tasks, so it was agreed upon that they would all meet at the store on Sunday. Elizabeth was flattered to be invited to spend the afternoon with the ladies, her friends. Flora had Annette prepare some small sandwiches and cakes, and Mum had brewed a pot of tea before Elizabeth arrived.

"Tell me, ladies: what do you think of this trial?" Flora said as she chose a sandwich and settled back into her seat.

"What trial?" Mum asked.

"I think Flora is referring to the Susan B. Anthony trial, of course. What other trial is as interesting as that one?" Olivia replied.

"Olivia, do fill in the ladies," Flora said.

"Well, Miss Anthony has been fighting for women to get the right to vote. She simply got tired of waiting for those men at the Capitol to take action, so she decided to just show up and vote. Then she got arrested for doing so."

"Why on Earth would women want to vote?" Mum earnestly asked.

"Ms. Anthony has been trying to win women's suffrage since the early 1850s. That woman has attended conventions, has made speeches, and has traveled around the country for more than twenty years—and goodness knows how much else she's done."

"Single women shouldn't be traveling around. It's just not proper. What good is the vote anyhow?" Mum said, waving her hand in the air.

"If you cannot vote, then you have no power of representation. So any law can be passed that condemns whoever isn't being represented. If you're a minority, then why should the majority, who holds power, allow you any rights?" Victoria explained.

"Mum, do you see that the job that you have in Flora's shop has afforded you some power over your own life?" Elizabeth asked.

Mum made sure that the next adornment was placed properly on the hat she was working on. She secured it with a few stitches before responding, which also afforded her a few moments to think over the question.

"Well, yes. Olivia and I earn our money; we budget and purchase what we need and, sometimes, what we simply want."

"Do you think that the money has given you more power, or that the authority you have over your money has given you more power?" Elizabeth responded.

Everyone could see that Mum was giving this question additional thought before venturing an answer.

"Being able to make my own decisions makes me feel more in control of my life. Before, I used to hand my money over to Da, who would sometimes go down to the pub and have a great night. My money was being handed right over to the pub owner. That made me feel helpless." Mum was intently looking down at her darning while speaking, shaking her head sadly.

"Mum," Olivia said, "you never told me that."

"Ya, but what could I do? He was my husband and I had no right." Suddenly, Mum put her darning down. Her face lit up as she understood the meaning of what she just said. "Yes, I had no right! He said that my money was really his money, just ask any police officer!"

"Mum! Here, have some more tea!" Elizabeth exclaimed, embroidering her own pillow.

"Oh, don't misunderstand. I loved my husband deeply. He was a good man, but, ya know, men sometimes have to prove they're the boss."

Elizabeth looked up and saw how each person around the table seemed so happy. Flora had always kept them busy debating and discussing topics. She made it appear as though the topic just came to mind, but Elizabeth had caught on that she chose a topic while reading the paper the day before and then brought it up as a way to prompt constructive conversation. Olivia confirmed to Elizabeth that this was Flora's habit. She often brought up current events to help pass the time while they were engaged in simple and mundane tasks. She always seemed so informed and knowledgeable.

Even though Elizabeth read the newspaper, she knew she didn't read it as Flora did. Elizabeth picked out headlines that excited her, such as "Attempted Suicide by Shooting" or "Arrest of a Horse Thief." She always skipped the columns that were labeled "Special Dispatches from Washington." She completely ignored the "Monetary Affairs" columns and went directly to "Situations Wanted."

But now that Elizabeth came by and participated in these informal talks, she forced herself to broaden her reading horizons in order to keep up. There was usually something interesting to discuss, such as what many of them considered the wrongdoings of the Society of Ladies for Faithful Women. This group of ladies only assisted women they considered "respectable." If a woman required assistance with her children or with her pregnancy, there would first be inquiries made about the woman's character. In some cases, a marriage license wasn't considered enough proof, so references needed to be provided. They wouldn't save women and their innocent children from starvation or homelessness or assist poor women to deliver their babies unless the unfortunate victim had the proper credentials.

Olivia told the group that she was horrified when she heard from Sister Britta that the Faithful Women's group had turned away a homeless woman in labor in the dead of winter because she couldn't produce her marriage license, which was lost in a fire the previous day. Olivia couldn't rest until she found the poor girl, and, after many inquiries, she had found that she'd been taken to the Alms House while Olivia was out. Ever since, she had nothing good to say about the Faithful Women and never relinquished an opportunity to voice her displeasure with them.

"They're the most wretched, self-righteous group of ladies you'll ever meet. I don't think they've ever worked a day in their lives," Olivia said with unusual venom.

"Olivia, why don't you tell us about the material that was delivered yesterday?" Flora said calmly. She was attempting to steer Olivia into a more productive conversation.

"Oh, I persuaded Mr. Rene Marchand—you know, the fabric importer—to sell me those eight bolts of old fabric he had stacked up in the corner of his warehouse, for the price Victoria and I had offered him several weeks ago," she said with a smile.

"You did!" Victoria exclaimed. "But how?" She looked at the women around the table in amazement.

"Well. . . ." Olivia looked quite pleased to have an opportunity to tell her story. "He was showing me a bolt of blue calico and was acting quite displeased that I was interested in something so inexpensive. I actually made him pull out a few varieties of calico and asked to inspect each one. After sufficiently annoying him, I told him that nothing interested me, stared at the fabric I really wanted, glanced at him, turned, and started to walk away. That's when it happened."

"What? What happened?" Mum asked.

"He called out to me, 'Oleeevia, how long will you continue this beeehaaaavior?'

"I said, innocently, of course, 'What behavior?'

"Then he looked down at the floor and said, 'What was your offer for that ole fabric? You've worn me out.'"

"Hmm," Flora commented. "Tell me, Olivia: how many times did you 'displease' Mr. Marchand during the past few weeks?"

"About—let's see—about four times, maybe five."

"Really, Olivia! This is so unlike you," Mum cried.

"Well, he was being so stubborn," Olivia said. "He is a dear man, so there were times when I did feel bad about my conduct."

"Hmm, really," Mum said under her breath.

"What did you say, Mum?" Olivia asked.

"Oh, nothing," Mum replied.

"Speaking of Mr. Marchand," Flora added, "I read in the newspaper that he gave a large sum of money to the Boys Club in Five Points."

Olivia's eyes widened. "Really? How interesting."

"Well now," Elizabeth said. "I'm not sure why people are so comfortable with giving so much of their money away."

Flora immediately replied, "How much money does one need?"

"What? I don't understand your question."

"Have you ever figured out mathematically how much money you really need?"

"No, have you?"

"Yes," Flora replied. "I've figured out that I earn ten times more than I actually need. Why should I have so much when others work just as hard but do not?"

"Your reasoning is very foreign to me. I grew up with the premise that you have to take everything you can."

"Yes," Olivia replied. "I understand that more than Flora. When a person begins with nothing, works hard, and then becomes wealthy, it's difficult to be generous. The fear of having nothing again is too great. In addition, they may resent and not respect those that didn't have to work as hard for their wealth."

"That's very astute. There aren't many people that challenge me as you women do," Elizabeth said.

"Challenge?" Flora replied.

"Yes. You seem to constantly force me to think in different ways. Being surrounded by women of different backgrounds is such an eye-opener. The women that I'm surrounded by are all, umm— how would you say?—cut from the same cloth. When I'm here, I see an entirely different world. Do you think you'll ever regret this decision of yours, Flora?--I mean the decision to share your profits."

"I don't think so. Do I really need to make more money if it causes Olivia and Mum to struggle? This decision of mine is a long-term strategy. I want Olivia's mind be free to create beautiful items for the store. Not be worried about her financial stability."

"Elizabeth," Olivia said. "The question is—do you ever regret your choice?"

"What?" Elizabeth was shocked that Olivia was so direct.

"Yes. You're alluding to the fact that we've challenged you; however, I feel that you're really questioning and challenging yourself," Olivia responded.

"Well . . . well, I don't know," Elizabeth replied, caught quite off guard. "I don't know any other way of life. What would I do instead?"

"You would first have to make a decision to change. I suspect that you may feel a sense of failure or defeat if you even take that first step," Olivia replied.

"Olivia, you're making Elizabeth uncomfortable," Mum reprimanded.

"No, she isn't. She's correct about my inability to even make a decision about my current profession."

"Elizabeth," Olivia said, looking into Elizabeth's eyes. "Please don't think I'm judging you. I'm not. I'm only saying that I feel you're in conflict with yourself."

Later that afternoon, as Elizabeth was preparing to leave, Olivia approached her and handed her a package. It was a set of chimes. The two women embraced and said their good-nights.

During her cab ride home, Elizabeth evaluated the conversation. She still couldn't understand why Flora would give so much money away and why she would share profits with her employees. But the shop had such a positive, joyful environment that she had never felt anywhere else.

Every other business consisted of someone who gave the orders and others who took orders. There was no discussion, collaboration, or cooperation involved, which resulted in dresses that were often unimaginative and that lacked creativity. Yes, Flora had a unique environment in which each member of her staff felt free to give an opinion.

Elizabeth wondered if that same formula would work for her business. If she gave her ladies more money, would they work with more joy in their hearts? She didn't think so. Her kind of work didn't generate that kind of bliss. What Elizabeth did for a living seemed to be fine until recently. Not too long ago, she stopped having sex with clients. She was more than happy to escort them out to dinner or to the opera, but that's where her services ended and the other ladies picked up.

The only person that she was now intimate with was Vince. They loved each other's company and respected each other's privacy. She asked Vince once if he had any other lovers, but he adamantly denied it.

"You're my only lover," he would say with his eloquent accent.

She almost believed him and pondered if she had asked this question because she loved him. Elizabeth wasn't even sure if she would recognize true love. But she did love his company and how he made her feel. The way he smelled of cigarette smoke and whiskey and the sensation of his stubbly beard against her face in the morning was comforting. She could imagine his arms around her at that very moment. A calm and protected feeling enveloped her. Keeping track of her schedule and watching over the girls were his responsibility. However, his most important job was to make sure that all the right people were paid off properly.

After Vince found out that she had stopped sleeping with her clients, he begged Elizabeth to marry him. But she wouldn't. How could she run her business as a married woman? Vince would chuckle and ask, "What does it matter?" But it did matter to her. Marriage would mean he would have control over her, and that was unacceptable, even though her whole business relied on the activities of this man. Elizabeth made sure that he was happy and content but couldn't bring herself to marry him.

Hmm. Asa never seemed to have these problems. Sleeping with clients never bothered her. On many occasions, Asa told Elizabeth that she loved the sex and couldn't care less about being rich. Elizabeth wanted the money and used sex to get it. In retrospect, she saw that these two philosophies were on opposite ends of the spectrum. Asa's philosophy enabled her to be happy in this profession for much of her life. Not Elizabeth. Olivia had correctly assessed that Elizabeth was weary of her choice.

"Oh well," she said as the cab pulled up in front of her home. "There's no use looking back now."

The East River Bridge

New York Anchorage

IN MAY OF 1875, CONSTRUCTION of the New York anchorage began right where George and Martha Washington lived when New York was the capital of the United States. Workers toiled at a constant pace of three shifts a day. Building the foundation of yellow pine, concrete, and limestone, and securing the four anchor plates were all completed within three months.

However, it took some five years to complete the Brooklyn tower. One year to lay the foundation of the *caisson* and four years to build the tower itself. Some felt that the tower took too long to finish, but others thought that high quality, solid construction shouldn't be rushed.

Flora

October 1875: Meeting Nathan

IT CANNOT BE POSSIBLE! Could it be that the same "beast man" from so many years ago is once again crossing my path on this very same boulevard? Yes, he's looking directly at me as he approaches. I'll look down at the pavement until he passes me by.

"Miss Pearl, how nice to see you again!"

Flora stopped right in front of him. She looked up into his mysterious eyes and wondered how she was going to get out of this situation.

"I'm sure you remember me," he said, tipping his hat and returning her gaze. "The last time we saw each other, you spoke of the bridge and how it was going to change the 'entire feel of the city forever.' Oh, please don't attempt to deny that you remember me."

Flora cleared her throat. "I do. . . . I mean, I do remember. The first and last time we met was on this very approach. Have you been away? I thought I would've seen you at least once during the past few years."

Oh, drat. Did she just say that? It sounded as though she'd been looking for him. How dreadful this situation was getting! Suddenly, she felt panic entering her throat. Then she started hoping that she wouldn't do something as horrible as blushing. *Imagine my whole face, throat, and chest turning beet red!* She tried to convince herself to stop thinking about how his voice had haunted her dreams. His face was exactly as she remembered it. She could simply lose herself just listening to his low voice while gazing into the deep, dark pools of his eyes.

"That Roebling keeps us engineers quite busy with bridge building. There are always numerous details to attend to, and it seems that even though our chief engineer isn't on site, he always has a long list of tasks for us."

Flora couldn't say anything. What made him think that she was at all interested in anything that he had to say? Actually, what did he just say? She wasn't used to being distracted by her own thoughts.

"May I walk with you?"

Speechless, Flora surrendered and continued walking in the same direction. It was another windy day, and the water in the East River was very choppy. If it had been a little colder, Flora wouldn't have ventured so far from home. But the sun was shining, so instead of pondering over her decision to go down to the market, she simply hailed a cab and left. Once she started her walk along this familiar path, she was happy that she did because the Manhattan tower looked complete—or almost complete.

"Look at that majestic tower," her walking companion said, pointing towards Brooklyn. "One could only imagine what the final product will be like."

"Oh!" Flora said, fishing through her pocket. "I still have the telescope that you let me borrow. Would you like it back?"

"Have you been using it?"

"Yes. See." Flora pulled it out to show him. "I always have it with me. After you gave it to me, I scolded myself for not thinking of getting one."

"Then I would've missed out on the pleasure of supplying it to you. Please, keep it as a gift from me."

They continued to walk several slow paces without exchanging any conversation; however, it didn't feel uncomfortable to her. Flora watched the bottom of her dress move back and forth with the movement of her legs. Then she started to worry that she should really think of something to say—anything.

"When you look at the towers, it's difficult to imagine how different the construction needed to be on each side of the river," Nathan said.

"How so?"

"Brooklyn was full of rocks and hard-packed clay. Digging even an inch a day seemed an impossible task. Manhattan, on the other hand, has more sediment. Its soil was much softer, and it contained fewer rocks. It was so much easier to dig. However, there seemed to be no end in sight. We kept digging but never hit any bedrock. So the chief engineer had to take a huge risk and stop our dig downwards. Too many people had become sick."

"Sick?" Flora had heard of caisson disease, the illness that seemed to be affecting many of the workers, but she wanted to hear what Nathan had to say about it.

"Yes, over one hundred cases of caisson disease have been reported, and I believe one man died."

"What about you? Have you been down there?"

"I have, but only a couple times." Nathan slowed his pace even further. "Once, we had hit some quicksand, and a group of us engineers went down to assess the situation. Then I was part of another group that took measurements seventy-eight feet down, the final depth. The senior engineer of the group made us take the measurements several times, just to make sure they were accurate." Nathan was shaking his head. "We never did hit bedrock. We knew Roebling was trying to decide whether to stop digging or not. Imagine having the weight of that decision on your shoulders?"

"I never would've thought of it like that," Flora said in amazement. "To think that if he made an incorrect decision, the tower could potentially fall over one day." This Nathan fellow had completely enthralled her with his bridge stories.

"Yes, I don't think I would have the fortitude to make such a ruling."

"Have you ever met Mr. Roebling?"

"I was only introduced to him when I first started."

"He must be very intelligent."

"He is—and so, so, intense. I would see him quite often talking to the senior engineers, his face very stern and confident. Mind you, this was before he fell ill. You could tell how astute he was just by looking into his eyes. Oh, I never had the opportunity to converse with him and am glad for it. I would've been afraid that he would ask me a question that I couldn't answer!"

Flora smiled at his humility.

Again, more walking, no talking.

"I always love coming down to these piers. I like it even more now that the bridge is here. It's a source of entertainment for me. My father used to own some buildings in this neighborhood, and I used to join him when he came to check up on things." Flora sighed. "But he isn't in that business anymore. He said it became too much work for him."

"What does your father do now?"

"He's on a trip right now in Europe, for leisure. He really doesn't have to work anymore. And I'm financially independent now, so he doesn't have to worry about me."

"When will he be back?"

"I'm not sure. I haven't received a letter from him in some time."

"So how are you financially independent?"

"I own my own dress shop. It's called 'The Pearl.'"

"You own a shop? I didn't know that women could manage such an endeavor."

"I think you're teasing me, Mr. Gibson." Flora stole a sideways glance.

"You do remember my name! Please, call me Nathan. May I call you Flora?"

"If you must."

"But seriously—how did your business fare during the panic?"

"I've found that wealthy people don't know how to stop spending their money. They're intent on making it look as if they aren't impacted."

"I was lucky. I have my account at the East River Savings bank, and it didn't seem affected."

"So do I!" Flora exclaimed.

"I did have some railroad stocks, which haven't fared so well."

"Yes, I know. I hope you weren't heavily invested in them," Flora said.

"No, I don't know much about investing, so I was being conservative."

"Oh, Nathan," Flora said, enjoying the use of his name. It made her heart flutter a little when she did so. "Look at the sky. It's going to be spectacular—the clouds are formed in a straight pattern in the sky." Flora was facing towards the setting sun, her finger pointing along the row of clouds. "They'll be very pink across that expanse of clouds, but I predict that they'll not turn vibrantly red. I believe the sky will continue to be blue in between the layers of the clouds. See how they run horizontally, as if a child smeared them across the sky."

"I've never heard anyone describe a sunset like that."

As they continued their walk towards Market Street, Flora felt very much at ease.

"Flora, may I be honest with you?"

"Yes, please do."

"After our first meeting, I've seen you many times on this walkway, but I hadn't the courage to approach you again. See that alleyway between those two buildings over there? That's where I would sometimes be when you passed by. Not every day, mind you, but sometimes, I'd be walking and would see you in the distance. It was as if we were bound to meet again. I'd think to myself, 'Should I run up and say hello?' But, as I said, I didn't have the nerve."

"Why today then? What makes today different than any other day?" Flora asked, looking up into his face.

"I realized that four years had quickly passed since our first meeting, yet my memory of it is as vivid today as it was then. At that point, I panicked a little. I was certain that you would be married by now—but I don't see any ring, so my assumption is that you're not. Maybe some fool has broken your heart or you're not a believer in marriage. I hear that some very independent women think that."

Flora noticed that Nathan ran his hands through his hair while he spoke—a sign of nervousness.

"I haven't met the right man yet. Don't ask me what the right man is because I don't have a list of qualifications. But I'll know the right man when I meet him. Most men don't seem to approve of women who can manage their own businesses. They like to have . . . um . . . have control over their wives."

"I like that you have a business. Tell me: do you make the items yourself, or do you employ people?"

"Well, we do make dresses and other accessories like hats and purses. My sister, Victoria, knows many importers. She buys things that she thinks our clients will find interesting, such as hatpins, jewelry, figurines, and mirrors. And if you have a good relationship with your importers, they give you the opportunity to purchase items before anyone else."

"Really?"

"Yes. It's important to be the first store that stocks a popular item. Sometimes, in order to keep up good relations, you may have to buy something, once in a while, that you may not want to. But most of the time, our arrangements are mutually satisfactory."

"What of your customers? I assume they're mostly women, unless you also sell men's hats."

"My clients are well-to-do ladies who need assistance in putting together outfits for social evenings with their husbands and business acquaintances. And New York City is just the perfect place to have a store. My father always said that everything changed in Manhattan after the Erie Canal was opened in 1825."

"When did your father come to America?"

"My grandfather came, I believe, in 1810. My father was born around 1822, somewhere in New York. It was very different back then, I'm told."

"Do you think there were many Indians in this area back then?" Nathan asked.

"Why do you ask?" Flora realized that she asked with a little too much emphasis, but Nathan didn't seem to notice.

"As a boy, I always thought that New York must have been an exciting place back then. I imagined Indians roaming around in the forest, ready to pounce!"

They both laughed at this.

"No, I don't think there were many Indians close to New York at that time. And you? Where are you from?"

"I grew up here. My parents—well, they weren't really my parents; my real parents died."

"I'm sorry."

"Kyle and Erin pretty much raised me. They owned a pub not far from here."

"What do they do now?"

"Oh, they have passed also. They died several years ago when their pub burned down."

"I'm sorry, Nathan. To lose so much family. . . ." Flora stopped walking, placed a hand on Nathan's arm, and shook her head in sympathy. "That must be difficult for you," she said as she looked into his eyes.

"Flora?"

"Yes."

Nathan paused before he said, "I would like to see you again. Would that be possible?"

Flora didn't answer but turned to start walking again. After a good five paces, she said, "I think that would be agreeable."

"I would like to take you to dinner at Delmonico's."

"I love that restaurant. I haven't been there since . . . well, for a long time."

"It's the perfect place for our first real date."

"All right, then. I live above my shop at 935 Broadway, up near 23rd Street."

"I'll be there at eight o'clock on Friday. Is that acceptable?"

"Yes."

After strolling for a while longer, Nathan assisted Flora into a cab and sent her on her way back home. The sun was starting to go down, and as the cab pulled away, she noticed the perfectly pink stretch of clouds across the bright-blue sky, just as predicted.

The East River Bridge

Towers Complete

BY JULY OF 1876, BOTH THE MANHATTAN and Brooklyn towers were completed and dominated the New York City skyline. In all, it took six years to complete the two towers.

Nathan

July 1876: Asks Flora to Get Married

NATHAN WALKED NEXT TO FLORA, looking at the ground and reflecting on the past several months that they had spent together. They had just finished an early dinner at Delmonico's, their favorite restaurant, and decided to take an evening stroll along the East River.

On their first date at Delmonico's, Nathan realized that the waiters and owners knew her and were happy to see her again after a long absence. He realized that she used to go there with her father, but she still hadn't acknowledged his death.

He'd seen this behavior before in the tenements—the denial that a loved one was dead. But it usually did not last long.

He wasn't sure if he should say anything to her about it. She was working and supporting herself just fine. Every other aspect of her life seemed to be intact and normal, so why should he confront her? But during their first dinner together, it distracted him. She did seem a little nervous, but it was their first date. She wore a dress that could only be described as "straw colored." The low, scooped neckline exposed her chest and the top of her shoulders. On several occasions, he found himself studying the front of her dress, which had the smallest amount of lace and intricate flower-like adornments along the edge. Her hair was tied up behind her head in a complicated knot, leaving the back of her neck exposed. He was truly enchanted.

Since then, they went back to Delmonico's about twice a month. Nathan could easily afford it, since he was a well-paid engineer. He enjoyed watching her order her dinner with such enthusiasm, but she always had trouble making a final decision about what to have. This dilemma always made him sit back and smile at the serious look upon her face. Nathan was quite familiar with the offerings on the menu, so he would steer Flora in the right direction. She always complied with a grateful smile. Then she would insist that he try a bite or two of her meal to prove that he made the correct recommendation. He started to feel spoiled by the high quality of the food at this restaurant and found it difficult to eat anywhere unless it was of equal caliber.

Tula's Restaurant, near Central Park, also served delicious fare. They went there for lunch several times during the cooler days of spring and then took walks in Central Park. Once, they went to the zoo, but Flora was too dismayed over the animals that were kept in cages. He didn't see anything upsetting about it, but she claimed it was cruel and couldn't bear to witness their incarceration.

One of their most pleasurable outings was when he took Flora, Victoria, and Olivia to the World's Fair in Philadelphia. Nathan arranged everything. Flora closed the shop, and they all spent one night and two wonderful days in Philadelphia. Mum wanted nothing to do with the trip and said she would watch over things until they returned.

Olivia voiced amazement over the entire trip and couldn't talk about anything else for days. It was the first time she had left the city, which made Nathan feel bad for her. While Flora and Victoria had gone on small trips with Flora's father to Niagara Falls, and once to Boston, Olivia had never seen anything but New York. During the trip, Olivia told Nathan in confidence that when she married, she would insist on having a honeymoon at Niagara Falls.

He looked up and realized that he was thinking about Flora so intently that he lost track of where he was. They had walked much farther than he realized.

"Nathan?"

"Yes, Flora."

"You seem so far away. What are you thinking?"

"Flora, why don't we get married?" Nathan asked in earnest.

Flora's face suddenly turned ashen, as if she was about to faint. "Well, I don't know. You've taken me by complete surprise."

"Why? Why don't you know?"

Flora walked alongside Nathan and looked steadily at the ground. In fact, they were walking on the same path as the one where they had first met, the same path where Nathan asked if he could court Flora. Since then, they had spent a lot of time together. Nathan was at the shop almost every night at closing time. He did stay away when Flora and the women had their get-togethers, but other than that, Nathan was a part of their routine now. Olivia and Mum just loved him, and Annette even confided to him that it was wonderful to have a man around the house. The time Nathan spent with this group of women became one of his greatest joys.

"I don't know if I can explain this."

Nathan was silent.

"When I'm with you, I feel very secure but afraid. I'm afraid that I won't be able to love you completely. There's always something that's holding me back from surrendering myself to you. What can it *be* that makes me so incomplete? Other women don't have any problems conceding to their husbands. No, that isn't correct. Is *conceding* the correct word?"

"Are you afraid that you won't be able to continue working in your shop? That you'll lose your independence?"

"No, I don't think so. You seem to like my working at the shop."

"I think it's a wonderful profession. You're so passionate about it, which is something I lack with my work."

"You may not be as passionate about your work, but you seem to be passionate about me."

"Yes, that's true." Nathan kicked a rock. "I used to harbor anger towards people. Almost all people—but when I lost Erin and Kyle, I began to see that my anger prevented me from loving other people. The question is—what's preventing you from doing so?"

166

After a few moments, Flora stopped and pointed towards the bridge.

"Nathan, you once asked me why I was so obsessed over this bridge."

"Yes?"

"Well, when I first read about the bridge being built, I was at. . . . Well, I was at a point in my life where I was. . . ."

Flora paused.

"Don't be afraid, Flora. Tell me."

"Look, Nathan." Flora stopped walking and faced the river. "This incomplete bridge looms over me. Those massive columns of granite, which you helped build, have the strength to weather one hundred years or more. It will continue to stand strong, even with the deep currents of the East River crashing against it day after day. But the two towers stand completely alone with their arches empty."

Flora turned towards Nathan and continued, "I feel that there's a connection between the bridge and my life and, now, our relationship. How will life change when the two towers finally unite?"

Nathan suddenly reached out and grabbed Flora around the waist and pulled her close to him. Flora, taken by surprise, was breathless, and for a moment, she looked frightened, but she made no sound. There weren't many people around, but this kind of physical contact wasn't normally seen in public. It was also not a normal occurrence between the two of them, even in private.

"Flora, let me make something very clear to you," Nathan said very softly. "I'll wait as long as you wish. I'll patiently wait for you as long as it takes."

He could feel Flora's sweet breath upon his face. Her eyes were wide open and locked with Nathan's, but in hers was an expression of surprise. It made Nathan feel powerful to hold Flora up against him, with one arm around her slender waist. Her chest was pressed against his, heaving with fear. She held onto his arms firmly, without resistance. He could feel wisps of her hair on the left side of his face, and he fought the desire to kiss her fully on the mouth. Instead, he let his lips move ever so close to hers as he spoke.

"You need to make this decision willingly. You need to want me, and you need to desire me so much that it will last for the rest of our lives. I'll never leave you and am totally dedicated to you. That won't change. Do you understand?"

"Yes," Flora said, her eyes brimming with tears.

Nathan took a handkerchief out of his pocket and gently wiped her tears with one hand as his grasp around her waist relaxed.

"I do love you, Nathan. As much as I'm capable of."

"I know, I know, Flora."

Aria
(Earth names, Anna and Olivia)

The Soul World: Not Going Well

ARIA SAT BACK AND SIGHED. The relationship between Nathan and Flora wasn't going well. Time was running out. Even though Nathan had other ideas to win Flora over, Aria was still nervous, just the same. This behavior wasn't surprising. Flora had waited for her husband to return from long voyages time and time again as Jillian Bristol, so this residual in their present lives was understandable. Flora would make Nathan wait this time.

Council Summary of Julya's life as Jillian Bristol, written by Councilor Creek:

Soul Julya—or Flora, from her most recent life—was married to Aiden in her life in Manhattan as well as in her previous life in Provincetown. In Provincetown, their names were Jillian Bristol and Kelvin Massey. Kelvin was a sailor with whom she was in love, even though no one, including herself, understood why.

They lived in a two-story home that Kelvin had built on a bluff close to the bay. The little whitewashed cottage had a small sitting room overlooking the street, a separate cook's room, a dining room, two upstairs bedrooms, and a small balcony. It wasn't a treacherous walk to get down to the beach, but the bluff provided just enough of a barrier to protect the house from the waves. The tall, sharp grasses around the house served to shelter nests of piper birds. Jillian enjoyed watching the birds scampering up and down the beach alongside the bubbles that fringed each wave. The couple had a perfect view of Cape Cod Bay, and when they stood on the balcony together with the wind whipping their hair, they were content and happy.

Kelvin wasn't a deckhand or a captain but a second-in-command and highly respected by his peers. But was the respect earned by intimidation? Jillian suspected that his crew feared him because he had such a quick temper. He had no reservations about brawling with someone over a simple misunderstanding. However, Kelvin's temper never seemed to stop men from entering into a contract with him for long voyages. She'd overheard these sailors say that he was a hard man, but one who would never turn his back on anyone in need.

He never struck her, but the fear of being struck affected her all the same. This anxiety hovered in the dark corners of their life together. When she had to tell him that she owed money to the tailor because she purchased a new dress, his fist would curl up onto a tight ball—but it never left the tabletop. Tentatively, she would place his dinner in front of him next to his tense fist, awaiting a blow. But it never came.

She hated asking him for anything, even to fix a broken hinge. Yet she knew that he would do the task sometime before he took his next leave. If he asked her opinion about something, she was frozen with fear. What answer did he want? Instead of responding with confidence, she meekly stated an opinion that she thought he wanted to hear. It wasn't evident in his actions, but she could feel his pent-up rage; this prevented her from being totally honest with him about her feelings. It kept her from trusting him. Her distrust was as if an invisible line was drawn between them.

Jillian was a soft-spoken woman, with a face horribly scarred in an accident that had happened shortly after their marriage. Kelvin wasn't handsome, but he was rugged looking and strong. He drank too much and boasted too much. He had no real friends, but that didn't stop him from going to the pub and having a good time. He was generous with his money, especially after a couple shots of whiskey warmed his stomach.

Kelvin's longest voyage was six months. Every evening, if weather permitted, Jillian would walk up the stairs to the widow's walk and gaze over the bay to watch the sun set. This was her habit whenever he was away.

The sunset always began with a few shafts of light and then blossomed to glorious shades of pink, red and orange while she watched. At times like these, she missed her husband, who she considered her closest friend. It confused her that she missed and cared for the man that frightened her. She did love him but felt that her emotion was from afar, on the other side of that invisible line.

Jillian would peer though her glass balcony door, eyes scanning the horizon for his approaching ship. Never once did she actually see his boat come into port, but, instead, he would burst through the front door unexpected or sneak up to her at the market or crawl into bed right before the sun came up. Each time, she welcomed him with open, warm arms. The days she spent with him were memorable ones, in which the time waiting suddenly became inconsequential, only to come crashing down when he left for the piers to start his next journey.

Then there was that last journey. Sailors from another ship told her that they had heard that the ocean took her husband's ship. She just pretended that his journey was taking a little longer than usual and kept up her nightly vigil on the widow's walk. After eating her evening meal, she would take a long walk down the beach with her Bible *in hand, watching the tide and listening to the ocean sounds. Eventually, the sound of the waves hitting the beach began to fray her nerves. The crashing sound on the sand never ceased, whether she lay in bed, made her meals, or mended her clothes in front of the fireplace that Kelvin built.*

When she believed that she might go mad, she took off her shoes, picked up her small Bible, *and walked along the shore. The sun was slowly starting to set, causing the light to sparkle across the expanse of ocean that lay in front of her. She could see whales swimming in the distance, their spouts spraying water into the air, as she bent over and picked up a large stone and hurled it into the ocean.*

She shouted, "I pray that your waves come crashing through my bedroom and pull me into the sea! Stop this miserable life of mine! Why did you take my husband? My hatred cannot be eased." With that, she threw her Bible *into the waves, hoping that her prayer was heard. She previously denied her fate. Now it turned to pure anger.*

Jillian changed from a pensive young woman to a bitter person filled with hatred. Her sister treated her with indifference. Isabella must have decided that there was nothing to be done. Though she never admitted it to the Council, she seemed to have been relieved when Jillian died from a severe fever a few weeks later.

The East River Bridge

Final Cabling

WASHINGTON ROEBLING PLANNED the final specifications of the cabling in 1876. Each of the four cables would consist of an unbroken strand of wire that would traverse from one anchorage to the other, nineteen times. The wires would be six times the strength needed to bolster the bridge. Zinc coating would protect the cables from the salt in the air.

What will be more majestic about the East River Bridge—would it be the massive towers or the seemingly intricate web of cables that would extend from the anchorages across the river, making their way between the two towers and then gracefully curving downwards?

Olivia

July 1876: Dreams

OLIVIA OPENED HER EYES. For a moment, she didn't know where she was. The room was completely dark, but then she realized that she was in her home. Several times in the past, she had awakened in the same way: confused about *where* and, more disturbing, *who* she was. It was the strangest feeling.

Rain tapped against both the window and the outside wall. For several minutes, she just stared up at the black ceiling, unmoving, enjoying and relishing the complete relaxation. The sound of the rain outside seemed familiar, but she didn't know why. Something in the back of her head made her throat ache from trying to think too much. It was as if she was trying to remember someone's name or a certain word. The information was there but just out of reach.

Maybe it was related to the dream she just had. She was dreaming that she was a tall woman with long, tan legs, walking through thick grass. Her straight, wet, black hair lay heavily down her back. She must have gotten wet in a downpour. Drops of cold water hit the backs of her strong legs. She was almost the complete opposite of her present, small, pale self. As Olivia continued to stare into the darkness, she tried to unearth more details of her dream but could only remember a peaceful, open feeling that was buoyed by the strong, warm, and fragrant wind. The sound of water could be heard flowing across rocks in a nearby stream, and there was a child's faint giggle.

She heard a fleeting, spontaneous call, "I neeeeed you." It sounded like a child who may have only wanted to show her the petals of a flower or to point out a frog leaping in the grass. It was a call of joy but also one of longing.

She dreamed about this child before. Maybe the child represented Olivia's childhood fear of being abandoned. No, no. Olivia was certain that she was leaving the child behind. During the dream, she felt fleeting stabs of sorrow, and, from somewhere within the dream, she heard a voice making a vow of patience and faith. A change seemed imminent, and there was a longing to hold on to the stability and love of this child as long as possible.

Instead of going back to sleep, Olivia started to think about when she had this dream before. Finally, she recalled that she hadn't had a dream like this one since right before she met Flora. Yes, it was the morning she met Flora. That too was a morning when she had awakened, her eyes opened, and she didn't know who she was. It was as if she had left her body for a moment, but then reality set in. She realized how cold she was and that her bladder was full and that she was achingly hungry. A dreadful pain traveled from her abdomen to her throat. She was too cold to get up to use the pot and too tired and hungry to expend energy even to make something to eat. It would be something meager anyway, so she just stayed in bed for a moment or two and tried to forget her problems.

Her physical discomfort got in the way of her thinking deeply about the dream that morning, but she could still remember it. Olivia was standing on a bluff overlooking a river. Again, she wasn't the plain, skinny Olivia but a robust, strong woman. She could hear birds singing and the movement of the water below. Olivia remembered that she didn't want to move. She just wanted to savor the feelings she experienced in the dream.

Also, in the dream, there wasn't only a child's laughter but also the child herself, sitting at Olivia's feet. She looked down at the child and sat next to her, and they admired the view together. She then peered deeply into the child's eyes. It was then that she realized that she had been holding a beaded necklace in her fist. When she opened her hand, the child's eyes blinked wide and sparkled with emotion. A huge smile crossed her face. The pair hugged, and Olivia whispered something in the child's ear in a barely audible voice. She wasn't even sure if the child had heard her. She had said, "We will meet again."

That was when Olivia had opened her eyes with the word "agaaaa-in" floating in her ears, along with the noise that grasses made when the wind blew over them. For a few moments, she strained to hear the word once more. Finally, she got up, with dread, once the sunlight filtered into the room. There was no more oil for the lamp, so waiting for the sun to come up was the only option. Her body was so thin that it barely seemed there, and her arms and shoulders ached from sewing all day.

Slowly, she stood, shivered a few times, and relieved herself in the pot. Afterwards, she started to assemble what she could for breakfast. What she would do for a pot of Mum's coffee or an apple dumpling! No, today it would be porridge, again. No coffee. No wood for the fireplace. No pay for another three days. Little did she know that her life would change that day, since it was on that very day that she had met Flora.

Thank goodness she met Flora. Her life was totally different now. Today, upon awaking, her nose wasn't cold, and her feet were toasty warm under a mountain of blankets. There was a bucket full of coal near the stove that was all hers, just waiting to be burned for warmth. Olivia reached over and lit her lamp so that it gave off a soft glow. It wasn't difficult to remember those nights where she and Ma had been freezing and hungry. Because of the lack of food, Ma had rapidly changed from being plump in all the right places to being too thin.

Ma had always had a nice figure. This set her apart from her six sisters, who had all been very slender. The only other characteristic Olivia could remember about them was their crackly, annoying voices. Her aunts were always gossiping about other people, but they never looked at themselves with the same critical eye. Thank goodness Olivia never had to see those selfish, wretched witches again. She smiled, recalling how Da used to say, "Ma must have come from another Da because she's so unlike her sisters."

Ma, who always tolerated Da's comments, hit him across the back of the head gently. They were living in Poland in a very small, but comfortable, house, where tiny Olivia used to sleep in front of the fireplace in a cot that Da built into the side of the wall. It was her favorite place in the world.

"You'll never live down that comment if it's overheard by one of them," Ma warned, pointing towards the door with a grin on her face and a chuckle in her voice.

Da would say, "We'll be away from here very soon—off to America! So don't you worry about that nest of hornets you call your sisters."

Ma and Da had been so happy together; Olivia sighed. Since Da died, she was always worried about Ma. Oh, Ma was a hard worker and bravely agreed to stay in America after Da died, but Olivia worried about her emotional fragility.

Through the curtains on the window, Olivia could see that the sun was starting to come up, and the rain had stopped. So finally she pulled herself out of bed and started to get dressed.

"Ma?" Olivia said softly.

"Yes?" Ma mumbled in her sleep.

"I'm going down to get apple dumplings. Is that OK, or do you want something else?"

"Oh ya, apple dumpling is good. I'll make coffee."

Olivia easily ran down the stairs and out into the damp air. When Olivia was employed as a pieceworker, bent over a sewing machine for twelve hours a day, she started to walk with a hunched back. The muscles in her arms were so pinched that it was difficult to stretch them out. Olivia didn't know how Ma made it through that horrible year. She must have been in pain also, being older, but she never complained once.

Olivia now spent only the mornings at the sewing machine. By the time they broke for lunch, her sewing would be done for the day, and the rest of her time would be spent waiting on customers. But what she enjoyed most was designing new items for the store—dresses, purses, hats, scarves, shawls, and even handkerchiefs. When she sat down with a client to pick out the material and pattern for a dress, she could never just make the dress as it looked on the pattern. The more she got to know her clients, the better she was at modifying dresses to suit their figures and personalities. She created accessories to go with the dresses as well, which her clients couldn't help but purchase.

The best part of her job was being able to control the schedule for her work. She could tell her customers that their dresses wouldn't be ready for weeks, and they would never complain. Flora helped her plan these arrangements. When Olivia first started working for Flora, she would stay up late in order to complete a dress as fast as possible, but Flora put an end to that.

"Olivia, they will wait for one of your dresses," she said. "If you wear yourself out, you'll be no good to me."

It had never occurred to Olivia that she could slow down. Flora arranged to have other seamstresses do the more strenuous work of cutting and pressing outside of the shop. Over time, Olivia learned how to balance the work of their group with outside help. There was an art to deciding who would do what and when it should be done. Once Flora taught her the basic concepts of outlining a schedule, she used it to her advantage.

Olivia went to the bakery two blocks away and picked up several small apple cakes. Before Olivia entered their building, she stopped and looked around. At this hour, she was one of the few people on the block that went to the bakery early. Down the street, she watched people entering and leaving the bakery. Down the other side of the street, she saw no one. Yet she felt as though she was supposed to see something, something important. She took a deep breath and opened the door, hoping that Ma had made some coffee. As she was about to step into the hallway, she heard a voice behind her say, "Miss Oleeevia?"

She knew immediately who it was and slowly turned around to see Mr. Marchand standing a few feet away, his hat in his hand. His suit fit perfectly, as usual. His gray pants were flawlessly pressed and matched his white waistcoat and dark-gray coat. His gray-and-blue paisley tie complemented the entire outfit. That was his knack: adding just that little bit to pull something together, whether it was an ensemble or a negotiation. As he stood, looking down and seeming so alone, Olivia's immediate thought was that something was wrong.

"What's wrong, Mr. Marchand?"

"Oh, nothing is wrong," he said, nervously looking down the street. "I . . . I wanted to tell you that I have a nice shipment of fabric coming in next week."

"All right," Olivia responded skeptically. "Are you sure that's why you came up here? At such an early hour?"

"Well, Miss Oleevia," Mr. Marchand said, taking a few steps closer to her, "you know that I've been a widow for quite some time."

Olivia couldn't believe what she was hearing. She had conducted business with this man for years, and she never once considered that he was interested in her. She estimated that he was about ten years her senior, and did know that he was a widow without children. Once, he told her that he didn't think he could have children.

Olivia always felt that he had a lonely air about him. He didn't seem to be depressed but just had a very calm, and balanced, perspective on life. He bartered in good faith, and she was always satisfied with the outcome. The only time he wouldn't budge was when they bartered for those bolts of fabric a few years back. Olivia had always suspected that he liked the extra attention she gave him during that barter session, and now she knew that her instinct was correct. She always thought he was handsome—but never considered that something would come of it.

"Yes, I know," Olivia said, pushing him to get to the point.

"I came by early, thinking that I would seeee you and maybe get to talk to you alone. I wanted to ask you if you would like to have dinner, or maybe lunch, with me on Sunday."

Olivia took a couple steps closer to Mr. Marchand and looked up into his blue eyes. He was about five inches taller than her. "I would be honored to have dinner with you, Mr. Marchand."

"Oh, pleeease, call me Rene," he said, his expression gleeful. "I'll come by at four o'clock and will need to meet your mama, of course." As he spoke, he took several steps back before he turned around and rushed away. Olivia smiled broadly as she opened the door and proceeded up to the apartment.

"You look like you're glowing," Ma said as she inspected Olivia's package. "Apple cakes! These are better than the dumplings, and they seem to be Victoria's new favorite."

While they finished getting dressed, Olivia filled Ma in on Rene's invitation to dinner. She was delighted to learn that Olivia had a man ask her out, and she seemed very pleased that it was Mr. Marchand, even though she hadn't met him. With a pot of coffee and the cakes in hand, they went downstairs.

"I can't remember. Were they going down to the piers today?"

"No, I think they will be down at their usual time. Could you help me for a moment with the fabric?"

Ma assisted Olivia in unrolling some paisley fabric on the table and helped her pin a pattern on. By the time they were done, Victoria and Flora were there and calling them into the kitchen to eat. Flora got a new pot of coffee percolating, and the women sat down, ready to devour the apple cakes.

Ma immediately told everyone about Olivia's date with Rene. Everyone was quite happy and a little taken aback by the sudden actions of the Frenchman; however, in retrospect, everyone agreed that the man obviously had a soft spot for Olivia for many years.

Olivia looked across the table at Flora, who was uncharacteristically picking at her cake. "What's wrong, Flora?"

"Oh, Olivia," Flora said, looking back at her and then around at the other women. "I'm hopeless."

"What?" No one had ever heard Flora speak that way about herself, and every face showed concern. She was obviously upset about something.

"Since we're speaking so freely of our relationships, I must confess that Nathan asked me to marry him."

All three women started to chime in with their congratulations but quickly realized that something was amiss when Flora just sat there, looking at her cake and shaking her head.

"I told him no. I told him that I was . . . that I was incapable of loving him."

"Flora, no!" Olivia quickly said. "That can't be true."

"Flora, are you sure you don't love him? It appears to everyone that you do," Victoria added. "Mum, what do you think?"

"I think that you'll know when the time is right. These girls are being romantic. Who here has been married? Flora, only you'll know when the time is right."

"Mum, you may have been the only one here that was married, but you cannot disagree that Flora has a problem letting herself feel emotions. Most women carry their hearts on a platter, waiting to serve it to someone. Flora has hidden hers so deep that she cannot even find it."

Flora sighed and took a sip of her coffee.

"Sorry, Flora," Olivia murmured.

"No, you're correct," Flora agreed, stabbing her cake with a fork again. "I don't know why. It's as if you know you're about to cry, so you start taking short breaths, and then with each breath, you swallow the bad feeling and try to replace it with something else. I've replaced that feeling, and the replacement is permanent. It's gone."

Flora paused, looked up at everyone, and sighed. "I'm not sure if it would be fair to Nathan if I married him. He gives so much of himself to me. He tells me everything about what his life was like with Kyle and Erin, the people who took care of him after his parents died."

"Do you talk to Nathan about yourself?" Victoria asked.

"Well, just mostly about the store and things that the four of us talk about."

"Why don't you try to tell him something about your feelings or what you like about him?"

"How can I know that? I don't even know what my favorite dish is at Delmonico's."

"Really, Flora! Tell me something that you like about Nathan right now, anything at all. None of us are going to say another word until you do," Olivia said.

They all started to slowly eat their cakes and drink their coffee in silence. They were all almost done when Flora finally spoke, looking down at her lap.

"I think Nathan has the most exquisite, insightful, dark, and mysterious eyes that I've ever seen. When I look into them, I feel as if they encircle me. They fill my soul with a mist that protects and relieves me of my fears." Flora raised her eyes and looked around the table. "Does this mean everyone can speak now?"

"That's the most beautiful thing I've ever heard you or anyone say," Victoria said, awestruck.

Nathan

August 1876: Words

SUMMER IN NEW YORK WAS SUFFOCATINGLY hot. The morning atmosphere was heavy, the humidity relentless, and, most of all, the unmoving air was odorous. That kind of weather was especially hard on people in the tenements. Nathan could recall the terrible smells oozing out of every crevice; it sometimes caused people to throw up on the side of the street. The lack of sanitary facilities was a disgrace to the city, and Nathan wondered if the situation would ever get better. On days like these, Flora would tell Nathan that she was seriously considering moving out of the city. She would sell everything she owned, she said, and just move to some other town that had fresh air to breathe.

It made Nathan nervous when she spoke like this, but he was certain that whatever plans were being devised in that brain of hers, they would involve him. He knew that she loved him, but did she love him enough to marry him? Not a day passed that they shared angry words, but there were plenty of days in which Flora couldn't express an opinion or make a decision about anything.

Flora could easily make every decision at work with ease and confidence, but when asked if she wanted to go to Delmonico's or the Oyster Hall, she would look dumbfounded. "Where would you like to go?" she would ask in earnest, as if the decision was too much for her.

"Do you want to walk over the bridge when it opens? Would you like to go to the theater?" These were questions posed by Nathan that she simply couldn't answer.

Bee told Nathan that Flora wasn't accustomed to sharing her life with a man. "Maybe she's afraid of what you will think of her decision."

"That's just plain silly," Nathan replied. "She competently makes hundreds of decisions at work."

"But Nathan, she's the owner. She has power over everything in that store. I'm sure she feels the opposite when she's with you."

"You mean *powerless?*"

"Yes," Bee replied.

As he helped Flora unpack some lead vases that were delivered to the store early in the morning, Nathan was beginning to agree with Bee's assessment. While Flora stood in this store, all decisions came rapidly and confidently. When alone together, she became full of indecision.

"Thanks for helping me," Flora said as she wiped her forehead with a handkerchief. "Let's go upstairs and rest for a bit. Olivia and Mum will be down soon. They'll open the store."

After they settled at the dining room table, Nathan looked over at Flora while she drank her coffee and read the paper.

She was concentrating on a story that she was reading. She wore a lightweight peach dress that she'd worn before. Nathan had called it orange but had been corrected—this was peach, not orange. Nathan knew that this dress was of the lightest material, but in this heat, any material would be difficult to wear.

He smiled as he looked about the dining room. Both Flora and Bee had an affinity for collecting things. Flora loved to collect glass paperweights, and Bee liked her spinning globes. They both loved paintings, but Bee tended to have more floral paintings while Flora liked pastoral scenes, especially those with cows and chickens. It seemed that every space available in both of their homes was adorned with artwork.

A recent purchase that Nathan and Flora had made together hung on the wall right across from the table. It had caught Nathan's eye in the window of a new art gallery, but Flora was unsure about it, perhaps because it was unlike any other painting in the house. Two ships with great white sails floated across a body of water in the painting, with mountains and a sunset in the background. Flora often spoke of sunsets and the beauty of cloud formations, so this painting had struck a chord in him. The gallery owner told them that it was a Hudson Valley River School painting. The members of the Hudson Valley River School believed that nature provided a healing force and that their paintings inspired that spirit.

"Flora, if you had to choose one word to describe yourself, what would it be?" Nathan asked, folding his napkin. "Personally, I've reduced my personality to one word. Mind you, I didn't come to my conclusion at once, but it came to me over a period of time and aided in the understanding of my self. You should give it some consideration."

"My, my, Nathan," Flora said, looking at him quizzically. Her delicate eyebrows were furrowed, with little creases running in a vertical pattern between them. "Where did this come from? I've never contemplated summing up my whole being into one word. Well, what would it be? Do you have an opinion?"

"I do."

"What is it?"

"I couldn't possibly tell you, since it might influence your choice. It's irrelevant anyway. My word would most likely be far from your own assessment." Nathan continued, "We'll each write down our word and reveal them to each other tonight after dinner, while having a drink. You must write down a word that describes yourself and a word that describes me. I'll do the same for you. I already know the word that describes me, but I'll need to come up with one that describes you."

"Why must I also describe you?"

"Because that will let me know your perception of me."

"Oh, I see." Flora looked amused.

Nathan gazed at her and said, "You must be serious about this, OK? Promise?"

"All right; I promise, darling."

"It's time for me to get back down to the shop. Are you leaving for work too?"

"Yes, let's go."

On his way to work, Nathan wondered when, or if, they would ever get married. On several occasions, Bee had asked Nathan when he would marry Flora, but he would just shrug his shoulders and shake his head as if the whole affair of marrying was foreign to him.

"Make an honest woman of her and marry her!" Bee would exclaim.

"What do you know of her reputation?" Nathan would tease back.

"I know *your* reputation! I hope you take the proper precautions so you don't embarrass her."

"Bee, this won't work. You've attempted to get this information from me in many different ways, but I won't succumb to your manipulative ways!"

They both laughed, but Bee became serious again and asked how much Miss Pearl knew about his childhood. "How much have you told her about your past?" she asked.

"I've only told her about my life with Kyle and Erin. Nothing else."

"Do you think that's wise?"

"What should I tell her that I haven't?"

"How your real parents died, where you and your real parents lived, how you spent your time before Kyle, your feelings about not wanting to be an engineer, your—"

"I get the picture," Nathan said, interrupting Bee.

"Does she mention me to you during those meetings you ladies have?"

"No," Bee replied.

"Are you sure? Are you withholding information?"

"You seem awfully interested in idle gossip," Bee said. "But if you must degrade yourself by being interested in and apprised of the latest talk, the only thing she says about you, in my company, at least, is something like, 'Mr. Gibson and I are still getting to know each other.' "

"What?"

"Yes, that's what she says, which amounts to absolutely nothing. She isn't one to gossip."

Nathan had to laugh out loud with Bee.

"Now, what's the real story? What's going on with you two? When will you ask her? Or are you not ready?"

"I've asked her, and she has said that she isn't ready."

Bee sat back with an amazed look on her face.

"I'm not often surprised, but I am now."

"At what part?" Nathan asked.

"The part about you actually asking her for her hand in marriage. I thought you were just going to continue with the arrangement as it stood."

"What arrangement?"

"You know what I mean."

"I do not."

"Oh, all right. You got me again—trying to pry very personal information from you."

Nathan surmised that Bee didn't know just how much he loved Flora. But Nathan was very serious about her. He mulled over Flora's single-word description all day long. He found it difficult to concentrate on work. He also chuckled over Bee's statements about Flora's honor. Little did she know, he and Flora had never even kissed in a passionate manner. Up until this point, they had just had friendly "hello" and "good-bye" kisses. Nathan wondered what made him love this woman so much that he was willing to wait. He remembered Kyle's words that Erin "had a grip on his heart," and now Nathan understood what he meant. Flora seemed to have more of a gravitational pull on him than a grip. Yes, *gravity*. That's her word.

"Gravity" has several meanings. It's defined as seriousness, and that certainly was Flora, a person with a serious nature and outlook on life. And as an engineer, Nathan knew that gravity is also a natural phenomenon by which physical bodies attract each other with a force proportional to their masses. Yes, Flora was his gravity.

Nathan left work and slowly made his way home—actually, to Flora's home. But instead of hopping on the bus, he took a detour and ended up walking through noisy and smelly Five Points and then on to the block that used to be home to Kyle's Pub.

He stood there for a while with his hands in his pockets, reminiscing about life at the pub. He missed Kyle. Nathan would've liked to have asked Kyle's opinion about Flora. If she only had known Kyle and Erin, they would surely be married by now. Kyle would've broken her down with his infectious love and inquisitive nature, and Erin would've given her powerful hugs. Reluctantly, he pulled himself away and started back to Flora's home.

When he arrived, he could hear that Flora was talking to Annette in the kitchen.

"Nathan, how are you, my darling?" As usual, Flora had a huge smile on her face, which always cheered him up, no matter how horrible his day. She always heard when he entered the apartment, and no matter where she was, she would immediately seek him out to give him a proper greeting. And if he left without a proper good-bye, her disapproval would be evident on her face whenever he returned. She would admonish him for sneaking away without so much as a good-bye. He found it a compliment to his ego when she scolded him.

Flora never complained about the day-to-day issues that she certainly faced at work. She seemed able to leave the problems behind her when she walked through the front door. And if she did talk about her day, it was always with patience and humor. Nathan, on the other hand, always seemed to be perturbed about something and would tell Flora—at length—about any dissatisfaction with his coworkers. This usually bordered on complaining, but Flora never seemed to mind listening to his stories.

They chatted about current events throughout dinner, especially the news that the bridge's towers would be united the next day. Since Victoria was spending the evening downstairs with Olivia, it was just the two of them.

When they retired to the sitting room, Nathan made them both a drink and asked Flora what her word was. At first, Flora seemed extremely uncomfortable. She took a sip of her drink and sat back in her chair. Nathan could tell that this task was difficult for her, so he gave her a moment to compose herself.

"I've given this considerable thought all day. It was a slow day, and I was mostly performing tasks that allowed my mind to wander. There were several times that my eyes welled up with tears. You see, you've forced me to look at myself and do an assessment of my life as it relates to you. I've never analyzed myself in this way before. I find that I—that I live outside of myself, almost removed from myself."

Flora paused to take another sip of her port. Her eyes barely moved from the floor as she continued her soliloquy.

"The more I thought about it, the more upsetting it was. You see, Nathan, I've come to the conclusion that my word is '*lost.*'"

"No, that can't be true," Nathan said, sitting straight in his chair.

"Yes." Flora shook her head. "My heart is truly lost. But there's more. When I think about how I feel when I'm with you, a different picture emerges. I had to look past my fears because they seem to get in the way. And still, my fears keep me from loving. But I'm tired of being afraid to love you, Nathan. You're my granite. That's my word for you: *granite.* My lost heart has found a secure place. The brickwork has been laid slowly, layer upon layer, like the great arches of the bridge that I admire so much. Now I know that I trust and need you. And I've found that what I fear now isn't living with you, but losing you. Because if you suddenly disappeared from my life, I would be lost again."

Nathan was truly taken aback about what he was hearing. How Flora spoke about her love for him touched him deeply.

Flora looked up at him and asked, "What are your words?"

Nathan suddenly felt very vulnerable. It took him by surprise, but he couldn't back out of the deal now that Flora had bared her soul to him.

"My word is '*solitary.*' " It was now his turn to gaze at the floor.

"I've been alone for most of my life. I have never been able to take care of myself and never put any effort into doing so. However, when I first met you, I didn't think I was capable of having a relationship with you."

"Why?"

"I was irresponsible. And I was angry during most of my life."

"Angry? Angry at what?"

"It doesn't matter anymore. What's important is that the anger eventually turned into reflection, improvement, and, finally, forgiveness. And that has freed me to be with you. And the word I think of when I think of you is *'gravity,'* an inexplicable attraction around which my life now revolves. Revolves around you."

"Nathan?"

"Yes."

"Look at me."

Nathan looked into Flora's eyes.

"Will you marry me, Nathan?"

The next morning, Friday, August 25, 1876, Nathan, Flora, and Victoria watched E. F. Farrington, master mechanic of the East River Bridge, zip across the towers on a wire looped between the arches of the East River Bridge. Then they went to city hall and got married.

Aria

(Earth names, Anna and Olivia)

The Soul World: The Intervention

MELA WAS ATTEMPTING TO MEDIATE when Aria approached. "Mela, you're needed in Flora's dream on Earth," Aria said.

"Is it that time already?"

Aria had briefed Mela earlier that a dream was necessary to boost a crucial part of Flora's life plan. Mela, when he was Flora's father on Earth, had been responsible for creating some of the problems that Flora was experiencing, so he was more than happy to assist.

"Yes, it's time," Aria said.

"Then let's be on our way!"

"Mela, have you ever intruded on a human's dream before?"

"No. I guess I was never really close enough to anyone to make the effort."

Aria knew it was true. She worked closely with Mela writing notes on his life, which would be placed in his Life Almanac.

Aria's notes on Mela's life (written with Mela's assistance):

Many people simply ignore what's happening in their lives, as Mela did when he was Edward Pearl. When his wife had died, he was supposed to prove he could continue on the path of humility. Instead, he went right back to his greedy ways.

During his life as Mr. Pearl, he may not have had friends, but he seemed content with how he raised Flora and Victoria. Upon his death, he told me that he was relieved to know that they were independent and would be fine. He was involved in bringing up Flora and Victoria. He educated the girls, believing that this would ensure their security throughout their lives.

During his younger days as Edward on the island of Manhattan in the 1840s and '50s, before Flora was born, he was a cocky and spirited man who carried himself as if he was an English aristocrat. But he lacked the manners of that station. New York City had scuffed his English polish; he was loud and obnoxious and never had a kind word to say to anyone. When he walked into a room, people turned to look because he made a pleasant first impression. However, as soon as he started talking, it was apparent that he was self-centered. His favorite topic of conversation was how he was going to make money.

Although Edward was better off than many, he wanted more. His father had been a trapper, but that didn't appeal to him. So he persuaded his father to purchase some land in the Catskill Mountains in order to start a logging business. This turned out to be a very successful endeavor and gave him the opportunity to travel and be free of his father's watchful eye.

Edward Pearl's life with Anna

Edward met a young woman named Anna. Her family owned a store in a small town that stood on the banks of the Hudson River in New York. Anna was gentle and striking, and they instantly fell in love. During his trips, he usually rented a room from her family for a few days and then went on his way. Over time, he started to stay longer and longer because he was infatuated.

He felt so much love towards this woman, who, besides seeming so sensible, also had firm convictions that couldn't be swayed. Her morals and beliefs were so different from his, but he couldn't resist her hypnotic energy. It seemed that she loved him as well, but their views of the world made it seem as if it, the relationship, would never work out. However, to their surprise, they found a common love that only grew over time.

After they married, Edward seldom returned to New York. He started to become less and less enthusiastic about hearing his father's latest money-making schemes. He told his father that the future of the logging business in the Catskills looked dim, and the profits would soon start to dwindle. Of course, this was a lie, but he didn't want to spend so much time taking care of the business. His father was making enough money for both of them in some unsavory ways. Edward told his father that he would go back and attempt to sell the business.

He didn't tell his father that he had married. He was afraid that his father would want to meet his new wife. Edward knew that his father wouldn't approve of Anna and would be furious about Edward marrying someone that he hadn't met. So Edward kept it to himself. Sooner or later he would have to abandon his father and disappear with his wife forever.

Then Anna became pregnant. They were overjoyed at the prospect of having a family. He knew that Anna would be a caring mother.

Edward began to work at his wife's family store. Because of his negotiation and sales skills, the store began to thrive. He also tried his hand at trapping and caught several beavers. Once, he gave Anna enough pelts to make some coats for herself, but to his dismay, she only kept enough pelts to make one and gave all the others to people in the family. At first, he was very angry with her, but she patiently explained her feelings.

"Why would I keep more pelts than I need? In fact, I already have a coat but kept these to make a new one, just to make you happy."

"But why? You could have made other clothing for yourself with those pelts."

"That's silly. Why would I need more coats? Should I walk around with several coats to wear when my niece and nephew have none? That would be shameful."

She said it with such sincerity and innocence that he just couldn't argue. It seemed pointless to try to convince her that she shouldn't give valuable items away. When he told her about his plans to build a large home overlooking the Hudson River, she simply shook her head. Again, her need for simplicity was clear.

"Why do I need a large home away from my family? Doesn't this home provide you with everything you need? We have our family around us, and the store is right here. Why would I want to live away from everyone, all alone?"

"I thought you would like to have a larger home for when our baby comes."

"Why would I want more than I need?"

Again, these simple statements struck a deep chord that he remembered, but didn't necessary follow, for the rest of his life. During the years he spent with Anna and her family, he sometimes felt that he was just humoring her. He was thrilled when his daughter was born, but at the same time, he was disappointed that it wasn't a son. But once baby Flora reached out for him, he fell in love with her. She was his child.

Edward Pearl and his daughter, Flora Pearl

Flora was a lovely little girl. She was sweet, like her mother, with her mother's dark eyes. Mother and Daughter were inseparable. Even after Flora started walking, she stuck right by her mother's side, always peering up at Anna's face and studying the smile that was constantly spread across it. If Anna was carrying her, Flora's hand ferociously held on to her mother's dark, thick hair. She wouldn't let go of it, even when Anna tried to put her down. It always made Edward laugh.

"When will we have more children, Anna, my love?"

Anna, still struggling with Flora's grip on her hair, turned her head as best she could to look at him.

"You act as if I've control over this."

"Well, don't you?"

"Maybe I don't want a little you running around here. That's all I need is two men in the house, bossing me around," she said with a laugh.

"I think you're hiding something from me."

Anna stood up straight, having extricated herself from her daughter. She walked over to her husband and sat in his lap.

"I am. How can you tell?" she lovingly asked.

"I know when you're keeping something from me. You have a look of mischief on your face, as though you're trying to decide when and how long to torment me."

"Well, I like to share my information slowly, to build up your anticipation."

"Well, come now—what have you to say?"

"I'm pregnant."

"You see how easy that was! I knew it!"

With that, he lifted his wife and twirled her around the room, practically knocking over the chair.

"Me too!" Flora cried, with her arms held up over her head.

But the baby was never to be. A few days after telling him about her pregnancy, Anna fell ill with a high fever and died. At first, Edward was completely overcome by grief but then realized that he had to make a decision about what to do next. Without Anna, he felt out of place in the village, almost like an intruder. It wasn't that people treated him as one, but he just didn't feel at ease.

Edward Pearl in Manhattan after his wife's death

He traveled back to New York by himself in order to have his home on Washington Square Park renovated. He sold some land and purchased more buildings, which he then turned into tenements and rented out. The more his already-large accounts grew, the happier he became. He began to revert back to the self-centered and greedy person that he had suppressed during his time with Anna.

But her words seemed to haunt him: Why do you want more than you need? *That was his nature; he wanted more and more, and over the course of time, Anna's influence mattered less and less. He couldn't resist. It seemed so easy to take advantage of the poor immigrants who littered the area.*

Flora and Victoria Pearl

When Flora was about eight, Edward started to worry about her future. After consulting with some acquaintances, he decided to find and hire a handmaiden for Flora so she wouldn't be alone. Finding and inviting Victoria to be a part of the family was the best decision he had ever made. He got great joy out of having two daughters and watching them share their life together. He made sure that Flora and Victoria were instructed in everything that a woman needed to know. But the one skill that both developed a passion for was sewing. They couldn't get enough of it. Suddenly, they became experts at analyzing people's clothing and had long discussions about fabric, colors, and patterns. They were both appalled at overdressed women and couldn't understand why simple, elegant clothing wasn't available.

Edward always brought Flora and Victoria along with him to see his property manager. His intent was to start training them about how to manage the properties, but it became apparent that his daughter didn't inherit his lust for property, and Victoria cared even less. Whenever they went downtown to collect the rent money, Flora would become agitated. When he finally confronted her about this behavior, Flora looked away and expressed her distaste for the large sums of money that he was collecting.

To his amazement, Flora seemed to have an outlook similar to her mother's about the accumulation of assets—she was disturbed by the situation.

Dreams of Anna

About a year before his own death, he dreamed of Anna. It was a clear, shocking dream. She was in the dress that she wore when she told him about her second pregnancy. Her long, black hair was loose and hung down to her waist, and she sat upon on his lap. Edward held her close, with his arms wrapped around her and his hands tangled in her thick hair. She peered into his eyes, and in a very serious manner, she told him to simplify his life.

When he opened his eyes, he could smell his long-departed wife's hair and could feel it in his grasp. He lit a lamp to see if she lay beside him. He could still feel her body close to his and hear an echo of her wonderful voice. Anna hadn't said this in the dream, but he had the distinct feeling that she communicated to him that his life was coming to an end. Time was short, and he had failed her miserably. He knew the disappointment that Anna would have towards him if she were alive. But there was still time.

He immediately and swiftly made the decision to sell all of his properties. His investment manager was shocked, but Mr. Pearl simply stated that he was going to make another purchase and needed cash.

After the property was sold, a great weight was lifted from his shoulders. All he was left with was the money in the bank, a vast number of securities that would be easily managed by his stockbroker, and his home on Washington Square Park. The building uptown belonged to Flora and Victoria.

Post Death

After his death, Mr. Pearl checked in on Flora occasionally, even though he couldn't control the events of her life. During his Council meeting, he recounted his evil deeds while he was on Earth. He was ashamed of how he had hurt people. His teacher and the Council assured him that the horrible deed of arson was a destined one.

He had no control over it. It was needed in order to strike a balance between those involved. It would cause Aiden, known as Nathan during this life, to be presented with the choice of pursuing a path of retribution or one of forgiveness.

"Mela," Aria said. "We're here, at Flora's home. I'll assist you in entering Flora's dream."

"Thank you, Aria. I'll need it. I've never done this before, but you seem to be good at it," Mela replied.

"Yes, those dreams that you had as Mr. Pearl were powerful, correct?" Aria said.

"Oh, yes, you did a good job coming back to me as Anna." Mela chuckled.

"I know it was part of the plan, but I still feel badly about how I treated Flora. You know, forcing her to forget about her mother."

"It was part of the plan," replied Aria.

"I know."

"Remember, Mela, many people have used childhood experiences as an excuse for failure. But they're placed there on purpose so the hurdle could be cleared."

"Yes, I'm glad I'm here."

The East River Bridge

Cable Shoe

ON JUNE 14, 1878, E.F. FARRINGTON was supervising the lowering of the 60th strand of wire into the anchorage when the rope holding the cable strand's shoe, which secures the cable to the anchorage, suddenly snapped. The iron shoe catapulted into the yard, behind the New York tower, and crashed atop a pile of stones. Then the weight of the unrestrained cable strand was yanked over the tower, where it splashed into the East River, just missing a ferryboat. Two men working with Farrington were killed, and two others were seriously injured. Farrington was uninjured. It was perhaps the most terrifying accident to occur during the construction of the bridge.

Skepticism over the safety of the bridge spread. Some even feared it, not only because of rumors that the bridge would interfere with commerce on the river, but also because of a perception that the structure was doomed to fall unless additional support systems were placed in the middle of the span.

Victoria

July, 1878: Taking Care of Flora

VICTORIA WOKE AND SAT UP IN BED, wondering how Flora was feeling. She knew that Nathan had probably already left for work, so Flora would be alone in her bedroom. She quickly got dressed and went to Flora's room.

She knocked on the door softly and opened it a crack. "Flora, are you awake?" she asked. Every morning for the past several weeks, Flora's room had been dark when Victoria entered. But earlier this week, Flora had started to open the curtains in the morning. Each subsequent day seemed better than the previous one. On Monday, she opened the curtains and was reading the paper in bed, and by Tuesday, she hadn't only opened the curtains, but was reading the newspaper in the overstuffed chair. On Wednesday, she agreed to take a proper bath, and Victoria had scrubbed her hair clean. She even agreed to let Annette come up to clean her room, strip her bedclothes, and replace them with fresh ones. On Thursday, she got out of bed and dressed herself. And today, she was out of bed, completely dressed, and sitting in her chair as though she was just waiting for Victoria to come in.

"Victoria! How are you this morning?" she heard Flora say in her usual chipper voice.

Victoria quickly examined Flora from head to toe. "You look like you're ready to go out," she said.

"Yes, I'm feeling so much better. I'm actually getting bored, and this morning, I wandered around my room organizing everything, including my armoire."

"Would you like something to eat?"

"Yes, in the dining room."

"Let me go tell Annette. She will be thrilled."

When Victoria returned, Flora was still sitting in her chair with newspapers strewn about her.

"I dreamed of my father. It was several nights ago, I think, but it was so intense that I can't stop thinking about it."

She paused for a few moments, but Victoria said nothing.

"It was the most vivid dream that I have ever had. When I woke, it was as if I hadn't really awakened but simply opened my eyes. It's difficult to explain." Flora paused, fiddled with her hands, and began to explain her dream.

"We were sitting in the parlor of our old house at the park. The fire was roaring in the fireplace as we sat in our usual chairs, but the chairs were positioned so that we were facing each other. I gazed at my father and told him how I missed him. He gave me a big smile, which, as you know, he didn't bestow very often. He had his favorite cigar in one hand and a glass of whiskey in the other. I could smell him, feel him, and hear him clear as a bell."

Flora paused in her story. She gazed into the distance as if she was seeing the scene right in the room.

"He told me that he was very happy that I felt better. He said that he could see my heart. It had been opened, and he hoped that I would find peace in the future by trusting and sharing my feelings and love instead of repressing them. He was proud of me, and, more importantly, he said that my mother would be proud of me."

Flora stopped and took a moment. She dabbed her eyes with her handkerchief. Victoria started to think that Flora hadn't yet fully recovered. *But Flora may never go back to who she was before losing the baby. That person may not exist anymore.*

"Then he told me something strange." Flora shook her head ever so slightly and squinted her eyes. "He said that he was glad that . . . that I had forgiven myself. What do you think he meant? I know it's just a dream, but I dreamed it."

"I don't know what it means."

They both sat for a moment in silence.

Victoria said, "Do you think he may have meant that you have forgiven yourself for not accepting his death at first? That maybe you felt guilty that you hadn't grieved for him. That now you're sorry for the way you acted but are ready to move on?"

"Yes. You told me so long ago that I didn't even cry at the funeral and that, while he wasn't even your father, you seemed to be more upset. I know we've already talked about this, but. . . ."

Victoria said, "We did talk about it in the past, but I feel that we now understand it better."

"Yes. I do feel more at peace now."

Flora's eyes were distant, but then she looked directly at Victoria and asked, "Do you think—oh, this is silly—but do you think that it was our father's spirit that visited me? That it wasn't a dream. It just felt so real."

"I don't know. We should ask Mum. She's always interpreting Olivia's dreams, and she has a lot of them." Victoria didn't know how they all would've coped without Mum and Olivia over the past several weeks.

When Flora found out she was pregnant, her first reaction was fear, especially since her mother died in childbirth. Everyone doted over her during the entire pregnancy, which Flora found annoying. She just wanted to pretend that she wasn't pregnant, but everyone around her kept reminding her of the situation.

When her contractions began at the store, Mum ordered her to go up to her room. Flora started to protest, saying that they were probably just some early false contractions, but Mum persisted, and Flora finally gave in. Mum followed Flora and Victoria upstairs, got her undressed, and helped her lie down on the bed. She felt Flora's stomach all around. She then looked up at Victoria and walked slowly to the corner of the room.

"I think the labor is starting. Of course, it's too early."

"Should we call for the doctor and for Nathan?" Victoria asked, a little scared.

"No, no, nothing is happening yet, but let's get prepared just the same. Nathan will be home in about an hour, so that's fine. Go down and tell Annette that Flora's labor has started. Tell Olivia to make sure we have tea, my special tea. Get the towels ready. Make sure they're clean. And…and yes, go find the doctor and let him know we may need him later tonight."

"Mum!" Flora cried, obviously in pain, "I'm scared."

Mum rushed to Flora's side. "I won't leave you, child. I want you to just try to relax and rest right now. You're going to need your strength."

Victoria rushed out and did everything that Mum told her to do. By the time she returned, Nathan was home, looking worried.

"The doctor's upstairs," Nathan said.

Victoria ran upstairs and burst into the bedroom, practically bumping into the doctor, who stood in the doorway.

"Ah, Victoria," the doctor said. "I'm leaving now but will be back tomorrow to check in."

"Check in?"

"Yes, this is her first baby, and she will probably be in labor all night."

"But," Victoria said, lowering her voice, "do you think it's too early?"

"The baby will come when it comes. There's nothing I can do about it," the doctor said loudly, talking to Victoria as if she were a child.

Victoria was offended that the doctor said this in front of Flora. She knew that Flora was scared and that the prospect of an early delivery and an all-night labor would make her even more frightened. She looked over at the bed and saw that Flora didn't seem to be paying attention, but that was Flora's usual way of facing unpleasantness.

*****

Nathan named the baby Kyle; he and Flora had often discussed what they would name the baby if it were a boy, and the name Kyle was agreeable to Flora. As Mum said, Flora's labor had taken place too soon and then it had taken too long. Once her contractions became stronger, and were eventually just two minutes apart, the doctor was called back. However, after an hour, nothing seemed to be happening, so the doctor left again for dinner. Mum and Victoria had been there since the previous evening and wouldn't leave her side for a moment. They washed her down with cool cloths and prodded her to sip tepid tea, but neither one of them could bear to eat or drink, even when Olivia and Annette had insisted that they take a break.

Finally, Mum and Olivia delivered the baby boy just as the doctor walked in. Flora had lost a lot of blood and was totally exhausted and feverish; she also started hallucinating. Victoria immediately went downstairs to tell Nathan that Flora wasn't doing well and that he should come up. Victoria never forgot Nathan's face as he ran up the stairs, through the apartment, and into the bedroom. He was pale and shaken when Olivia handed his son to him. She was crying and whispered to him that he should hold his son before he left.

"What do you mean 'leave?'"

"He . . . he isn't going to make it, Nathan," she said, through her sobs.

Nathan looked at his son and held him close.

"Hey, Kyle," he said ever so softly.

He looked at the doctor as he tended to Flora. When he walked over to Flora, the doctor said, hardly looking at him, "You shouldn't be here."

"Don't listen to him, Nathan," Olivia said. "You're his father and her husband, and this is your house. You have as much right as anyone to be here."

The doctor glanced at Olivia with a sneer and then started to pack his bag. "I'm sorry, but neither one will be making it through the night."

Victoria saw that this message didn't register with Nathan. He just looked down at his son and then took a seat in the chair next to Flora's bed. Before the doctor reached the door, Nathan said, with total confidence, "My wife will live."

Baby Kyle died quietly in Nathan's arms within an hour of the doctor's retreat. Olivia tentatively took Kyle away from Nathan, and he fell to his knees with his face in his hands, weeping. Victoria knelt down, and the two of them clung onto each other in their grief for the baby, but both knew that they were needed at Flora's side. Victoria helped Nathan back up into his chair and went to Mum.

"Mum, I'm going to need you tomorrow morning. You should go down and get some rest," Victoria said quietly.

"Yes. Come with me, Olivia," Mum said, taking a long look at Nathan as he knelt at Flora's bedside, and slowly turned away with tears rolling down her face.

Victoria and Nathan kept vigil at Flora's bedside. She was so hot, but even through the fever, she asked to see Kyle. Victoria knew that Flora would quickly surmise what had happened. She was too smart for them to trick, so she and Nathan decided that they should tell Flora what had occurred. That's when Flora broke down. Her grief was so painful and filled with guilt and anger that it frightened Victoria. Victoria thought that they had been incorrect, that they shouldn't have told Flora. Victoria couldn't bear it if Flora died, so she pushed that from her mind and concentrated on caring for her.

For five days, Nathan, Victoria, Mum, and Olivia took turns looking after Flora. Finally, when they were confident that she would pull through, they decided that they could leave Flora alone during the day with Annette, so they re-opened the store, and Nathan went back to work as well.

After Victoria made sure that Flora ate something in the morning, she went down to the store. But she was still worried. Flora was eating—not a lot, but she was eating, just the same. The unnerving thing was that she wouldn't talk. Her only means of communication was crying.

Olivia worried about her behavior too, so she went upstairs to talk to Flora. Olivia never told anyone what she said to Flora, but she finally began to speak. Nathan started to look after her every morning before going to work, and Victoria left work early every afternoon to sit with her before Nathan got home from work.

Victoria would bring her a glass of port to calm her nerves. Since Flora refused to drink alone, Victoria had to join her in what had become a little evening ritual. While drinking their ports, Flora would talk nonstop for hours. She talked about her father, about Nathan, about herself, and about the baby. Her talks covered a whole range of emotions, from fear to pain to denial, and, finally, to forgiveness.

On a few occasions, she pled with Victoria to forgive her. As Victoria had suspected, Flora was unhappy that her father's attention had been so equally divided between the two girls. However, she knew it was petty, so she kept it to herself. Her hurt was assuaged by wielding control over Victoria. Flora finally seemed to realize how wrong her behavior was.

"Did you see Nathan this morning? He usually stops by the shop before leaving for work, but he didn't this morning," Victoria said.

"You know that I always get angry with him if he doesn't say goodbye to me before he leaves the house. I'm worried about him—I never thought I would see him so overwrought. When I was really sick—you know, during those first several days—he kept saying how proud he was of me for being so strong and brave. He held my face, my hands, and my body while I was in such pain. He said he would do anything to ease my suffering, but I knew that this agony couldn't possibly be from just the physical pain of delivering my baby. It was also mental distress so great that it had overtaken me. He kept repeating over and over again how he loved me and was there for me. But even though I love this man devoutly, I always feel that I don't know him completely. We've hidden things from each other, but now I feel that I've truly shown him my soul. I continue to wonder when his truth will emerge."

"He was so distressed," Victoria said, "that every morning, he just sat in front of his breakfast but couldn't touch it. Even drinking coffee seemed to be a task too great for him. Annette told me that he's been pacing around the building. She's a light sleeper and could hear him and see him from her window."

"I . . . I didn't know that. Why didn't you tell me?"

"You needed to take care of yourself and not worry about Nathan. Olivia told him to go back to work. She said that he needed to get some normalcy back into his life. Olivia always seems to know what to do and when."

"Olivia's been a godsend. During the first few weeks of your illness, she came here every afternoon to watch over you, sending me downstairs to try to work. She has an innate way of knowing what people need. She tended over you as a mother would and told me every day that you were going to pull through. She gave Annette strict instructions to make you drink this special brew of tea every hour."

"Yes, I remember Annette and Olivia waking me up constantly to make me drink sweetened tea. I wasn't happy about being awakened all the time."

Suddenly, Flora got up from the chair and said to Victoria, "It's time to face the world again." Arm in arm, they went to the dining room, and for the first time in a long while, they ate breakfast together.

Flora then asked, "What's happening at the store?"

"It's been quite subdued without you. You breathe life into that little space of ours. Oh yes, business is certainly good. Olivia and Mum have been busy. Rene is in France but should be back home soon. We got four dress orders on Monday, practically one right after another."

"How is Elizabeth?"

"She's fine. She stopped by early yesterday, but Annette told her that you were sleeping. Olivia said that she stops by the shop every evening and asks how you're doing. She gave me a note late yesterday and asked me to give it to you. Let me get it."

Victoria rummaged through her pocketbook and handed it to Flora.

"Could you read it to me?"

Dearest Flora,

You've most likely been briefed on my visits to check on you and your welfare. I sincerely miss you and our interesting conversations. Your sensibilities and forthright way of speaking have often been helpful to me, and I continue to look forward to our meetings. On another note, I need to speak to you as soon as you're well enough; I'm very worried about a mutual friend, and your advisement is greatly needed.

*Sincerely and with love,
Elizabeth.*

"Victoria? Do you know what this is about?"

"No. We don't even have any mutual friends. Except for Rachel. But you don't even know her, and she's away in Provincetown."

"Strange," Flora said. Victoria handed the letter back. "Well, let's go down, shall we?"

After having breakfast, Victoria and Flora went downstairs to the boutique. Olivia broke into tears and hugged Flora. Mum ran from the back room and gave Flora a great motherly hug, tears brimming in her eyes. Flora returned the hugs as her eyes welled up with tears and spilled onto her cheeks. It was the first time Victoria saw Flora so emotional in public.

"How are you, child?" Mum asked.

"I'm doing much better. What you two have done for me—I'll cherish for the rest of my life."

Flora pulled a handkerchief from her sleeve and wiped her eyes. She said to Mum, through her tears, "I wanted to let you know how much I love you and Olivia."

With that, Mum threw her arms around Flora again and swayed her back and forth, as a mom does with her baby in her arms. She patted Flora's back, told Flora that she loved her and that everything would be all right.

After everyone settled down, Flora said, "Let me know when Elizabeth comes by," and retreated to her office.

Victoria busied herself dusting off shelves, checking inventory, meeting with Olivia, and completing a list of items that needed to be ordered. She and her mother always seemed to be chatting while they sewed, with Olivia on the machine and her mom either cutting patterns or performing some manual tacking. But today, they were silent.

Elizabeth suddenly appeared just when Victoria came to the door to lock up.

"Flora is here, isn't she?" Elizabeth asked, breathlessly.

"I'll get her."

But before Victoria could take a step, Flora appeared. Silently, Elizabeth, Victoria, and Flora gathered around the table.

"Where are Olivia and Mum?" Elizabeth asked.

"I sent them home, upstairs," Flora replied.

Elizabeth slowly took her hat off and placed it on the table.

"Flora, I have two things to tell you. One is a confession and the other is information I would normally never reveal, but now I have to."

Elizabeth was obviously under stress. It appeared as though she hadn't slept, and there was a whiff of wine on her breath.

"Your husband and I grew up together."

Flora's faced showed her emotions changing from concerned to confused.

"Are you referring to Nathan?"

"We were and continue to be very good friends. We're friends, not lovers. We're like brother and sister, but we aren't related."

"Elizabeth, you know that Flora is still very weak and vulnerable," Victoria said.

"I don't want to hurt you, Flora. I don't know what you know—and don't know—about Nathan. I've only told you this because it's the only way that I can prove that I know what I'm talking about." Elizabeth suddenly paused, as if she regretted being there.

"Go on," Flora said.

"Let me preface this by stressing that this isn't idle gossip but verified fact."

Flora got up, went to the back office, and returned with a bottle of port and three glasses. Victoria noticed that Flora's hands were a little shaky, so she took the bottle from Flora and poured the drinks—nice, tall ones. They each took a healthy sip, and Elizabeth continued.

"There has been fraud at the bridge. All of my acquaintances have agreed that the bridge project has been run with relatively little fraudulent activity, but that has all changed. As you know from our previous conversations about the bridge, the wires will support its entire span. Each roll of wire is inspected by an engineer."

At the word *engineer*, Flora squirmed in her seat and took another sip of port.

"The wire that passes inspection," Elizabeth continued, "is marked, loaded onto a wagon, and brought to the work site. Somewhere along the way, the good wire is being replaced with inferior wire that didn't pass inspection."

Elizabeth paused, cleared her throat, and took another sip of her port.

"One of the people involved in this scam bragged about it to one of my girls. He boasted about how they keep outsmarting the bridge inspectors. The inspectors are aware of the problem, but every time they believe that they have shut down the fraud, the perpetrators find another way to switch the good wire with the bad. They have been getting away with this by pure bribery."

Flora suddenly stood up. Elizabeth instinctively looked down at her lap and said nothing. Slowly, Flora sat back down and kept silent.

"It's not what you think. I believe that Nathan has been helping the authorities in investigating this fraud. He would never accept bribes. He's not like that. Instead, I think he has been placing himself in danger by posing as an engineer who would take the bribes. I believe that this, coupled with the stress of your illness, has been too much for him."

Elizabeth took another drink and looked around the table at the ladies.

"At times, he has had a problem with addiction. He has always liked to live on the edge. He spent a lot of time in the Points and—"

Suddenly, Flora interrupted, which was not like her at all.

"What do you mean that Nathan has a problem with addiction and . . . and that he has spent a lot of times at the Points? His parents owned a pub down near the piers."

"I'm sure you know that Kyle and Erin were not his real parents. They did take care of him and educate him, but he spent every spare moment at the Points. In fact, he spent the first nine years of his life living in Five Points with his real parents. Then, after his parents died, he was homeless—that is, until Kyle and Erin took him in."

"I . . . I just don't understand. Nathan told me that he was an orphan."

"Did you ever ask him if he knew his real parents?"

Flora paused. "No, I guess I just assumed that he was orphaned as a baby."

"As I said, I don't know how much you know about Nathan's past and what he has told you."

"Who were his real parents? Where did they live in the Points, exactly?"

Now it was Elizabeth's turn to be silent. She obviously didn't want to answer that question.

"I don't remember exactly where he used to live."

"You're lying."

"What does it matter? The point is that Nathan is in trouble. He's in jeopardy of losing his job and reputation."

"But you said that he was helping with this investigation. And why didn't you ever tell me that you and Nathan knew each other?

You've crossed paths many times in this shop, yet you two never indicated that you had already known each other. Why hasn't Nathan ever said anything? I talk about you all the time with him!"

"Where was Nathan last night?" Elizabeth asked quietly.

"What?" The question took Flora by surprise and silenced her.

"Has he been away from the house at night for long periods of time?"

Victoria had to speak up. "Yes," she said, clearing her throat. "He has been leaving the house at night. It seems that as Flora got better, the longer his lapses have been."

"For once in my life, I'm afraid of what I'm going to be told," Flora said very softly.

"Flora, you and Victoria must come with me right now."

"Where?"

"We need to get your husband and bring him home. You need to come see where he is."

Obediently, Victoria went to the back room and fetched their wraps and pocketbooks. They went outside and found that Elizabeth had a cab waiting, with Vince at the helm. As they climbed in, Flora said that her knees had started to shake and her mouth had become dry. She didn't ask where they were going but instead totally surrendered her fate to Elizabeth.

They headed into Five Points, stopping at the corner of a seedy-looking alleyway. Vince helped them out and led them farther down the alley, where they paused in front of a stairway going down to a basement apartment.

"Aye! What are ye people doing here?" asked a filthy, smelly man, barely as tall as Victoria, who appeared quite suddenly from the shadows. It seemed to Victoria that he was standing guard.

"Let us by," Vince said. "We're here to pick someone up."

"Why should I let ye by? Ye have no business here. Everyone here wants to be here."

Suddenly, Vince grabbed the short man by the shirt and practically lifted him off the ground. He threw him aside like a shovelful of dirt. He towered over the man and gave him a couple of swift kicks in the stomach. They didn't seem to be hard kicks, just enough to get the man's attention.

"Do you know who I am?" the man cried, writhing around on the ground.

"Yeah, do you know who I am?" Vince replied, leaning over him. "I'm going down into that den and getting Mr. Gibson. Do you know him?"

"Of course I do. He's one of my best friends."

Flora couldn't help but gasp. Victoria instinctively put her arm around Flora's waist, pulling her close.

"Well, best friend, I'm going down there, and I'm pulling him out. Where might he be? I don't want to have to disturb more people than I have to." With that, Vince put his hand in his pocket and pulled out a handful of coins, dropping them onto the man's stomach.

"Aaah, now ye're talking! He's in the corner under the stairs. He likes to see who is coming and going." With that, the scruffy man scurried around in the dirt to retrieve all of his coins. He stood up and waved Vince in.

Vince turned to Elizabeth and said, "I'll be right back."

"Be careful," Elizabeth replied.

Within minutes, Vince came up the stairs, dragging an incoherent Nathan alongside him. Flora took up Nathan's other side, and they all walked down the street back to the cab.

During their ride home, Flora held Nathan's head on her lap and told him it was going to be all right.

Aria

(Earth names, Anna and Olivia)

The Soul World: Success

MELA AND ARIA WERE RELIEVED TO SEE that the dream had worked. All her worrying and planning finally seemed to pay off, so far. The fact that Flora took her place at Nathan's side and helped him into the cab signaled that the intervention had worked for Flora.

But now it was Nathan's turn. His test of forgiveness was imminent. It's one thing to say that you've forgiven, but another to actually show your forgiveness.

It was no use trying to play out either outcome. Aria knew what would happen in either case. In addition, she didn't have the power to accurately predict what Nathan would actually do. He also had his addictive behavior to contend with. Now Aria was worried all over again.

"Aria," Mela said, "don't worry yourself. You've done everything you can."

"Thank you, Mela."

The East River Bridge

Wire Fraud

AS EARLY AS JUNE 1878, THE ENGINEERS of the bridge started to suspect that a fraud was being perpetrated. They noticed that piles of rejected wire seemed to be decreasing instead of increasing. From the first days of construction, the chief engineer had stressed the importance of testing every ring of wire before it was transported to the bridge for use. He was shocked to find that anyone would compromise the quality of the bridge for personal profit.

Washington Roebling estimated that approximately 221 tons of rejected wire had already been woven into the cables of the bridge. The chief engineer was therefore faced with a crucial decision about the integrity of the bridge. However, after much deliberation and careful analysis of the facts of the investigation, he concluded that the cables had been designed to be six times stronger than needed, so the bridge would still be safe, regardless of the bad wire.

On October 5, 1878, the last wire was run across the bridge. However, the wire's wrapping, which would squeeze all strands of cable together to create a cylindrical form, still needed to be completed. A rotating machine that was operated by men in wooden "buggies" was used to traverse down each of the four cables. The wire would be wound so tightly that it would be virtually impossible to pull any length of wire out.

Elizabeth

July 1878: Surprised

ELIZABETH HAD NEVER EXPECTED that Flora would react as she did when Nathan was rescued from the opium den. From the moment he was dragged up those stairs, Flora decisively acted to care for her husband. Elizabeth had seen many women turn their backs on their husbands when faced with addiction or dishonesty. She respected Flora for her loyalty towards Nathan.

When they arrived at Flora's home, Vince, Flora, and Elizabeth helped get Nathan into his room. Elizabeth and Flora undressed and put clean pajamas on him. The whole time, Nathan just lay there and stared into space. After tucking blankets around him, Flora motioned to Elizabeth to leave. They both made their way into the parlor, where Elizabeth found the liquor and poured them all drinks. For a few minutes, no one said anything.

Elizabeth had prepared herself to be dismissed from the house forever. She envisioned Flora pointing to the door and demanding that she and Vince never show their faces at her home or shop again. But instead, Flora asked everyone to sit for a moment. Annette came in and brought a tray of finger sandwiches. Before she could take her leave, Flora asked her to sit with them. She would be needed for what lay ahead.

She tentatively sat down and asked, "Was Mr. Nathan ill?"

Instead of responding, Flora closed her eyes and dropped her head back, as though she was looking at the ceiling. Slowly, she opened her eyes and looked at everyone seated about the room.

"Everyone in this room loves Nathan dearly, correct?"

"Yes, of course, Flora," Victoria replied.

"As I was lying in my room during the past several weeks, my husband's words of love and support drew me back from sure death. I feel this is all my fault."

"No, it isn't your fault. It's something that's haunted Nathan his entire life," Elizabeth said.

"You said he was addicted to opium. How did you know? Tell me how this started. Who *is* my husband?"

"I cannot tell you."

"Why?"

"He must be the one to tell you, not me. Right now, I must let all of you know about the withdrawal process. He will be feverish and may hallucinate. He may get violent, but I've been through this with him before, and he didn't get violent. I can tell that he hasn't been at it long, but with opium, it doesn't take long. It's a lifelong addiction that must be fought every day. The pain will be severe. He will sweat, have stomach aches, and—"

"How did you know?" Victoria interrupted.

Elizabeth looked around the room and decided to just try to tell everyone as much as she could without betraying Nathan too much. "He hadn't been by to see me in a few weeks. I didn't think much of it, since I knew that Flora was ill. However, I heard what he was up to from mutual friends."

"Like that man that Vince beat up?" Victoria asked.

"No, not him. I happened to see one of his old friends, and he took great pleasure in telling me about it. But this person is not really a friend. None of these people are his friends. They're just people who have assisted Nathan down this road in the past. They enjoy seeing people suffer. You see, this readily happens to people when they're vulnerable. And, as I said, once you've felt the effects of this drug, it's always with you. It's an escape route when life gets too difficult."

Elizabeth continued, "He will probably be ill for about five days, but it will take longer to completely recover. Make sure he drinks a lot of tea."

"Please, Elizabeth, tell me who my husband really is," Flora pleaded.

Elizabeth stood and walked around the room to think. She gazed at Flora's paintings and baubles.

"You should at least feel free to tell me of his character," Flora pleaded.

"You see, Flora, there's the old Nathan and the newer Nathan. The Nathan of old started to change when he saw you on that fateful day along the East River. Change is not the correct word. More like 'evolve.' Your husband has spent his entire life looking for something. I thought he found it in you; however, there's something that's still missing, and I don't know what it is. I'm sure that he didn't volunteer to investigate the wire fraud. I believe that his coworkers could tell that he was more knowledgeable about the unsavory aspects of the city. Maybe he was told he didn't have a choice. Regardless, it isn't like Nathan to put himself in that kind of position."

Elizabeth paused and looked at Flora.

"Go on, Elizabeth," said Flora.

"He lived on the fringes of life when he was younger. He never wanted to be an engineer and said that he was forced into being one by Kyle; he then felt obligated to continue in that career. Perhaps it was because Kyle educated him, and Nathan felt like he owed it to him, even though Kyle is long deceased. And . . . he dislikes police officers, so my guess is that this investigation really rubbed against his character."

Flora cleared her throat and whispered, "I had no idea that he didn't like being an engineer. How could I've missed that?"

"Don't fret. If you had asked him, he would no doubt have told you that he loved it."

"If so, why do you think otherwise?" Victoria asked.

Elizabeth

"Because he told me on many occasions. I knew Nathan before he went to school." Elizabeth stopped short. She didn't mean to go down that path in Nathan's life. "Vince and I must go now."

Elizabeth rose, and Annette retrieved her wrap.

Flora stood and walked over to Elizabeth and Vince and gave them both large hugs.

"Thank you; thank you both."

Nathan

July 1878: Awakened

NATHAN HAZILY LOOKED AROUND and couldn't for the life of him figure out how he had gotten home. He was in bed in his own bedroom, which he primarily used for dressing. It was small, but comfortable, and contained his more personal items. There were two chairs in the corner around a small table used for taking tea and light meals.

The last thing he recalled was entering the den for a quick escape. *Just one more time.* How foolish of him to think he had control over this drug. He'd been through withdrawal before and couldn't bear it right now, but he had plenty of time to go back before the onset of the horrible symptoms. When he opened his armoire, he saw that it was completely empty. Too late! Someone was opening the door. It was Flora, carrying tea and food on a tray.

"Nathan, you're awake. How are you feeling?" Flora asked.

"Fine. But I need to go."

Flora put down the tray and stood up straight, with a determined look on her face. "You're not going anywhere. You'll stay here until you're better."

"Better?"

"Do you remember what happened last night?"

"No, no, I don't. I must have had a little too much to drink."

"Sit down," Flora replied, "and have some tea and something to eat. You'll need your strength." Flora sat down, poured tea into two cups, and looked up at him.

"Strength for what?" Nathan asked.

Nathan

Flora took a sip of her tea and gently placed the cup back in its saucer.

"I know where you were last night. Elizabeth, Victoria, and I rescued you from that . . . that place. Well, Elizabeth's friend Vince actually went in and got you, but we assisted."

Oh, God. What a nightmare. His worst fears had come true. There was no hiding. Nathan sensed that Flora was looking at him very carefully. Every inch of his face and body was being evaluated. Why did Bee bring them to that horrible place? Why would she do that, and worse yet—what did she tell them?

Flora looked straight at him without wavering and said, "Elizabeth said that you two are good friends."

Nathan looked away and pushed his hair back with his fingers.

"She said that you lived in the streets of the Points until you were nine. She also said that you like to live on the edge, but I'm not sure what that means. I guess my first question is why you never told me you knew Elizabeth."

Nathan now felt beaten. He should have never kept this information from Flora for so long.

Flora looked down at her hands and then back up at Nathan and said, "While I lay sick in my room, thinking that I would die, you held me, listened to me, and soothed my fears. You told me over and over again how sorry you were because you knew that my father had died long ago. Yet you allowed me live this lie. You said that you felt helpless, but you were anything but helpless. At first, I hated you for making me face up to my lies. Hmm, remember when I threw my tea at you? But I have to ask you, Nathan. Why didn't you shake me and tell me to stop pretending before all that?"

"I . . . I was afraid that if I confronted you, you wouldn't like it and would leave me." Then Nathan said, softly, "And that day, when you threw your drink at me, I was afraid to come back."

"But Nathan, you did come back. Every day that I spent in that room was a day that I thought that you wouldn't return to it."

"Me—leave you? Flora, that's impossible. I might have been afraid to come back, but I would never just leave you."

"Please, trust me," Flora replied. "Let me help you. Please, tell me about your real parents and about Elizabeth. Tell me everything. What were your parents like? Why didn't you tell me about them? You said that you were orphaned as a baby and never knew your real parents."

"Well, I never really said that."

"No. . . . I guess you never did."

Nathan finally took a seat on the edge of the bed and sighed.

"My father was a ragpicker. He had his own territory and made a decent living." Nathan shook his head and looked at the floor. "He was a ruthless person. If anyone came into his territory, he would brutally beat them as a warning to others. My mother, on the other hand, was very sweet. She worked at a bakery really early in the morning, and she helped my father go through garbage when she could. But they both drank too much. There was always food to eat, and my clothes were the best they could find, but they loved the beer halls and ended up there too many nights a week. My father got into a lot of fights. He loved to get drunk and brawl. I think he fought for money; you know, that's what men sometimes do when they sit around getting drunk and bored. I've seen a lot of fights like this but never understood why. How much money can you make doing this?"

Nathan paused, and Flora said, "A lot of people fight like that when they feel they have no control over their lives. Or, they may have no other recourse; they just need the money."

"This is something I lack," said Nathan, shaking his head and looking at Flora.

"What? What do mean? What do you lack?"

"You don't seem to judge people," Nathan said. "Why don't you ever have a cross word to say about anyone? Why don't you pass judgment or jump to conclusions or simply hate anyone?"

"How could I?" Flora shrugged. "I've never experienced what you have or what your parents may have had to endure. Who am I to judge whether a person needs to go through the garbage of others? I've purchased items from ragpickers, so I've, in essence, purchased other people's garbage."

"I know you have. I've seen you do this."

"When?" Flora asked.

"When I used to follow you."

"When you saw me near the piers? Or did you actually follow me?"

"I followed you all around—after learning that your father had died. I knew your routine of going to Market Street, the Alms, pastry shops, and at the pier. Both before and after our first meeting."

"I—I just don't know what to say. Why, Nathan? Why?"

"I . . . I used to see you in your father's cab when you came to Five Points with him to collect rent. That . . . that first meeting of ours was no accident. I sought you out. No, no, that's not right. I wanted to meet with your father. Kyle's Pub had burned down, leaving me homeless again, and it just brought back all that hatred. So I looked for someone to take my revenge on. Since I had no one to blame for the fire at the pub, I went back further in time to when it all began. I resurrected the hatred I had for him, your father."

Nathan stared at Flora, but she said nothing, so he continued, "I found your house and knocked on your door, asking to see your father. I found out that he had died. I crossed the street and faced your house, trying to figure out what to do next. Moments later, you arrived home, and the thought of revenge against you entered my mind."

"But why, Nathan? What did my father do to you?"

Nathan hesitated. He got off the bed and walked over to the window to gaze out.

"My family rented a room in one of his deplorable tenements. I believed that he was taking advantage of the poorest. How could he rent out such horrible spaces? I saw neighbors thrown out into the streets when they couldn't pay their rent. He would intimidate and scare people who were late."

"He was a greedy person, my father," Flora said in a low voice.

Nathan turned to face Flora.

"I know he was," Nathan replied, "and I believe he took great pleasure in taking advantage of people. I used to hear your father and his goons talk about their experiences when they collected rent. They laughed at our poverty and discussed who was going to be evicted, the repairs that they were not going to make, and whose rent would be increased based upon who they thought was making more money. It sickened me."

Flora wiggled uncomfortably in her chair.

"Yes, I know you're correct, Nathan," she said softly. "He made a lot of money on those tenements. He was heartless in his love for money. It's the one thing that I . . . I—"

"What?" Nathan asked impatiently.

"I despised him for it!" Flora spit out.

Nathan was shocked to hear such a harsh and strongly spoken statement from Flora.

"You see, Nathan, I'm capable of hatred. I actually loathed his love of money. How he dragged me down to the stockbroker and to that nasty Mr. McGuire. To think he wanted me to share his lust for . . . for . . . well—I don't even know what to call it. He was greedy and heartless. Whenever we were at Mr. McGuire's office, I felt so . . . so dirty. He used to look at me. You know what I mean, Nathan—that look that men give women to . . . to make them feel ashamed."

Flora's face was red with anger. Nathan could tell she was reliving her experiences with that nasty man.

"This is why I spend a lot of time thinking about what to do with all of that money. How do I get rid of it in a responsible way? This wealth suffocates me with guilt."

After a few moments of silence, Flora looked up at Nathan's face. "Nathan. Are your real parents really dead?"

"Yes."

"How? How did they die? Were they ill?"

"No, they died in a fire."

"No, I mean your real parents."

"My real parents died in a fire, as well as Erin and Kyle."

Flora's face went completely pale.

"Flora, put your head down. You look as if you're going to faint."

Flora did as she was told and took several deep breaths.

"Nathan, what year did your parents die?"

"In 1854."

"Oh, my God!" Flora started crying. "Now I know. . . . I know why you hate me. I think I've sensed this from the beginning."

"I don't hate you, Flora."

"Yes, how could you *not* hate me? I know what my father has done to you. I always knew that my father's sins would catch up with me. I've kept his secret. He didn't even know that I knew his secret."

"Flora, please stop! I . . . I'm not sure I know what you're saying."

"Nathan. What I'm saying—" Flora raised her head, tears rolling down her face, and answered, "—is that I know that my father set that fire."

Nathan was shocked. All along, he knew in his heart that Mr. Pearl ruthlessly set that fire for the insurance money, but he never had proof. Bee kept telling him that he was mistaken, that no one would set fire to a building in the middle of the night. But nevertheless, hearing it from Flora was shocking. It was even more shocking that she confessed her knowledge without even being asked.

"You do? Are you sure?" Nathan asked.

"He never said that he did, but I know he did. I specifically remember the night when Mr. McGuire knocked on our door. He never came to the house. My father didn't know that I was close by, but I couldn't help overhearing Mr. McGuire say, 'The deed has been done. By this time tomorrow, we'll be rid of that property once and for all and will soon thereafter have a check in our hands.' Then I distinctly remember him asking for half. Oh, my father was so mad at him. He told him to go home, that he should have never come by in the first place. He said, 'This business could have waited until morning, but no, you had to come over and gloat over what we've done.' I never heard my father speak so harshly to anyone before, and it scared me. That's probably why I remember the discussion so vividly. But I didn't really know what he meant. Even when he told me that one of his buildings had caught fire, I just didn't put it together that he had caused it."

"Well, you must have suspected."

"Yes, you're correct--I did suspect that the 'deed' was the burning of the building. But I had just assumed it was an old, empty building. Yes, that's right. He told me that it was of no concern because the building wasn't being used. But now I know. We only lost one building to fire, so it had to be yours. How could he be so cruel?"

Nathan came over and sat in the chair next to Flora. Flora dried her eyes and put her head in her hands. After a few minutes, they both drank tea, trying to regain control over their emotions.

"Nathan, how will you be able to look at me with love after this?"

"Flora, Flora, look at me."

Flora lifted her head.

"You needn't ever think that way. I know that you aren't your father. You're trying to make up for the damage he did."

"Tell me what you were thinking when you introduced yourself to me."

"Well, one day I decided that I would speak to you while you were walking along the water. I ran ahead and then started walking towards you. As you approached, I couldn't take my eyes off you and couldn't believe that I was finally going to meet you face-to-face. I still imagined how would I take my revenge. But as you approached, your face was so soft and your eyes so warm. As soon as you spoke to me, I simply fell in love with you. I believe in my heart, Flora, that we were meant to be together."

Nathan reached out and took Flora's hand in his and kissed it. "The role your father played in my life was meant to be. The revenge that I had in my heart would never have been addressed without meeting you."

"How many years went by before we met again? I forget."

"Four or five, perhaps. That's how long I kept away from you in an attempt to improve myself. Well, not at first, but eventually it just happened . . . with Bee's help. I tried to stay away from my old friends, who only wanted to see me fail. I obsessed over the fires, which Bee called '*signs*.' I followed you during those years. Finally, I gathered enough courage to face you for a second time, and the love I felt towards you was strong."

"So—why keep Elizabeth a secret?"

"Can you believe that you and Bee met by happenstance? You met her before you met me. When I told Bee that I had fallen in love with you, she told me that she was a patron of your store. I told her that I was afraid that you would think . . . well, you know . . . that you would think that Bee and I had more than a friendship."

"Did you keep her a secret because she's a prostitute?"

"Yes. I thought you would think ill of me. We've been friends since we were children."

"Nathan, Elizabeth told me that you were helping the police investigate the wire fraud at the bridge."

Nathan couldn't believe that anyone could have discovered this piece of information. "How did she know?" Nathan said under his breath. "She seems to know everything. I wanted to tell you but was afraid."

"Why don't you trust me?"

"It's not a question of trust. For some reason, I thought that if I told you, it would put you in danger. As soon as I agreed to take the job, I felt that I had put you in danger. I'm so used to the ways of the bowery, but these criminals are different than the ones I'm used to. They were nothing to be afraid of. They were only interested in making extra money for their bosses. They weren't interested in hurting family members, as a gang would."

"Nathan, I have to be honest with you. When Elizabeth, or Bee, as you call her, brought me to that horrible alleyway last night, I couldn't believe it was really happening, but I forced myself to readily accept it so I could help you. Please tell me why you ended up there."

Nathan pondered how to evade the question but then quickly realized that he needed to trust his wife.

"I've had experiences with opium before. It's a terrible, addictive drug, and I regret that I ever tried it. It's a form of escape for me. Once, when I knew that Kyle wanted me to go to college, I ended up in the den. Bee found out, of course, and went to Kyle for help. She said that he came straight away, as angry as a raccoon, and forced his way in. As you know, there's someone guarding the entrance. You're supposed to give him money to protect your privacy. But from what Bee told me, Kyle simply took a hold of the man and gave him a good punch in the face!"

Nathan smiled. In his mind, he could even picture Kyle delivering the punch.

"He went downstairs, found me, threw me over his shoulder, and brought me home. I never told Kyle why it happened. Yes, I told him that I was nervous about school and even blamed my so-called friends, but the real reason was that I just didn't want to be an engineer."

"I can only blame myself for going to the den. Seeing you so sick, thinking that you would die, having to pose as someone who would take bribes—which would ultimately compromise the bridge that we both love so much—was all too taxing. As you got better, I allowed myself to escape just once. Then, once I did it just that one time, I was immediately hooked again."

"I think you should quit your job," Flora said.

"What? No, no, I couldn't do that. What would I do?"

"I don't know, but we'll think of something."

"Well, there will be no quitting until you do."

Nathan started to feel an intense headache approaching.

"Please, eat something."

They both ate. Then Flora tucked him into bed, promising to return in a few minutes.

Victoria

October 1878: Moves Out

VICTORIA WAS READY TO TELL FLORA that she wanted to take the vacant apartment on the same floor as Olivia and Mum's. She needed to build a life for herself that didn't revolve around Flora's. She stood next to the entrance of Flora's office and hesitated for a few moments.

"Victoria, is that you? Is there something the matter?"

"Flora?" Victoria stepped into the doorway. "I want to talk to you."

"Come in. Have a seat."

Tentatively, Victoria sat next to Flora's desk.

"What's wrong, Victoria?"

"Flora. I don't know how to communicate this to you." Victoria looked down and played with one of the buttons on her dress.

"Come now—you can tell me anything."

"Well, I would like to move into the vacant apartment next to Olivia."

Flora looked at her accounting book and then took a sip of the tea that sat on her desk.

"You wouldn't have to pay me anymore for being your handmaiden," Victoria blurted.

"Nonsense!"

Victoria's whole body jumped at Flora's loud reply. Olivia poked her head into the doorway and asked if everything was all right.

"Yes, Olivia. Everything is fine. Victoria just took me by surprise."

After Olivia was out of earshot, Flora said, "I don't think of you as my handmaiden, Victoria." She paused. "You're my *sister*, for goodness' sake. You deserve every penny you get for your efforts. I think you know more about the details of running our business than I do. You aren't under my employ."

"But Flora—"

"No buts. I know it's been uncomfortable living with Nathan and me."

"I thought you would be angry."

"Angry? No, it's a relief knowing that you've decided to move out on your own. It was something that I talked over with Nathan when that apartment was first vacated last week. But how was I even to suggest that you move in? You would be right next to Olivia and Mum, and I know that Mum will watch over you. You don't want to leave the shop, do you?" Flora said, looking a little frightened.

"No. I would never leave the shop."

"You're going to need furnishings. You can take whatever you want from your room or from the entire house, for that matter. Let's make an assessment tonight, and then we can go out tomorrow to order anything you need."

"Thank you, Flora."

Victoria left Flora's office, feeling as if a load had been lifted from her shoulders. Her insecurities about leaving Flora disappeared. She seemed to be a different person since her illness. She no longer held a secret magical power over her, at least not anymore.

Victoria looked up and saw Elizabeth approaching.

"Hello, Victoria. Is Flora in her office?"

"Yes."

"Can you call her? I need to talk to both of you."

"Why don't we both go back? Olivia can take care of things."

Elizabeth followed Victoria to the office.

"Flora, Victoria. I've decided to leave New York and move to Provincetown. Rachel has invited me to stay with her until I find my own accommodations."

Flora sat back, completely shocked.

"Elizabeth—why are you leaving? What will happen to your girls and the house?"

"I've told my girls that the house is closing one week from today. I refuse to sell it as a business and am simply letting the lease expire."

"Are you sure? You don't seem very happy with your decision. Is there something wrong?"

"You see, ladies, it seems that I've syphilis."

Flora stood up, circled the desk, and put her arms around Elizabeth.

"Oh, Elizabeth. I'm so sorry," Flora said with tears in her eyes. "But why not stay here and receive treatment?"

"No," Elizabeth said, retrieving a handkerchief from her purse and dabbing her eyes. "Both Vince and I are going to the ocean to be with Rachel. She has written me many times over the years, urging me to leave the foul air of the city to be with her. The atmosphere is calm and scenic. I may even recover fully; I don't know."

"Does Nathan know?"

"No, I haven't told him yet. I should have listened to him those many years ago."

"Please, come upstairs," Flora said. "Let's go up now and wait for him. That way, we'll be there for you when he tries to talk you into staying."

"Oh, thank you, Flora."

The East River Bridge

Vision

SOME PEOPLE HAVE VISION, and some have an enduring vision. Washington Roebling envisioned a long and durable future for the bridge. As the years passed, he made numerous decisions about the use of new technology and materials. He offered innovative ideas, such as adding a train to the bridge, which gave him the excuse to add even more strength and stability to the entire structure.

Always conservative in his published estimations of what the bridge could bear, he considered the real capacity and strength of the bridge to be a well-guarded secret. Whatever engineering feats he accomplished, his primary goal was clear: to create the most spectacular bridge in the world.

Washington didn't introduce intricate carvings or obvious artistry; the art was in its simplicity. He purposely didn't reveal that that the bridge was three times stronger than necessary. If he did, the board of directors would have demanded that he cut down on some technologically advanced materials or questioned how costs could be lowered in order to make the bridge simply meet—and not exceed—the requirements of the time.

He was at the cusp of accomplishing what he selflessly devoted himself to: a majestic symphony of granite and gravity.

Flora

April 1880: Necklace

FLORA OPENED HER DRAWER and retrieved the object hidden in the back, behind a book, and wrapped in cloth. As she unwrapped it, she thought of how she hid it so many years ago in the pocket of her wrap, denying to her father that it was being transported to New York.

Every so often, she would hold and study this precious piece from her childhood. It represented so many things to her; not only did it evoke memories of a past life that she had largely forgotten, with the assistance of her father, but it also reminded her to try to live in the present and to look forwards to a future with her husband. Most of all, this piece represented the lies that she had perceived as reality for much of her life—especially that first lie. Although it was a lie created by another, she had accepted and lived with it. She could have spoken of it when it no longer mattered, but her realization of the truth didn't emerge until she was ill. She sighed, thinking about how many other things her father may or may not have lied about. She wasn't innocent of this little habit; in fact, she learned it from him.

No one knew how old she was when she lost her mother, because her father had concealed the truth—it was so easy for him to do. Flora didn't know how her mother died but discerned it was very sudden and unexpected. There was something wrong with her stomach, and she distinctly remembered someone discussing a pregnancy while her mother was being buried.

She also recalled standing at her mother's grave and reaching out for her. Then, someone touched her shoulder, causing Flora to look back. She turned around and saw it was her cousin. He took both of her hands in his own and brought them to his chest.

"Don't worry, Flora; she will always be with you. You'll meet her again."

It was her cousin who gave her comfort that day and in the days to come. He spoke to her long into the evenings when she was staying at his house. She had no idea where her father was during this time, but her extended family was looking after her.

Flora unwrapped the necklace, leaned back in her chair, and peered at her secret object as if it was the first time she had laid eyes on it. It was a simple necklace constructed from purple and white beads made from shells. It wasn't very long, since it was made for a child. Flora was careful in her treatment of it because it was so old. The string that held it together didn't look as if it had much strength.

Her mother gave the necklace to Flora when they were seated on a bluff. The wind was strong and fragrant, and she could feel the moist grass beneath her. Her mother said, "Look what I made you." She opened her hand and showed Flora the necklace. This was the necklace she wore every day before leaving—forever.

When Father came back from his trip, he took her to the home she shared with her mother and father. He made a fire, sat down, and picked at some bark, breaking it apart piece by piece and throwing it into the flames. *What was he thinking?* Finally, he said, "We're going back home. To my home in New York. I have a dress for you to wear. This is the only item that you'll be bringing back with you. Do you understand? Nothing else is coming."

Flora nodded, her eyes brimming with tears. She loved her father very much. He was kind and gentle, but she missed her mother. She didn't want to leave.

The necklace seemed to help link the past and the present. With the object in her hand, she could recall the corn dolls and the dresses and coats made of beaver pelts, all of which were left behind.

Her father said that they would be moving to another place down the river, but, as it turned out, it couldn't have been more different from the one they had left. Their house was much larger, but it was run-down. Her father employed many people who worked on it every day to restore it to his liking. He hired Annette and other people to assist in running the household. Everything seemed to move quickly in the city, including time.

The first instance she heard her father tell a lie was when one of Flora's teachers asked her where her mother was from. She was standing over Flora and looking down at her in a demeaning sort of way. Her father, who was standing right next to her, spoke up.

"Her mother died giving birth to Flora. She wouldn't know."

"Oh, I see," replied the woman, peering down at Flora through her glasses.

The woman was discharged shortly afterwards. She seemed to be obsessed with whom and what Flora's mother was. Flora was relieved when her father lied, because that made it easier than to be questioned about her mother. It was painful to be asked, and she didn't understand why people wanted to know. With time, the lie was fully ingrained and became almost real. However, when she was ill, she finally faced the question that had been waiting deep in her soul. Why did her father say that her mother had died in childbirth?

It took her some time to realize it. Her memories had to be dismantled and realigned in her search for the truth. She took out the necklace and pressed it against her chest as she searched for an answer. And then, with a jolt, she realized—her mother was part Indian. She was told never to breathe a word about it to anyone. Flora kept asking him why her mother died. Was it a sickness or an accident?

"Father, what was she like? Do I look like her?"

"Flora," her father said sternly, "I don't want to speak about your mother. You have to stop asking these questions!"

"But, Father! What of my cousins? I miss them!"

"Don't you understand, Flora? You aren't to speak of her or her family. She's dead, and you have no memory of her," he yelled. "You're to pretend she never existed, that she's away forever! I don't want to see you crying over her death!" He reached out and grabbed her by the shoulders.

"But why?" Flora cried.

"Because it will be easier to pretend you never knew her than to try to explain who she was. People may kill you if . . . if they found out what you are! I won't be able to educate you or find a husband for you!" He shook her, yelling, "Do you understand?"

When he turned away, Flora heard him mutter, "I'm happy that you don't look too much like her."

What he said struck fear in her heart. Would people kill her because of her mother?

"But she loved me," Flora said, through tears and sobs. "Why? Why would they care what she was?" she cried.

"Because . . . don't you understand, Flora?" he said, turning back towards her. His eyes looked tired. "People hate the Indians. They have been forced out of much of the country. Others like your mother are only accepted in small communities where there are people like her. I loved her dearly, but we must forget about her now."

She cried, but her father never hugged her or comforted her. Instead, he made her fearful. Her anger at being unable to talk about her mother turned into fear. So each time she started to imagine her mother's hair or the way she spoke, fear overtook her, and the memories were forced out.

Flora took a deep sigh. She no longer needed to hide the necklace. She opened the small music box that Victoria had picked out years earlier and placed the necklace inside. It was a perfect fit. Flora smiled, thinking of the long-ago argument with Victoria about how the music box served no purpose. Now she loved the little thing.

Flora

May 1883: Crossing the Bridge

CROSSING THE BRIDGE WAS ONE of the most exciting moments in Flora's life. For a person who couldn't stand the stuffy, hot, malodorous air of New York, being on the bridge and looking over the expanse of the East River was breathtaking.

Nathan had been across the bridge hundreds of times, along with the other engineers who were in charge of placing the walkway across the span. Almost all of the engineer's wives had been on the bridge at some time before opening day, along with family members and friends. The engineers enjoyed showing their families the result of all their hard work—some had toiled on the bridge for the full fourteen years.

"Tomorrow . . . will be mayhem," Nathan said.

Flora was grateful to be able to take in the beauty of the bridge the evening before the grand event.

As night began to fall, Flora looked down upon the boats that were making their way up and down the river. People were now accustomed to seeing boats traveling under the bridge. Flora had watched them from the shore many times, but being above them and peering down at their decks were quite astonishing to her.

"Nathan?"

"Yes, Flora; what's the matter?"

Without taking her eyes off of the view, she said, "I would like you to come work at my store."

"And do what?"

"I need someone to help me keep the books, find merchandise, and deal with the suppliers at the piers. It's getting too difficult for Victoria and me to manage on our own."

Nathan leaned on the banister and looked down at the river.

"Am I insulting you?"

"No, not at all. I would love to work at the store. I love the store, and I hate being an engineer. But—"

"But what?"

"Am I really qualified to assist ladies into their dresses?"

"You have very good taste. And you won't be assisting ladies into their dresses," Flora said as she suddenly understood Nathan's little joke.

Flora looked at Nathan's face and saw a devilish smile. He looked so handsome, with the wind tossing his hair and that boyish grin on his face. How she loved him. She stepped forwards and slid her arms around his neck, and he welcomed her in turn by wrapping his arms around her. Then he picked her up and twirled her around.

"Maybe we could expand into men's hats."

"Maybe," Flora said, laughing.

"Hey, what's so funny?" Victoria said. She, Olivia, and Rene were walking up quickly to join their happy group.

"Oh, Nathan was thinking that we should start selling men's hats."

"Oh, I would love to do that!" Olivia said. "Men would come into our store! Why hadn't we thought of that before, Victoria?"

"What's this about men? Is this what I'm up against?" Rene exclaimed with a big grin on his face. "Well, are you going to tell everyone?"

"Before we tell Ma?" Olivia replied.

"Tell us what?" Victoria asked.

"That Rene just asked me to marry him!"

Everyone whooped and hugged each other, while Nathan shook Rene's hand and then pulled him in for a hug.

After everyone had settled down, Rene said, "I think men's hats would be a fine addition to the store."

"Well, if the decision to sell men's goods has been finalized, then I have to say yes, Flora. I'll start working at your store immediately!"

Victoria and Olivia were stunned.

"Nathan working at the store? What a wonderful idea, especially since he's there all the time anyway!" Olivia exclaimed.

They all walked towards New York and hailed a cab once they reached the street.

The East River Bridge

Official Opening

THE BRIDGE WAS ALREADY FOURTEEN years old on the day of its official opening, and a spectacular event would commemorate it. The festivities would begin as the sun rose on the morning of May 24, 1883. All businesses in both Brooklyn and Manhattan would close for the event, with everyone taking a holiday except for the hundreds of street vendors planning to make a fortune selling food, drinks, and souvenirs.

The celebration would take place on land and on sea. Hundreds of vessels in the water surrounding the bridge would gather as thousands of people massed along the riverfront.

Special invitations, printed by Tiffany's, had been distributed to hundreds of people. In addition, seven thousand blue tickets were sold to the general public for five dollars apiece to provide entry onto the promenade during opening day, and six thousand important guests received yellow cards embossed with a picture of the bridge, which would allow entry inside the Brooklyn terminal. There would be several speeches followed by a huge hour-long fireworks display. A little before midnight, the bridge would open to the public. Anyone could then cross the span upon payment of a one-cent toll. As it happened, two-hundred-fifty-thousand people crossed the bridge within the first twenty-four hours of the great premiere.

Washington Roebling considered the celebration excessive. He simply wanted to place a sign on the bridge that announced its opening to the public, without fanfare, fireworks, pontification, or mob scenes.

Corin
(Earth name, Elizabeth)

The Soul World: Life Almanac

EACH SOUL'S LIFE ALMANAC CONTAINS details about every life it has lived. Touching a specific sliver of light opens the Almanac instantly to the life the soul desires to view or analyze. The information can be illuminated in a number of ways; it can be projected onto a wall, into the sky, as a small pamphlet, or as a huge volume. Instantly accessible, the Almanac is most useful when discussing an event for verification or review with a fellow soul mate. Each conversation from the past can be replayed, discussed, and debated. The Almanac also contains vital notes from teachers and Council members.

Corin had been pondering the entries to her Life Almanac for some time. She was disturbed while reviewing her most recent life in New York, where she was known as Elizabeth "Bee" Shannon. She felt like a failure. When she communicated this to the Council, they seemed quite pleased.

Councilor Creek said, "Corin, we've never seen you feel regret over a life before. This is good."

"Yes," Councilor Pedor added. "I suggest that you study your Almanac carefully and reflect."

This was agreeable to her because she didn't feel like meeting with her soul mates yet. The seclusion was good; her attention wasn't divided, and this allowed her to search for the reasons she made the same faulty decisions over and over again.

Teacher asked Corin to come up with a plan for her next life and then left her alone to contemplate it. In the past, Teacher and, most recently, Aria, had worked closely with her in the meticulous planning of each life, but this time, she was told to take more responsibility for the plan. However, Corin found this to be a difficult task and wished for help. It was painful to review all of her lives—not only because she could see each detail, but also because she could see what could have happened if she had made different decisions. These glimpses were the most difficult for her to register.

In many of her lives, Corin took the path that would result in greatest monetary rewards. Once, she was a man, part of a group of hired soldiers who would indiscriminately destroy towns; moreover, they looted, killed, and raped many of the people who lived there. This happened many, many lives ago, but Corin continued paying for the consequences of those actions in numerous other lifetimes. She wasn't alone in her path. Almost every soul has been both the victim and the perpetrator of horrible actions. Since part of the lesson was to experience every part of human existence, these scenarios were planned and balanced across the universe. She had raped and had been raped. She had stolen and had been stolen from. Killed and had been killed. Each side had its own lesson.

Her core group of souls had played many parts through many lives: parent, child, friend, wife, husband, employer, and even jailer. The roles of husband and wife began to solidify for Aiden and Julia, who gradually began to plan their lives together, always as husband and wife.

Corin's role during the past several lives was happily that of a friend. Occasionally, she would plan a marriage with someone outside of her immediate soul group, but these marriages were always short-lived and ended badly.

One of her marriages was with a member of a different soul group. This particular soul was a great artist with an affinity towards painting floral arrangements. He was falling behind in his studies, and his life lessons didn't seem to meld with anyone else's from his own soul group. Corin liked to help members of other soul groups in situations like this and agreed to be his wife in order to help this soul learn the lesson of remorse. The marriage did end badly; however, both had achieved what they needed.

Now she turned her attention to her own deficiencies. When Aria had suggested that she concentrate on some of her own problems in preparation for her New York life, she was at a loss. But Aria took time to assist her in choosing a life that would be shared with Aiden and Julya. She was placed with a family that was destitute. She was to overcome her challenges by hard work, first as a waitress in a pub, Kyle's Pub, and eventually by opening her own little pastry shop. She would meet a man who knew how to make wonderful chocolate confectionaries, and they would fall in love. She wasn't to become rich but instead would learn the value of work and the joy of true love. However, Corin didn't choose that path.

Teacher's notes on her life as Elizabeth "Bee" Shannon in Manhattan:

Corin has gained great insight into the human spirit while on Earth. Unfortunately, these insights aren't being put to good use. She gives of her time as a friend and always offers good advice, but she cannot resist the lure of wealth, even if means that she must sell her body. If she put more energy into positive aspects of human life, her soul growth could improve significantly. At the end of her life as Elizabeth, she suffered greatly from syphilis. I believe that this will carry over to her next life, and she will be less prone to continuing sexual activities for monetary gain.

"Corin, I see that you're reviewing your Life Almanac in great detail."

"Yes, Teacher. Why didn't I listen to Nathan when he tried to persuade me not to be a prostitute? Why can't our goals be more obvious while on Earth? Aria intervened when Julya wasn't attaining her goal. Why didn't she do something to try to get me to change my mind?"

"Aria was monitoring your progress very closely. She did consult with me; however, we decided that even though you didn't make the optimal choice, the long-term effect of your dying a painful death because of your choice would ultimately be more effective. These intense experiences are quite effective in steering you in a better direction the next time."

"But why didn't I ever listen to my soul mates? While I was Elizabeth, Flora befriended me. Why didn't I listen to her or Olivia when they tried to show me that money shouldn't be one's motivation in life?"

"Did you respect Flora?"

"Respect her? Why, of course I did," Corin answered.

"Are you sure? Do you think that perhaps you didn't listen to her because she had always been rich? Did you not take her seriously because you thought she didn't understand that your thirst for money would never be quenched? How could she understand this thirst when she never felt it?"

"Are you saying that I really didn't respect her? That I stood in judgment of her?"

"Yes. Did you consider what Olivia said about your internal conflict?"

"Well, she asked why I couldn't make up my mind."

"You should review that interaction. I believe she actually asked you if you regretted your choice and if quitting would equate to failure."

"I don't remember that," Corin responded. "But what about Nathan? Do you think I was too harsh with him before he left for college?"

"You used his weaknesses to cover up your own. You accused him of being needy, but you never assessed your own character flaws. You understood why he was going to school and understood completely why he wanted you to go with him."

"Yes, he wanted to use me as a crutch."

"Yes, but did you really understand why you were becoming a prostitute instead of working at the pub?"

"For the money, of course."

"Are you sure? Take a moment to think about it. Your own soul mate pointed it out for you," Teacher said slowly.

"Teacher, I just don't know. Your questions are too difficult. I still believe that I just wanted to make money in order to escape the slums."

"You wouldn't work at the pub because you thought it was beneath you and would have to rely on Kyle and Erin for a job. Asking for help would've gone against your grain. It would've meant a loss of control. Just as marrying Vince would've meant a perceived loss of power."

"No! That can't be true!"

"Yes, you had the same thought patterns as your mother. She was too proud to take advice from anyone and felt she was too good to work hard."

Corin now saw that her real problem wasn't greed, but pride and control. Her mother was a terrible example to Corin throughout her life. Her mother had traits that she despised, but now she saw clearly that this was only a reflection of Corin's own surfeit of pride. Why didn't she see this on Earth?

"Take some more time to reflect on this. Specifically, review the time you spent with Nathan, Olivia, and Flora, especially when they were giving you advice. There were many positive pieces of advice you gave to them; however, you were unable to bring yourself to listen to them. Meditate on this, and concentrate your energy into being more trusting."

Corin began internalizing these lessons in an attempt to recognize signs in future lives. It took patience and practice to create a stronger sense of intuition. But if she developed these techniques, she knew that her next life might be more successful.

Victoria

June 1883: Elizabeth Dies

"FLORA!" VICTORIA SOBBED.

"What is it? What's wrong?"

"I just received a letter from Rachel. Elizabeth has passed away!"

"Oh no!" Flora said, hurrying over to the sofa where Victoria sat. "Do you think Nathan knows?"

"I don't know. He might. Rachel probably wrote to all of her friends."

Victoria was afraid for Nathan. What would he do when he heard? They all knew that Elizabeth was ill and that her treatment wasn't going well. In the last letter that she wrote to Nathan, she made it clear that her time was coming to an end. She even went so far as to say that she was transferring all of her assets to Rachel and Vince and that she mourned that she hadn't done something more constructive with her life.

She wrote that being ill left her with memories of what had been, and allowed her to wonder about what might have been. In a separate letter to Flora, she expressed concern about how Nathan would react to her death.

Both Victoria and Flora waited for Nathan to come home. He was meeting a new supplier but neither knew where. Finally, at 11:00 p.m., Flora told Victoria to get dressed to go out.

"Where are we going?" Victoria asked as Flora flagged down a cab. Flora wouldn't respond. When they climbed in, Flora gave the cabby instructions. To Victoria's surprise, they pulled up to the old alleyway outside the building where they had rescued Nathan years before. Flora had a look of complete determination on her face as she climbed out of the taxi. With her hands in her pockets, she stepped right up to the guard of the stairwell.

"Ah, you again," the despicable man said. "Where's your friend?"

"I'll not be needing him. You know why I'm here. Is Nathan down there?"

"Ya."

"Then let me by."

"My patrons don't wanna be disturbed."

"All right. Maybe I'll go home. Nathan will show up there sooner or later. But when I see him again, I'll tell him how you accosted me."

It wasn't what Flora said but the way she said it, leaning fearlessly towards the man.

"Do you know of Nathan's reputation?" Flora demanded.

The guard nodded his head. "Ya, he kicked my friend's teeth out—when we were kids."

Flora didn't react at all to this information but leaned in, whispering, "Then you know better than to make him angry."

"Just go in and retrieve him. He's more trouble than he's worth," he said, waving her in.

"No, you retrieve him!"

"Flora, I'm right here!" Nathan exclaimed, walking up the stairs.

Flora whirled around. "Nathan!" she cried.

She quickly ran down the stairs to meet him and embraced him so hard that he had to grab the rail in order not to topple down the stairs.

"It's all right."

Flora looked into Nathan's eyes and saw that he had been crying. She took his hand and led him up the stairs so she could see him better in the moonlight. His hair was askew and the back of his suit dirty from sitting on the floor of that godforsaken den, but he looked unblemished. He smelled of beer, but Flora cared not at all as she embraced him once again.

"Let's go home," she whispered in his ear, and he agreed.

In the cab, Nathan told the women how sorry he was. He went down into the den but didn't take the drug. He said that he had held the opium in his hands, paused, and looked into the dark room.

"I swear, I felt my Bee with me," he said, with a faraway look in his eyes. "Since she was there, I couldn't do it. And then I heard your voice and knew everything was going to be fine. Bee was making me wait until you got there."

"No, Nathan. You're the one who had the strength to resist. You're the one who chose to face your grief with a whole heart, not an anesthetized one."

Aria

(Earth names, Anna and Olivia)

The Soul World: Addiction

ARIA WAS SO HAPPY THAT NATHAN had finally overcome his addiction. She could tell right away that his future in this life held no more issues with that problem. He had to trust himself—there would be others dependent upon him soon, and with this challenge behind him, it appeared that her soul group would be successful.

Aria's notes on Aiden's life as Nathan Gibson for Teacher to review:

Nathan's immediate reaction to the deaths of his real parents and then of Kyle and Erin was typical. He immediately placed the blame on others, and his desire for retribution was strong. Even though it was his first response, he realized that it wasn't the answer.

The sacrifices that he had made during Flora's unplanned illness and the emotional support he gave her surprised everyone. This demonstrated Nathan's ability to give time and energy to another, breaking his long habit of selfishness. Even though he regressed in his addictions, he was there when Flora needed him, which in turn allowed her to be there for him.

Nathan picked up his signs readily and needed no additional coaching. He understood before incarnating that both sets of fires were needed. With Elizabeth's advisement, they were recognized as signs for Nathan to heed.

Julya

(Earth name, Flora)

The Soul World: Crossing Over

THERE'S A TIME WHEN THE HUMAN FORM crosses over into pure light and energy. It is then that all aspects of a human's incarnations come together with total recognition. Both the past and the future meld into a single perspective that cannot be fathomed by a mere mortal. This light and energy is the soul.

Soul Julya assessed each of her soul mates as she floated near the ceiling of her home. Her soul mates on Earth were so different than what they were in the Soul World. Olivia looked so weak and small in her human form. Olivia, or Soul Aria, was bold and full of energy in the Soul World.

Together, Julya and Aria had planned Julya's entire life as Flora. However, Aria warned the entire soul group—a human's personality has immense influence on what happens in a life.

During their many study sessions, Teacher would drop by to deliver one of her many speeches. This particular lesson kept running through Julya's energy. It was applicable to Aiden, but they all had to suffer through it:

"You may ask yourself why something keeps happening: why do I have a certain problem?—why do I have such bad luck? But instead of analyzing your own faults or attempting to understand what can be learned, you may believe that you're a victim and that others should be blamed for your unhappiness or misfortune. Perhaps the largest obstacles in the soul-maturation process are an inability to recognize lessons and a propensity towards blaming others."

But what is my goal? Her life lesson seemed just beyond her grasp. Her sudden death left her rattled, and she was frustrated with her inability to connect to Nathan before leaving Earth.

Nathan. The one with whom she had spent countless lives. *What was their relationship supposed to accomplish?* She yearned for the opportunity to say good-bye to Nathan. Her attempts to invade Nathan's dreams were unsuccessful; grief had shut him down. His dreams were haunted by childhood memories, of people chasing him, and of dark, rodent-filled alleys. Almost every night since Flora's passing, he dreamed that he fell off the bridge. She tried to soothe him into a more blissful slumber, but his memories were too strong, and his grief too painful.

Flora watched Victoria enter his room and place a hand on his forehead, whispering words of comfort, as a mother would. Victoria wasn't sleeping either. Her nights were filled with pacing in her old bedroom, crying, drinking long ports, and, finally, sleeping. Her slumber wasn't deep enough to penetrate, but Victoria cried out for Flora on many occasions. She spoke aloud—as if she knew that Flora's spirit was in the room—of her broken heart. She spoke about how grateful she was for the life they had together and how afraid she was to move forwards all by herself.

Flora floated in the corner of Victoria's bedroom and knew that Victoria would survive this event with courage and bravery, just as she had done when she was heartbroken as a little girl. Being a soul now afforded her the luxury of being able to peek into the future. Victoria would meet a lovely man who would walk into the shop sometime next year to purchase a hat. He would come by often and without any reason except to see Victoria. Yes, Victoria would be fine, as would her seamstresses, Olivia and Mum.

Flora decided to pay Olivia a visit. She floated about Olivia's room and saw that she was sleeping. Mum had given her a cup of tea with a good dose of whiskey and honey. Rene had his arm protectively around little Olivia, and they both seemed to be sleeping soundly. Flora took a seat at the end of her bed and watched them sleep for a while. Thank goodness Olivia had Rene, who worshipped her.

Flora knew that the couple would adopt and raise many children together, since they would be unable to have their own. Suddenly, Flora realized that Olivia was in a perfect state to enter into her dream. In the dream, Flora conveyed a message to Olivia to give to Nathan as well as her final farewell. It was time to go.

As she made her way back to the sky, she passed around the arches and wires of the East River Bridge. Exhilarated, she flew around, over, and under it. She examined it closely, from the tops of the great stone arches and down to the main cables.

The East River was actively churning, running in great swaths of water. She stayed at the top of the Brooklyn tower all night to watch the sunrise; the entire next day, she had still remained. The unmoving granite held steady against the tide and gleamed brightly in the last sunset she would see for some time. She felt the wind blow right through her as she watched the sun make its final descent, leaving behind a fury of red and orange clouds that bubbled up from the west.

Julya turned her face up to the sky and surrendered to its gravitational pull. Faintly, in the distance, she could make out the small outline of her teacher bobbing up, around, and within her own joyful energy, seemingly unaware she'd been seen. Upon her return, Teacher usually presented herself in her favorite Earthly form; however, this time she was simply a jubilant array of colors. Flora could tell when Teacher felt her approach. She suddenly stopped bobbing and remained completely still.

Their greetings were joyous. Leisurely, they intermingled for some time, enjoying each other's energy. Teacher hadn't had a life on Earth in many, many years and had expressed that she was going to be incarnating soon. She said there were an abundance of young souls about to burst upon the Earth and how more experienced souls were needed to keep a balance.

Finally, Flora had to ask: "Teacher, why was I taken so early? This life in Manhattan was vibrant. My lessons were surely not complete. How many long lives have I spent on Earth under less-than-comfortable conditions? This one was to be enjoyed."

"This life was supposed to be short and, as always, not entirely yours," she said. "Do you remember what your lessons were supposed to accomplish?"

"I'm unclear."

"I'll assist you in remembering when we get to the Council meeting. I can only assume that they have suppressed your memory on purpose. They're expecting you."

Peace was already making its way into Flora's energy. The sweet warmth, filled with love and compassion, was beginning to seep into her every cell. As they traveled, Flora began to feel troubled once again.

"Teacher, I believe I missed some signs."

"Yes, but you were redirected accordingly and were placed back on track."

She could see multiple gradations of colors in the background as the Council area started to loom before her. The majestic arched columns and layers of stairs rose up from the floor. As the two approached, the space between the archways appeared in a dark deep-purple hue, gradually fading away to the color of pale lavender. They entered the Council area beyond the arches. Flora could see them all waiting for her.

"Flora, welcome. You are now Julya, everlasting soul," said each Council member, slowly and clearly. Julya paused before each Council member to acknowledge the welcome as she and Teacher made their way to the center.

"I'm grateful, dear Council, for your kind welcome," Julya replied.

"Julya," Councilor Creek said, "your time on Earth as Flora Pearl was to be spent attaining two goals. You were to assist your soul mate, Aiden—or Nathan, as he was called in this life—in meeting his goal of trusting himself so he would have more confidence in making his own decisions. You, on the other hand, were to experience the effects of grief and compassion instead of denying them. Julya, please describe how you spent your time on Earth and whether or not you feel these goals were met."

The cloud of confusion began to lift, giving Julya the ability to make connections between her behavior on Earth and the planned lesson.

"Teacher and Nathan and me—no, no; it was Aria and Nathan and me," Julya said carefully. "We chose a life of wealth and security for me so that I could concentrate on my emotional growth—to face and feel an emotion rather than to suppress it, as well as to feel compassion and empathy for others. I was given the opportunity to embrace emotion, in the form of grief, when my Earthly father passed away unexpectedly. He was a good and stable father who provided an education and the tools to successfully manage my own business. Compassion was not one of his strengths; however, this was my lesson, not his.

"For a long time, I suppressed my grief. I know that I coerced my dear sister, Victoria, into enabling me to pass through most of my life within a façade that ignored this emotion. Our signal for an initial confrontation about this issue was my bedroom vanity mirror. It was a pivotal point in my life. Aria specifically explained to me that I had two lessons, but this one was the most important."

Julya recalled that Aria had pleaded, "Please, remember to grieve. This is how you show your respect for human life and compassion for others who shared your life."

"When Victoria listened to my plan to ignore my father's death, she was supposed to remember to confront me, whatever the cost, and to make me face reality. Victoria was supposed to cause the vanity mirror to break, but she didn't follow through on this."

"Yes," Councilor Ustrina said. "If the mirror had been broken, you would've sustained a major injury to your foot, causing so much pain that you would've been bedridden for several weeks. Victoria and you would argue, which would cause Victoria great distress. She would've borne the brunt of your fury for causing your injury; however, she would've cared for you while you experienced this pain, as well as the horrific fever that would ensue. She would never have left your side. When you awakened from your fever, you would have started your grieving process."

"But," Julya said, "the mirror never broke. We both neglected our lesson, and I continued to coerce Victoria into accepting my inability to confront my emotional problems. I had too much power over her and used it to my advantage."

Teacher began to elaborate, "Julya's lack of growth as Flora, and her continued suppression of emotions, caused us to create a second occurrence. She missed her first sign, so Aria suggested that we needed something more traumatic to occur in her life to force this process to occur. I believe it was successful."

"Julya, you seem disturbed by this bit of information," Councilor Inbur responded.

"Yes, I am."

"Can you see the value of this occurrence, even though it was unplanned?" Councilor Aer said. "It didn't disrupt your main life cycle and did assist you in attaining your goal, did it not? Please, look above." Councilor Aer indicated a viewing area used to reveal both actual and possible life events.

"You had the free will to choose a path in your life. We planned out the most efficient path, but as you know, alternative routes can always be sought and taken. Look at this day, June 27, 1867, in your room with Victoria: see the new vanity. See Victoria trying to help you in this process—to no avail. You aggressively chose to take an alternate route in your life. Now, if you had stayed on this alternate route, how would you've assisted Nathan later in life?"

"Yes," Councilor Ustrina said, "if you had continued on this route, it would've adversely affected Nathan. His whole lesson was in jeopardy. You see here?—when Elizabeth brings you to the opium den to save Nathan, you don't assist Nathan, but Elizabeth does. And here you place him in his room, where a relationship-ending argument ensues about his drug use. Nathan doesn't know what to do without you. He has lost you forever and eventually ends up dying of an overdose. This causes a rift in your entire group. Victoria is ashamed of how you acted, and Olivia is disappointed by your lack of compassion. Your store ends up closing, and you live a quiet life. Victoria never marries and lives with you in shared sadness."

Councilor Aer stopped a moment to let Julya take in all this new information. "You see why we had to present a situation that forced you back on track. This was actually Aria's idea. We normally don't like to interfere with your chosen paths, but in this case, Aria was very persuasive. Your illness caused you to be more confident and emotionally stable and, most important, to open your heart to empathy. You see how Nathan's life plan would've failed, because he wouldn't have been able to lean on you during his time of need. Do you see that marker on your life plan, Flora?"

"Yes. Nathan has the same marker on his life plan, at that very same time," Julya said, pointing over at Nathan's plan.

"It's at that point that Nathan needed your trust and understanding," Councilor Aer explained. "Because of your maturity, you were able to have complete faith in yourself. You were able to be honest, and later, you were able to communicate your innermost feelings to your soul mate."

"Julya, remember in a previous life when Nathan was a sailor and you were his wife?" Councilor Gens asked. "You didn't grieve when he was taken from you. You waited for him to return home, even though you were told that he was dead. You became angry when he didn't come home, which caused great internal conflict. Since you didn't grieve and forgive, your health declined."

Julya remembered this tragic mistake in Provincetown. She was still a lingering soul when Kelvin came home just a few weeks after her death to find his home empty. It was then that she saw the love that was truly in his heart, the love that she couldn't see when she lived beside him on Earth. But her husband quickly became angry and raised his fist into the air as he watched the sun set from their balcony.

"Why did you take her?" he yelled, looking up at the sky. "Wasn't I a good husband? I saw how she used to look at me—so afraid! Why was she so afraid of me?" After he was done ranting, he fell to his knees, crying, and doubted that he would ever be able to go on.

"Julya," Councilor Aer asked, "why were you so afraid of him?"

"I guess because I was never allowed to have any opinion. I didn't know how to be honest. My sister, Isabella, would never let me speak freely. She thought of me as unworthy and stupid," Julya replied.

"How do you think your life with Kelvin might've been different if you didn't die?"

"I don't know. Can you show me?"

"All right," Councilor Creek said. "Look—if you accepted that you had lost your husband, you would have mourned. During moments of intense loneliness, you would see that he never hurt you, and you would curse yourself for being so afraid. In your sorrow, you remembered how good he was to you. You would've recalled the way his eyes lit up when you walked through the door, as well as the gifts he brought to you—how he loved to watch your face when you unwrapped them. All of these moments didn't register while he was alive, but you were able to recollect them during your mourning."

"When he returned home," Councilor Creek continued, "your joy would've been intense. You would convince him to never go to sea again. Your relationship with your sister, Isabella, would have improved. Her control reduced you to someone who was incapable of independent thought. But, since you chose anger, you caused your own untimely death and ensured a life of sorrow for your husband."

"Since you weren't there when he returned home," Councilor Pedor added, "he had no one to take care of. He turned to alcohol and died a painful death. Both of you failed your lessons."

Flora now started to understand what had happened in New York City. "Yes, I see. Losing my baby did set me on a new course. After that experience, I began to trust myself."

Councilor Gens added, "Your lack of confidence in your Manhattan life was a residue from your life in Provincetown. This is a common occurrence. Previous lives affect current lives. Another example—you had trouble looking at yourself in the mirror in New York because your face had been scarred in Provincetown."

"Yes, I see," Julya said. "Isabella was so cruel to me when I was Jillian. I was afraid of what I would do to Victoria when we planned our lives in Manhattan. I didn't want to treat her with contempt. We worked together before incarnating in an attempt to fend off some of that 'residual' that could potentially follow us into our lives in New York."

"Julya, Teacher will now take care of you. Corin has placed herself in seclusion for a while."

"Is she studying her life patterns?"

"Yes."

"What of Aria?" Julya said. "I would like to see her."

"She's here as well as Mela. They would both love to see you," Councilor Creek replied. "We're very pleased with how Aria brought your group together, and Julya, we're delighted with the progress you've made during this life."

Nathan

April 1886: Acceptance

NATHAN WAS NUMB. He was surrounded by Victoria, Olivia, Mum, Annette, and Rene. There were also several others who were associates and friends of Flora. But he didn't hear a sound and couldn't feel anything. He was tired of asking himself why horrible things happened to him. Standing over Flora's grave, he asked himself why the most precious people in his life had been taken away from him. Flora, Bee, Kyle and Erin, his own parents. Why? But he knew the reason—according to Flora, that is. She had told him just days before she died that all he had or would encounter in life was there for him to learn. Bee had also had similar feelings about life, but she wasn't as positive as Flora. Bee believed in signs, but Flora believed in fate.

While they sat in bed one evening, she disclosed all of her feelings—communicated to Nathan that life was larger than what people knew. She proceeded to tell Nathan all about life with her mother, the woman who was half Indian. Her father suppressed any memory that Flora had of her mother by not allowing any reminiscing. But her mother's philosophy on life remained, which obviously had an effect on her.

"I haven't thought of these conversations until I took my beads out of hiding," Flora said. "Every time I have a moment, in the evenings, I take them out of this music box that Victoria gave me. This music box is a memento that reminds me that I'm not always right. Anyway, I take them out and look at them and hold them in my hands and try to remember what I was told to forget so long ago."

"Well, where are they? Where is this music box?" Nathan asked.

"Right there." She smiled, as she pointed to the vanity.

He could vividly picture her sitting in bed—her robe loosely tied about her. They had just made love, and her face was still blushing. Her hair the way he loved it—a wavy mess. She got up to retrieve the small box that contained the beads and showed them to him.

She whispered to him, as if it was a secret, "God is not in a church nor is He in an institution, but He's ever-present in all of us. He, God, doesn't sit in judgment. We aren't judged by just one, but instead, our lives will be assessed by all of those we've touched. Attention will be given to what improvements were made in our character and in how we reacted to our environment. Did we make excuses for our behaviors, or did we strive to make changes within ourselves? We aren't to be compared to all, but we'll be compared to ourselves, what we are versus what we could have been."

Nathan had been completely confused by what Flora said, and didn't like her talking in this manner. He wasn't a religious person but did remember Sundays in church as a boy. What Flora said was totally wrong, but he was surprised to react so strongly. He hadn't been to church since before college, yet his core beliefs were still there. God would judge you. It was very simple.

"I know what you're thinking, Nathan," Flora said. "But you need to build relationships with all, not just with God. This goes against the very teachings we've learned in church since we were children, but it's the very thing that has bothered me about the church."

Flora looked over Nathan's shoulder and shook her head, saying, "Why do you think we've been told that we're accountable to one entity?"

"I don't know," replied Nathan.

"I believe that we're told this because it allows an element of control to seep into our lives. Who would you worship if your life was measured by your own personal growth and assessed by all the individuals with whom you've interacted?"

"But there can't be many to judge you. How would a decision be made if many people had recommendations or opinions? Who would decide if you were going to heaven or hell?" Nathan asked.

"Correct—there would be no judgment by one. No single entity would have power over you. The many wouldn't decide your fate, and they wouldn't judge either. There's only an assessment—a recommendation for improvement. The source of these recommendations would be the many people that you lied to, stole from, treated badly, or simply ignored, as well as the people you helped or protected. You see, all of those people would simply provide the information necessary in order to proceed."

"Proceed? You mean proceed to heaven or hell?" Nathan asked.

"No, there's no heaven and hell. I don't think I've explained my feelings well, but it's the best I can do right now. You must empathize with everyone you encounter, and you must be caring to all."

It was fascinating to watch Flora as she said these words. She seemed so at peace with herself.

"How could you think that you don't follow these principles? As long as I've known you, I've seen great goodness and a giving spirit in you," Nathan said.

"Oh no, Nathan. I've been greedy with my innermost feelings. I've withheld love, especially from you, and I've denied grief . . . been mean and controlling to Victoria. Aloof to Olivia, ungrateful to Annette, and have ignored Mum's love. But I've been trying to rectify those actions."

Flora took the necklace and placed it back in the music box. "No one knows about my necklace, and no one knows about my religious feelings." She got out of bed, stood near her vanity, and looked at Nathan in the reflection. "My darling, I haven't told you my largest secret of all."

"Come back into bed and tell me. You said something about how everyone you encountered would decide how to proceed. What do you mean?"

She turned around, crawled back into bed, and placed her head on his shoulder. After a few minutes, Nathan prodded her some more. "Well, what is it that you want to tell me?"

"You'll laugh or . . . or maybe you'll think me foolish or stupid. I've never spoken about these feelings to anyone."

"No one? Not even Victoria or Olivia?"

"No, never. You see, Nathan," Flora said as she sat back up in bed. "I believe that the human soul doesn't die. It's assessed, as I said, and then must live another life. We're given more than one chance. We're given chances, one after another, until we get it right. Our previous lives affect our current life, and our current life affects the next. That's why no one has authority over our souls. We're all in this together and need to rely on each other for help in our advancement. That's what my mother told me. And she specifically told me that we would meet again."

Nathan took a deep breath and then said, "Did she mean that you would see her in heaven?"

Flora was silent for a moment, as if she was afraid to go on. Finally, she met Nathan's gaze and said, "She said that she would see me again on Earth."

"Do you believe that?"

"I don't know, but it's better to think that you'll be reborn if you've failed at being a good person instead of being sent to hell without being given a chance to improve."

"But," Nathan asked, "do you think she's here somewhere? Living a new life, here, with you?"

Flora laid her head back on his shoulder and ran her hand across his chest. Finally, she raised her head again, looked right into Nathan's eyes, and said, "Yes, I do."

She had spoken those words only days before her death.

Nathan couldn't help but feel despair over Flora's sudden death. A sense of helplessness overcame him as tears ran down his face. He walked away from Flora's grave and towards a large oak tree. As he leaned against the tree, he looked around at the group of people around Flora's grave. He assessed each one, wondering about Flora's theory. Then he shook his head in disbelief. How ridiculous he felt. Flora's philosophy was too unbelievable to even consider. *Had he lost his senses?*

He took out his handkerchief and wiped his eyes. It was odd that Flora shared her innermost feelings just days before her death. He looked over again at his friends and noticed that Olivia was staring at him. She started to move towards him, with Rene following closely behind, without ever losing eye contact.

"Nathan?" Olivia said. "I wanted to tell you something but am afraid you'll think that I'm crazy."

"Don't be afraid," Nathan said as he took Olivia's hands in his. "I've heard a lot of crazy before."

"Go ahead, Oleeevia. Tell him," Rene said.

"Well," Olivia said nervously. "I sometimes have these very vivid dreams. I don't even tell Ma about some of these dreams because . . . well . . . because sometimes I don't even think they're dreams."

Olivia looked up at the sky, letting small tears escape out of the corners of her eyes. Rene immediately took out a fresh handkerchief and handed it to his wife.

"It's OK, cheri," he said, placing an arm around her waist.

"Nathan," Olivia said in a very low voice. "This dream that I had has left me unnerved." After a moment, Olivia continued. "I'm standing on a cliff overlooking a great river when I hear a child behind me, calling my name."

"A child?" Nathan asked.

"Yes. I've had this dream several times. I turn around, and there she is, smiling up at me with her hands raised in the air. I kneel down, and she quickly grabs onto my hair and pulls me in close so she can kiss my cheek. I say to her that I have something for her, and her eyes light up as I hand her a necklace with white and purple beads."

"What?" Nathan's heart raced.

Nathan's interruption caused Olivia to look directly into Nathan's eyes.

"Yes, usually at this point I awaken with the words 'we will meet again' ringing in my ears. But this time is different. The child says, to me, 'Ma, put it on for me,' and I say, 'Yes, Flora.' " Olivia squeezed her eyes shut for a moment. "And then I say to her very clearly that we will meet again. That I'll leave for a while but will be back."

There was a few moments of silence before Rene said, "Oleevia, tell him what you *felt* when you awoke. Tell him what you immediately said to me upon waking. She was sobbing in her sleep, but I let her wake up by herself."

"Nathan," Olivia said, looking into his eyes, "I wouldn't tell you this since it's so unbelievable; however, during this dream, Flora stressed how important it was to tell you."

"Yes, Olivia," Nathan said, taking her hands in his again.

"I told Rene immediately upon waking that Flora told me that I, Olivia, was her mother reborn. That the child of my dreams was Flora, and I was her mother in a previous life."

Nathan looked at her with disbelief.

"Then, Flora said to tell you, Nathan, that you would see each other again and to . . . 'take the beads and hold them close.' "

Nathan then felt the earth move. Absolutely no one except he and Flora knew about those beads, and no one else knew about her feelings about her mother being reborn. No one.

"Nathan, are you OK?" Olivia asked.

Nathan reached out and gave Olivia and Rene a great big hug. "Yes, I'm fine. Thank you, Olivia! You don't know how much that means to me."

"Do you . . . do you believe that I was Flora's mother?"

"Yes." Nathan then recounted the conversation that he had with Flora only days ago, which made all three of them start crying all over again.

He thought Flora's ideas were absurd. Now he was ashamed. Instead of judging her, he should have asked what she thought of his character. He hadn't reflected on what she had said at all. But today was different. He wouldn't run to the opium den or to the nearest pub. He would go on without her because he had Olivia, Rene, Victoria, and Mum to look after. Flora left him the shop, and people were there to show him how to give back some of the love he had taken during his lifetime. Flora would be with him, whether she walked the Earth or not, and he now truly believed that they would be together again.

He couldn't wait to get home and press her beads against his heart.

References

David McCullough, *The Great Bridge*. Simon & Schuster, New York, NY, 1972.

D.B. Steinman, *The Builders of the Bridge*. Harcourt, Brace and Company, New York, NY, 1945.

Mary J. Shapiro, *A Picture History of the Brooklyn Bridge*. Dover Publications, Inc, New York, NY, 1983.

S. W. Green, *A Complete History New York and Brooklyn Bridge: From Its Conception In 1866 to its Completion in 1883*. The Chas M. Green Printing Co, New York, NY, 1883.

Jeff Hirsh, *Between the Rivers, Manhattan 1880 – 1920*. Arcadia Publishing, San Francisco, CA, 1998.

Alma Lutz, *Created Equal, Elizabeth Cady Stanton 1815 – 1902*. Van Rees Press, New York, NY, 1940.

Tyler Anbinder, *Five Points*. Free Press, New York, NY, 2001.

Jacob Riis, *How the Other Half Lives*. Seven Treasures Publication, 2009.

Christine Stansell, *City of Women Sex and Class in New York 1789 – 1860*. Alfred A. Knopf, New York, NY, 1982

About the Author

VIVIAN ELANI LIVES IN CONNECTICUT with her husband and two children. She graduated from the State University of Buffalo with a degree in Management Information Systems.

Currently, Vivian works at a small company in Connecticut as Manager of Software Quality. In the near future she will be retiring from testing software to concentrate on writing full time. Aside from writing, she's passionate about collecting antiques.

Vivian is currently working on her second book, which takes place during the late 1970's in her hometown, Kenmore, New York.

www.ingramcontent.com/pod-product-compliance
Lightning Source LLC
Chambersburg PA
CBHW021141080526
44588CB00008B/164